THE DOMESTIC DOMAIN

The Domestic Domain

Chances, choices and strategies of family households

PAUL PENNARTZ
ANKE NIEHOF

Ashgate

Aldershot • Brookfield USA • Singapore • Sydney

Published by
Ashgate Publishing Ltd
Gower House
Croft Road
Aldershot
Hants GU11 3HR
England

Ashgate Publishing Company
Old Post Road
Brookfield
Vermont 05036
USA

British Library Cataloguing in Publication Data
Pennartz, Paul
    The domestic domain : chances, choices and strategies of
    family households
    1. Family 2. Households
    I. Title II. Niehof, Anke
    306.8'5

Library of Congress Catalog Card Number: 99-72653

ISBN 0 7546 1011 X

Printed in Great Britain by Antony Rowe Ltd., Chippenham, Wiltshire

Contents

List of Figures

List of Tables

Acknowledgements

Working on this book was a stimulating and enjoyable experience. Nevertheless, writing is a rather solitary and time-consuming occupation. The moral support of our colleagues and our family households provided a valuable input in sustaining the writing effort, and we are grateful for that. There are a few people who played an important role in shaping the book, and to whom we owe a special debt. In the first place, our thanks go to Martin Southwold and Michael Price for correcting our English, a tedious but very essential job. In the second place, we would like to thank Marleen Verhoeven, Gerry van Nieuwenhoven and Riet van de Westeringh, whose assistance in transforming the manuscript of the book into a camera-ready copy was indispensable and most valuable. It goes without saying that we as authors are responsible for the book as it is, including the flaws that it might contain.

Paul J.J. Pennartz
Anke Niehof

Department of Economics and Management
Wageningen Agricultural University

The authors and publisher gratefully acknowledge permission from the following to reproduce copyright material:
. Prentice Hall, Inc. , Upper Saddle River, NJ. for figure 2.1, copyright ©, Ajzen, I. and Fishbein, M. (1980), *Understanding Attitudes and Predicting Social Behavior*, p.84.
. Open University Press for figure 2.2: Ajzen, I. (1988) *Attitudes, Personality, and Behavior*, p.133.
. SAGE Publications, Inc., for figure 2.3, copyright ©, Taylor, J.R. and Todd, P. (1995), *Environment and Behavior*, vol. 27, p.617.
. MacMillan Press, Ltd. for table 4.1, copyright ©, Pahl, J. (1989), *Money and Marriage*, p.95; with permission also of St. Martin's Press, Inc.
. The University of Chicago Press for figure 7.1, copyright ©, Murphy, P.E. and Staples, W.A. (1979), *Journal of Consumer Research*, vol. 6, p.17.

1 Introduction

1.1 Why a Book on Family Households?

Some institutions in every society fulfill general functions of production, reproduction, and consumption. Generally, family households embedded in and interwoven with social networks in their environment have an important, albeit non-exclusive, role. To some, the family household is going to be stripped of all but a residual function of consumption. In our view such a conception is definitely wrong. The private dimensions of human living and the inherent domestic activities have indeed been undervalued, partly for fear of further stereotyping gender differences. But we expect households as representatives of the private sector to regain a more significant balance in relation to the public sector and the industrial sector. Instead of serving both other sectors, households will move towards a more balanced position for interaction with them (Burns, 1975).

In addition to the fulfillment of its general functions, studying family households is important for other reasons. The research on and the resolution of many urgent social problems require consideration of family households in order to understand the existence and the causes of these problems. For instance, child labour in low-developed countries is generally considered a highly urgent social problem, but its emergence and its continuance are undoubtedly bound to the needs and strategies of households the children are members of. Social policy which aims at reducing the amount of child labour has to conduct a concomitant policy which aims at enhancing the households' economic welfare. In much the same way, general social problems concerning large-scale out-migration, emancipation of minority groups, gender inequality, or environmental pollution cannot be succesfully studied or resolved without considering the goals and strategies of the family households involved.

This book focuses on what goes on inside the 'black box' of households. Initially we intended to restrict ourselves to processes of decision-making within households, but what seemed well-defined in the beginning gradually appeared to be just the tip of the ice-berg: decision-making is a process which is indivisibly interwoven with larger and

1

encompassing processes going on within households and within the societal context. Therefore, we widened our scope and aimed at developing a comprehensive view of what is going on in what we term 'the domestic domain'.

We intentionally use perspectives from several disciplines so as to be able to catch the multiplicity of factors which influence the diversity and dynamics of households' functioning and to stimulate dialogue and interchange between different disciplines (Chant, 1997). The book also intends to generate terms, ideas, and perspectives that are appropriate to other parts of the world, despite the fact that they predominantly originate from Northern universities.

1.2 Definitions

1.2.1 The Domestic Domain

We derive the term 'domestic domain' from Goody (1972; Wilk and Netting, 1984; Jelin, 1991) who used the term for three main kinds of unit, namely the dwelling unit, the economic unit, and the reproductive unit. The dwelling unit pertains to a group that shares a living space (Wilk and Netting, 1984). The economic unit entails the persons who are jointly engaged in the process of production and consumption. The reproductive unit refers to biological reproduction, reproduction through domestic tasks for subsistence, and social reproduction, comprising the extra-tasks aimed at maintaining the social system. The domestic domain is closely associated with a web of emotional connotations, such as financial and emotional security, adult independence and freedom from control by others. It is also experienced as a place where family household members can experience togetherness (Pennartz, 1986; Richards, 1989; Cheal, 1991). However, as such it is a cultural ideal in liberal Western democracies which requires further critical investigation.

1.2.2 The Family, the Household, and the Family Household

Households are defined in most censuses as spatial units where members live in the same dwelling and share basic domestic and/or reproductive activities such as cooking and eating (Wallman, 1986; Schlyter, 1989; Chant, 1997). However, such a definition hardly will do. On one hand, a group sharing a dwelling is not necessarily sharing resources and expenses.

Extended families may share a compound or even a house, but do not necessarily share a kitchen (Niehof, 1985). The household itself may contain non-related persons more or less on a temporary basis, such as colleagues, friends, or lodgers (Chant, 1997).

On the other hand, in many cases a male or a female may leave the shared dwelling temporarily for seasonal labour migration (Anderson, 1980; Bentley, 1989). Children may leave the parental home for better opportunities somewhere else in the household's kinship network (Lloyd and Desai, 1992; Bruce and Lloyd, 1995). Many reproductive functions may be taken over by the wider networks of kin, friends, or neighbours (Chant, 1997). In short, the concept of 'household' is broader than just 'a group of individuals living together and sharing meals'. Boundaries around households are fluid rather than stable.

We derive a definition of the *household*, intentionally offering a main line rather than a clear-cut concept, from Wallerstein and Smith (1991, p.228), which runs as follows: 'a social unit that effectively over long periods of time enables individuals, of varying ages and of both sexes, to pool income coming from multiple sources in order to ensure their individual and collective reproduction and well-being'. Reproduction needs imply several resources such as food, shelter, and clothing. Decisive is having entered into long-term income-pooling arrangements, also if the member is an intermittent coresident. Members of a household are not necessarily biologically related and not always share a common residence. Generally, a household is embedded in a network, which is called a 'domestic network' (Stack, 1974, in Jelin, 1991), a vast kinship network comprising reciprocal relationships set up through children, marriage and friendship, which join together to satisfy domestic functions.

Interestingly, Chant (1997, p.281) notices that writers on developing countries more commonly discuss 'households', while writers in advanced communities often use the term 'family'. She argues quite convincingly:

> One possible reason why 'household' has been the preferred term in developing societies is because the members of individual residential units are often embedded within strong networks of wider family and kin and it accordingly makes little sense to confine 'family' to small domestic groups. Alternatively, people in Northern countries often have less contact with relatives beyond the immediate household or their natal families and so the concept of family becomes prioritised in a household setting.

Some authors (Levin, 1993) hold the equation of family and household to be somewhat outdated. Indeed, such a distinction remains useful. The *family* has a biological substratum and is based on alliance/kinship, related to sexuality and procreation (Coltrane, 1996). Similar to the way a 'household' is embedded in a 'domestic network', a family is embedded in a larger network of kinship relations (Jelin, 1991).

A further distinction is made between family-households and nonfamily-households. A family-household must have at least two persons: the householder who is the person who owns or rents the living quarters and at least one person who is related to the householder by either marriage or birth/adoption. A *non-family household* comprises either a householder who lives alone or one who is not related to anyone residing in the household (Cook et al., 1994b). While neither type of household deserves priority, for reason of brevity this book focuses on family households.

Rather than trying to further delineate household or family boundaries across different cultures, it seems more important and practical to delineate some mechanisms which result in existing or changing boundaries. According to Wallerstein and Smith (1991), cyclical patterns of global economic expansion and contraction exert pressures on the units of production, such as households. Cyclical rythms lead to a shifting rythm of modal household composition. Periods of expansion supposedly lead to relatively greater wage-dependence and to relatively narrower boundaries of inclusion. Periods of stagnation are supposed to lead to changes in the reverse direction. Wilk and Netting (1984) in more detail suppose that the simultaneity of labour requirements of major productive tasks and the diversity of productive tasks within a yearly cycle influence the size of household groups. Households actively respond to such changes and requirements by adjusting existing strategies or by developing new ones. In addition to economic factors, political forces are operating through laws and policies, primarily located in the multiple levels and forms of the state machinery. They may all entail consequences which directly or indirectly turn households toward expanding or contracting. Such laws and policies relate, amongst others, to the right to migrate, the degree of legal obligations of kin to each other, possibilities and requirements of co-residence, financial and legal responsibilities, fiscal obligations, the right to physical movement, and constraints on the physical location of economic activities.

1.2.3 The Family Household as a Relatively Autonomous Unit

Focusing on family households is like navigating between Scylla and Charybdis. On the one hand, a family household is viewed as a unified interest group living in close harmony: the bounded monogamous nuclear household with pooled economic resources and a common budget being the basic reproductive decision-making unit, as in the view of the New Home Economics school (Becker, 1981, in Fapohunda and Todaro, 1988). This view also nicely fits in with Functionalism in that it assumes that a society must somehow provide for the production, physical care, and socialization of children and cannot do without an efficient reproductive *unit* being the family (Matsushima, 1992). The family is also viewed as an agent of change in its own right, similar to the economic system, and processes of modernization or individualization.

On the other hand, a family is viewed just as a location in which the individual members engage in struggles about matters of gender and age, and where production and redistribution develop. This view criticizes the first one for not having identified and addressed the *sources* of conflict within a family's household life. It focuses on the differences between women's and men's experiences and interests within family households (Hartmann, 1981). The family household is not considered an agent of change in its own right, but it is rather the underlying patriarchical and capitalist relations among people that causes change. After having stated that it is not 'the family' that as an active agent resists or embraces capitalism or other social movements, Hartman (1981, p. 369) quite clearly states:

> Rather people - men and/or women, adults, and /or children - use familial forms in various ways. While they may use their 'familial' connections or kin groups and their locations in families in any number of projects - to find jobs, to build labour unions, to wage community struggles, to buy houses, to borrow cars, or to share child care - they are not acting only as family members but also as members of gender categories.

Within a functionalistic view, individuals may participate in the political system or in the larger society more generally, but they do not do so in their roles as family members. By consequence, families are considered to belong to what is called 'the affectional subsystem' in functional terms (Matsushima, 1992).

Instead, we prefer a view of individuals as being participants in the political system and the economic system and at the same time as being part of the family household, fulfilling its productive and reproductive functions. Ideology, culture, habits, and practices enter family households, are transformed when passing through and exert a certain influence on the larger society in turn. By consequence, we consider the family household to be an active agent. Despite being interwoven with its social and cultural environment and its individual members being involved in divergent social networks, the family household ultimately has to *coordinate* the preferences, practices, resources, and interests of its members, diverging as these may be. In addition, each household has some 'emergent properties' - for instance rules of accomodation or coordination - which cannot be reduced to the properties of individual members and which an explanation of behaviour cannote dispense of (Anderson et al., 1994b). We consider family households to be active agents that are able to perform some changes within broad structural constraints, that are relatively autonomous vis-á-vis macro-structural processes, and that act as mediating agencies between the individual and society (De Oliveira, 1991; Gilbert and Gugler, 1992).

1.2.4 Domestic Activities, Decision-Making, and Modernization

Embedded within the process of modernization, domestic activities were subjected to the rationalization of means and ends. Rationalization implied achieving greater efficiency in the use of time and money and to upgrade moral and physical standards of care. Activities such as cooking, cleaning, sewing, and child care - traditionally considered women's chores - became subjected to rational scientific management. At the turn of the century, experts from the Home Economics Movement played a crucial role in redefining domestic work. Traditional practices were considered to be inadequate. Emancipation was conceived as liberating individuals or groups from irrationalities in thought and action and to free people from repressive social constraints became a core issue (Green, 1996). The importance of conscious effort was emphasized (Gross et al., 1973), because 'without conscious effort family members can slip easily into a passive role, letting fate make decisions. Tradition, fate, or past experience can no longer be used as primary determinants of family affairs' (Paolucci et al., 1977, p.6).

Within Home Economics, as well as in Family Studies (Scanzoni and Szinovacz, 1980) and Economic Anthropology (Wilk, 1989), household decision-making became a main issue. It was defined as a process of evaluation in the choice or resolution of alternatives (Deacon and Firebaugh, 1988), and it was considered to be a crucial process underlying all functions of family resource management and essential to the quality of human life, the prospect of the family's continued survival within limited environments, and the preservation of the natural environment.

Several large-scale developments intensified the individual subjects' and family households' needs of decision-making and at the same time afforded enlarged opportunities of decision-making. The explosion of knowledge about cause-effect relationships and booming technology increased both the opportunity and the responsibility to make decisions. The rapidly changing environments became more complex and urged family households to stabilize and maintain the family's most important values. Family households should adapt to these changes and find room for personal growth and development. Further, in modern contexts key decisions gradually became freed from pre-established ties to other individuals and groups, while in pre-modern contexts:

> Kinship relations helped determine, and in many cases completely defined, key decisions affecting the course of events for the individual over the whole lifespan. Decisions about when and whom to marry, where to live, how many children to aim for, how to care for one's children, how to spend one's old age were among the most obvious examples. The externalities of place and kinship normally were closely connected (Giddens, 1991, p.147).

However, restricting the main issue to decision-making would result in a reductionist view of reality in family households' everyday life.

We prefer a broader view, which is supported by the following arguments: First, in most studies on decision-making, emphasis is placed on information processing to reduce uncertainty as to the management of resources while full attention is given to cognitive processes (Paolucci et al., 1977; Stafford and Avery, 1993). Meanwhile the impact of traditions, people's past experiences, their cultural expectations, processes of routinization, and occurring events are easily overlooked.

> People are presented as purposive, reasoning 'problem solvers', neither blindly seeking pleasure nor driven by inner passions, but making their own decisions in a complex and challenging world (Carroll and Johnson, 1990, p.9).

However, in everyday life choices are blocked or programmed by unconscious emotions which sets clear limits to feasible options (Giddens, 1996).

Further, within decision theories the main focus is on the individual as the decision-maker. Individuals decide in such a way as to minimise their costs and to maximise their benefits, and they will engage in interaction only in case benefits exceed costs. The household is considered a single entity with a 'joint utility function' (Becker, 1981, in Wilk, 1989) or the interactions between its members are subsumed under the cover of 'generalised reciprocity', while all that is going on within or between households is conceived of as 'exchange' (Wilk, 1989). By consequence, the issue of power among family household members is hardly explained and approaches prevent 'the micro-politics of domestic interiors' to come to the fore, as for instance regarding decisions on food (Mennell et al., 1992). Cheal (1991, p.135) calls this approach 'the most single-mindedly individualistic of the recent approaches in sociology that emphasises human agency'. We fully agree with his statement.

Third, while decision-making is being restricted to the intra-individual and inter-individual level, both structural and cultural forces remain out of view. Factors out of the hands of the subjects involved bind their choices. Indeed, in everyday life options for choice may have been enlarged considerably, at least in welfare states, but political and economic arrangements define and provide these very options beforehand. For instance, decisions made by the producer or designer of consumer products determine the choices which are open to the consumer (Giddens, 1996).

Finally, many decision-making studies fail in that a temporal perspective is missing. On one hand, decisions households made in the past influence their actual constraints and opportunities and - as a consequence - the options now available. On the other hand, many households tend to anticipate changes and events which may occur in the near or far future, and their behaviour may seem to be quite irrational and barely understandable, if such anticipating behaviour is left out of consideration.

All in all, decision-making analysis which assumes that subjects make rational choices among discrete options offers 'an extremely restricted framework for analysing the complexities of intra- and inter-household processes, and their implications for macro performance' (Berry, 1984, p.4). Therefore, this book offers a framework for analysing the complexities of these processes in a much more comprehensive way.

1.3 Structure of the Book

1.3.1 Selection of Theoretical Approaches

Each theory gives access to a distinctive aspect of the functioning of family households and thus contributes to a comprehensive view in a unique way. Approaches might have been developed within the field of

Family Studies or some related field, but might also have had their origin within an unrelated area. Most theoretical approaches are bound to larger intellectual traditions within the social sciences and draw on a range of disciplinary perspectives. Some contrasts between national traditions in family studies are salient. For instance, as Cheal (1991) noticed American sociologists of the family rarely mention Marxism as a scientific framework, but Marxism had a large influence on family studies in Britain and Canada. Exchange theory shows an inverse picture. In our view, these diverging practices imply and reflect more fundamentally different stands regarding an individualistic versus a collectivistic explanation of social phenomena. Aiming at comprehensiveness, both fundamental views are relevant and will be represented in this book.

The theoretical approaches we selected have generally originated from universities in the Western world and may, by consequence, unintentionally result in a certain partiality. We decided to counteract possible biases by inserting key studies which have been performed in non-western countries. Nevertheless, to some degree partiality may still operate throughout the several chapters. In that case, we hope the book evokes its counterpart from non-western scientific institutions.

1.3.2 Selection of Key Studies

All key studies pertain to issues which are highly relevant to understanding the functioning or malfunctioning of family households or the consequences of certain ways of functioning to society. We further aim at a certain randomness across countries and cultures to check the validity of the approaches and possibly to stretch their reach. However, the selection of key studies does not indicate the overall extent to which a theoretical approach and a research method have been applied. They rather exemplify the way such approaches and methods can be followed.

We selected our key studies considering the specificity of the theoretical framework, the consistency of application, the appropriateness of methodology, and the salience of outcomes. In some cases, the outcomes quite clearly and even surprisingly show the narrowness of a specific approach, as for instance in the key study by Chen (1996) on power within farming households, but consequently indicate quite convincingly new directions for research on the issue at stake.

1.3.3 New Directions

A number of proposals for 'new directions' on behalf of further discussion and further research will conclude each chapter. The purpose of these sections is not to discuss in detail the various issues raised, but rather to indicate the existence of certain gaps in the theoretical approach presented in the chapter and show the way the chapter's theme might be studied in a more appropriate and more advanced way. Suggestions for further reading are offered. In some cases we refer to studies which made use of different frameworks and which have recently been published elsewhere. In other cases we refer to theoretical approaches which are explained in another chapter of this book. Despite the divergence of the several approaches, the book consequently gains a certain degree of unity and each chapter contributes to the clarification of the main issue of one or more other chapters.

1.3.4 The Chapters

The chapter on the *Rational Choice Approach* (chapter 2) shares with most decision theories cognition or belief structure as its main issue: cognitions or beliefs ultimately determine a subject's behaviour. However, both theories in this chapter distinguish between 'behavioural beliefs' and 'normative beliefs' and - by consequence - introduce external normative influence apart from expected utilities, thus mitigating the pronounced individualistic base of most other rational choice approaches.

The application of the rational choice conceptual framework is exemplified using the theme of the recycling behaviour of family households. Households have an important role in the problem of environmental sustainability: a large part of waste is produced by households and the way they dispose of this waste largely determines the possibility of recycling. In addition, much research on households' recycling behaviour uses the conceptual frameworks we present in this chapter and shows both their strengths and weaknesses.

The chapter on the *Strategy Approach* (chapter 3) adds a different dimension to decision theory: whereas decision theory implies behaviours in the short run, the strategy approach introduces the temporal dimension. Only now are decisions studied as being part of or being embedded in future-oriented strategies of households. These strategies comprise one of the contexts in which specific decisions take place and can partly account for decisions made within households and the resulting behaviour of its members. While the Rational Choice Approach takes the individual as its unit of analysis, the Strategy Approach predominantly takes the household as its unit of analysis. Both approaches are grounded on rationality of behaviour.

The Strategy Approach will be applied to an important family household's function: income earning. It will prove to be helpful to studying work-related practices low-industrialised countries. Key studies consider in particular temporary migration by one parent as a main element in households' income earning strategies.

The *Organisation Approach* is dealt with in chapter 4. It criticises the assumption that the household is a unit and that those who bring money in will share it with other members resulting in a 'family wage' policy. The chapter brings different patterns of allocation of resources to the fore, the way these practices depend on household characteristics, and also inequalities regarding earning opportunities among household members. Insight into processes of allocation within households is important to social policy.

The Organisation Approach will be applied to the theme of the allocation of financial resources once these have entered into the family household. Finances are a key resource in most cultures and money allocation reinforces and is reinforced by prevailing power relationships. In addition, pooling or non-pooling financial resources appears to be significant to a household's ability to take advantage of opportunities for commercial investments and thus for a household's long-term welfare, particularly in less-industrialised countries.

The *Power Approach*, as described in chapter 5, also detracts from the ideal of the family household as a unit. But contrary to the Allocative Approach, it introduces a macro-phenomenon (i.e. ideology) as a factor to explain inequality within family households. The Power Approach further criticises the equation of decision-making and power, and conceives decision-making as just one level at which power operates. It does not deny the validity of resource-based explanations of the division of power, but rather it intends to explain existing inequalities among household members in access to resources, and to inequalities regarding the physical and psychological burdens.

We will exemplify the application of the Power Approach using the division of household production tasks between husbands and wives as the main theme. Obviously, many factors are relevant in this respect, but power relationships within the family household are undoubtedly significant. Demographic changes, increasing numbers of married women entering the labour force, unequal physical and psychic burdens strongly question the actual patterns of the division of work within households.

The *Opportunity Structure Approach,* chapter 6, also introduces external forces in order to explain decisions and practices within households. However, unlike the approach in the preceding chapter, the Structural Approach focuses on the social structure - comprising the network of social agencies and institutions - which the household is embedded in and which determines the opportunities the larger society offers to family households by means of provisions and services. The chapter aims at elucidating two important matters. First, social structure should not be conceived as a self-autonomous, closed and unchangeable system. On the contrary, it is rather a melting-pot in which several agencies aiming at divergent goals and interests compete and supply provisions, but not quite independent on the 'demanders' of these provisions. Despite the fact that these external agencies determine family households' opportunity structure, households are definitely not powerless and therefore are conceived again as active agents. Also in this chapter, power relationships are at stake again, but the focus is now on power inequalities between households and external social agencies.

The Opportunity Structure Approach will be applied to households' accessibility to the housing market and will further be exemplified using key studies concerning housing of women-headed households. The selection of the theme is far from incidental. Housing is a household's basic need and implies opportunities and constraints for many aspects of its functioning. Housing has unjustly often got low priority among other welfare provisions, implying an intriguing latent conflict with competence. Women-headed households comprise a substantial minority among all households, their housing conditions are found to be on a rather low level, and women appear to be most involved in as well as most burdened by insufficient housing conditions. Key studies from Third-World countries are elaborated in this chapter because problems are most salient here.

The *Longitudinal Approach,* as described in chapter 7, covers approaches in which the temporal dimension of family household phenomena plays a crucial part. Several important concepts which try to capture this temporal dimension are discussed. These include the concepts of cohort, generation, family life cycle, family time, and life course. The methodological problems that arise because of the fact that there is not just one temporal dimension receive ample attention. The authors whose work is presented struggle with the interrelationships and interdependencies between individual time, family time, and historical time. The chapter concludes by giving new directions for research on family households and indicating research questions in which the longitudinal perspective is integrated.

Two key studies are presented. The first one is a classical study in which the term family time was invented. It is a historical study which centers around the lives of workers in textile mills in Manchester (US) and their families, during the second half of the nineteenth and the first half of the twentieth century. The study's core is the analysis of the synchronisation of the individual life course, family time, and industrial time. The second key study applies a life course perspective to migration and relates migration decisions to changing household situations and changing socio-economic trends at a macro level. The three temporal dimensions and their intersections are part of the design of this study. The study differs from the first one in that it takes the individual life course as the unit of analysis. The other temporal dimensions, notably family time - in this study conceptualised as household career - become contextual.

The *Morality Approach*, as described in chapter 8, focuses on the moral dimensions in the organisation of family households and on the importance of kinship relationships for family reciprocity and family obligations. Care giving as an important element in the organisation and activities of family households, will be analysed for its moral and political aspects. Gender is shown to be an important issue in family morality and in care giving. Another aspect is what has been phrased as the moral economy of the family household. According to this paradigm, economic transactions in the family household cannot be explained by utility rationality only, but involve morality.

The Morality Approach will be highlighted in the selected key study. The subject of this key study is family obligations, both within the nuclear family and in the extended kinship network. The fieldwork for this study was done in Britain during the late eighties.

The final chapter 9 *Synthesis and a View Ahead* will summarise and integrate the divergent approaches and will highlight the consequences of ongoing social changes.

2 The Rational Choice Approach and Households' Sustainable Behaviour

2.1 Introduction

In rational choice theories, behaviour is assumed to imply a choice between two or more alternatives. Most rational choice theories assume that the subject makes a systematic choice among several alternatives after performing a utility analysis by cognitively structuring his beliefs about their potential consequences (Sheth and Raju, 1974). This subject's belief system about each alternative is assumed to be relatively stable. Because beliefs, in particular about potential consequences of choice alternatives, dominate in people's choice behaviour, Sheth and Raju call the mechanism behind this kind of behaviour the *Belief Controlled Choice Mechanism*. They explicitly contrast it to other choice mechanisms, such as habit-based, curiosity-based, and situation-based kinds of choice behaviour.

We select two allied theories which explicitly have a subject's cognitive or belief structure as their main issue and most clearly exemplify this version of the Rational Choice Approach: the *Theory of Reasoned Action* (TRA) and its successor the *Theory of Planned Behaviour* (TPB). According to both theories, for a full understanding of behaviour it is necessary to identify the beliefs related to the performance of each behavioural alternative. Since a person's beliefs represent the information he has about his world, it follows that a person's behaviour is ultimately determined by this information (Ajzen and Fishbein, 1980).

In this chapter, we will first shortly elucidate the relevance of both theories to studying the functioning of family households and the relevance of sustainable behaviour within households - more particularly recycling behaviour - which is an intrinsic aspect of the way in which households function. Then, we will offer a description of the Theory of Reasoned Action and the Theory of Planned Behaviour. Two key studies on recycling behaviour will exemplify ways in which each conceptual framework can be operationalized. Finally, we will formulate conclusions and elaborate a number of 'new directions'. These concern factors which are lacking in both theories, but which appear from other studies to be relevant for explaining recycling behaviour and - supposedly - for explaining other kinds of behaviour within households as well.

2.2 The Relevance of the Theories and of Sustainable Behaviour within Households

Both theories are important because they offer an - albeit limited - view into the 'black box' which mediates the usual 'demographics' of individuals and households as independent variables, and specific behavioural outcomes as dependent variables. They do not deny the meaningfulness of such demographic characteristics regarding the performance of a specific behaviour. However, these characteristics are considered 'external variables' which affect behaviour only to the extent that they influence the assumed real determinants of behaviour. Further, contrary to other approaches within rational choice theory, both theories attribute distinctive explanatory power to the subjects' social environment. To a certain degree, this addition mitigates the pronounced individualistic base of most other rational choice approaches. In consequence, they offer an opportunity to insert other household members into the research model. In addition, the Theory of Planned Behaviour considers to some degree the opportunities and constraints which may influence household members' intentions and behaviours. Because our focus is on the functioning of households in everyday life, and opportunities and constraints are part and parcel of the household's life-world, no study on family households can actually dispense with both these components.

   In order to elucidate the usefulness of both the Theory of Reasoned Action and the Theory of Planned Behaviour, we decided in favour of the issue of households' *recycling behaviour*.

   We considered that a large proportion of total refuse is produced by households and, in consequence, households have a main role in the production and disposal of refuse in society (Oskamp et al., 1991; Van Beek, 1997). Surprisingly, in view of the environmental issue, the research interest within the field of Home Economics, Family and Consumer Studies, or Human Ecology has been rather limited. Hill and Solheim (1993) analysed three environment-related journals in the 1960s, the 1970s, and the 1980s, and conclude that the number of articles was rather limited, and that the purpose of most articles was to disseminate technical information, offering 'prescriptive' and 'how to' information for management and conservation of resources. Only a few publications focused on life-style questions, and a rather limited number considered predominant values upon which household and decision practices are based. However, in other disciplines research on recycling behaviour is rather abundant, and researchers have often used the framework of the Theory of Reasoned Action or the Theory of Planned Behaviour, although in most studies other determinants have been inserted into the research model as well.

Recycling is defined as the process through which materials previously used are collected, processed, remanufactured, and reused (Schultz et al., 1995).

Materials include many different items, such as paper (Jones, 1990; Goldenhar and Connell, 1993), tins, or textiles (Daneshvary et al., 1998).

Recycling may take different forms and may vary as to the complexity of recycling behaviour, as in commingled programmes of recycling versus programmes in which several types of materials have to be separated (Oskamp et al., 1996).

However, the reader should be aware that recycling behaviour is closely related to the economic and political structure of the wider society. While in many Western countries recycling is predominantly a 'public society' affair, in other countries - particularly Third World countries - it is an authentic 'civil society' enterprise and is part of the informal sector of the economy (Corral-Verdugo, 1996). Here, it is often performed by people of the lowest social class, generally under unsafe and unsanitary conditions, and within the disposal site itself. In addition, in these countries recycling is often practised by housewives and other citizens who classify and store recyclable products at home to sell them to refuse intermediaries. People also separate some recyclables from other waste and offer them to garbage collectors who usually earn part of their income by selling recyclables. No public systems or programmes of recycling exist, no systematic campaigns have been developed so far.

The key studies selected (sections 2.4 and 2.6) which have been carried out in Western countries will hardly represent recycling practices in Third-World countries. We will return to this issue in the final section of this chapter.

2.3 The Theory of Reasoned Action

The Theory of Reasoned Action is concerned with both the prediction and the understanding of human behaviour. The authors (Ajzen and Fishbein, 1980) intend to demonstrate that behaviour of various kinds can be accounted for by reference to a relatively small number of concepts which are integrated into a single theoretical framework.

The Theory of Reasoned Action is based on several assumptions. First, human beings are assumed to be quite rational and to make systematic use of available information. People consider the implications of their actions before they decide to engage or not engage in a specific behaviour. Second, most actions which are socially relevant are assumed to be under volitional control and a person's intention is conceived as the immediate determinant of those actions. Except for unforeseen events, a person will usually act according to his intentions. Ajzen and Fishbein admit that 'there might be some human behaviours that cannot be explained by a theory of reasoned action'. For instance, emotional outbursts and performance of well-learned skills, such as turning the pages of a book or driving a car, are supposed to occur beyond reasoning. However, they hold that many behaviours may at first sight seem to be unplanned, but will on closer examination appear to be quite intentional.

Figure 2.1 summarises the Theory of Reasoned Action and traces the causes of behaviour back to the person's behavioural and normative beliefs. Each successive step in this sequence from behaviour to beliefs provides a more comprehensive account of the causes underlying the behaviour.

Step 1 A first step towards predicting and understanding a person's behaviour is to identify and measure the *behaviour of interest*. The researcher can decide on a single action criterion, a behavioural category criterion (i.e. an index based on a set of single actions), or a multiple-choice criterion (which usually involves a set of mutually exclusive and exhaustive single action alternatives).

Step 2 The identification and measurement of a person's *intention* to perform or not perform a behaviour. Because most behaviours of social relevance are assumed to be under volitional control, they therefore can be predicted on the basis of specified intentions. Obviously, to predict a behaviour from an intention, the level of specification of the intention should correspond to the level of specification of the behaviour. Important specifications of people's behaviour refer to action, target of action, context and time. The authors refer to a number of studies on topics which show strong correlation between intention and behaviour. The topics concern diverse issues such as 'co-operation in a prisoner's dilemma game', 'having an abortion', 'using birth control pills', 'breast- versus bottle-feeding', 'smoking marijuana', 'attending church during the Easter holiday', and 'voting choice in presidential election'. Correlation between intentions and behaviour appeared to vary between .72 and .96, and were all significant (p<0.05).

Step 3 The theory intends not only to predict behaviour but also to understand it. Therefore, the next step requires the identification of the determinants of the intentions. In this step a person's intention is considered a function of two basic determinants; one is personal in nature and the other reflects social influence. The personal determinant is the *attitude* towards the behaviour, implying the person's positive or negative evaluation of performing his or her eventual behaviour. The most crucial aspect of the attitude is 'evaluation' and the authors therefore suggest that attitudes be directly measured by a procedure which locates respondents on a bipolar evaluative scale (for instance 'favourable/unfavourable'). Again, the attitude should correspond to both the behaviour and the intention regarding action, target, context and time characteristics.

The second determinant of intention is the *subjective norm*. This concept is specified to refer to the person's perception that important others desire the performance or non-performance of a specific behaviour. This perception may or may not reflect what the important others actually think the person should do. As with other determinants, the 'subjective norm' has to correspond also to behaviour and intention as to action, target, context and time. It might be measured in terms of: 'Most people who are important to me think I should/I should not.....'. In short, individuals will intend to perform a behaviour when they evaluate it positively and when they believe that important others think they should perform it. However, the relative importance of the attitude and the subjective norm may vary in accordance with the intention under investigation and may vary from one person to another. For some intentions attitudinal factors may be more important than normative factors, while for others normative considerations may prevail. Therefore the *relative importance* of these two determinants should be determined in order to enhance the explanatory value of the theory.

With respect to a variety of different intentions, consideration of attitudes and subjective norms permitted highly accurate prediction, with correlation ranging from 0.73 to 0.89. In all cases both attitudes and subjective norms made significant contributions to the prediction of intentions. However, in eight of the ten cases, attitudes contributed more than subjective norms (Ajzen, 1988).

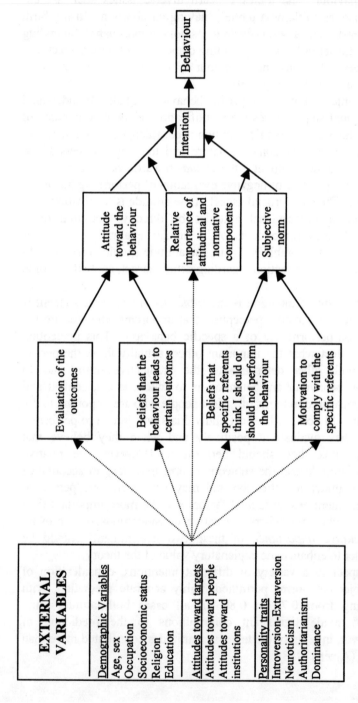

Figure 2.1 The Theory of Reasoned Action; indirect effects of external variables on behaviour

┈┈► Possible explanations for observed relations between external variables and behaviour

──► Stable theoretical relations linking beliefs to behaviour

UNDERSTANDING ATTITUDES AND PREDICTING SOCIAL BEHAVIOUR BY Ajzen/Fishbein, ©1980.
Reprinted by permission of Prentice-Hall, Inc., Upper Saddle River, NJ., p.84.

Step 4 In order to further understand people's intentions, an explanation is required why people hold certain attitudes and subjective norms. The way the Theory of Reasoned Action answers this question is crucial.

Attitudes are considered a function of beliefs. A person who believes that performing a given behaviour will lead to mostly positive outcomes will hold a favourable attitude toward it, while a person who believes that performing the behaviour will lead to mostly negative outcomes will hold a negative attitude toward the given behaviour. The beliefs that underlie a person's attitude toward this behaviour are termed *behavioural beliefs*. Under most circumstances a person can - supposedly - attend to only a relatively small number of beliefs, his so-called 'salient beliefs'. These 'salient beliefs' are assumed to determine his or her attitude. Therefore, an initial step requires an assessment of the 'salient beliefs'. Once this has been accomplished, the next question concerns how the different salient beliefs combine in determining the attitude toward performing the behaviour. To assess a first aspect of a 'behavioural belief', i.e. the *strength of a person's beliefs* (i.e. the 'subjective probability'), a person may be asked to indicate the likelihood that performing the behaviour will result in a given outcome. In order to assess the person's *evaluation of each outcome*, implying his or her feelings, (s)he could be asked to evaluate each outcome on - for instance - a seven-point 'good-bad' scale. According to the theory, a person's attitude toward a behaviour can be indirectly measured and predicted by multiplying the strength of each of the behavioural beliefs with his evaluation of each outcome and then summing the products for the total set of beliefs. The following example concerns a (fictitious) person's beliefs about smoking cigarettes:

Table 2.1 A person's behavioural beliefs about smoking cigarettes

Smoking cigarettes	Belief Strength	Outcome Evaluations	Product
Causes cancer	+1	-3	-3
Steadies	+3	+2	+6
Enables me to concentrate	+2	+2	+4
Gives me bad feelings	+1	-1	-1
Socializes	+2	+3	+6
Total			+12

This person's belief strength concerning the consequences of smoking varies from +3 to +1. Her outcome evaluations range from +3 to -3. Product outcomes vary more between +6 and -3, but result in a positive score of +12 which indicates a strongly positive attitude.[1]

'Subjective norms' are also considered a function of beliefs, namely the person's beliefs that specific individuals or groups think he should or should not perform the behaviour. These beliefs which underlie a person's subjective norms are termed *normative beliefs*. If important Others - in the subject's view - think (s)he should (not) perform the behaviour, the subject will feel pressure to (not) do so. As to 'normative beliefs', the authors distinguish between the degree to which *specific referents* (parents, friends, church etc.) would approve or disapprove of the respondents' performing the behaviour and his or her *motivation to comply* with them. A person's 'subjective norm' can then be predicted from the index which results first from multiplying his believed degree of approval or disapproval by each referent by his corresponding motivation to comply, and next from summing the products. By taking into account the motivation to comply, the important referents are given proportionally more weight in predicting the 'subjective norm'.

Table 2.2 illustrates the procedure concerning the way in which a (fictitious) person's subjective norm might be measured about smoking cigarettes.

Table 2.2 A person's normative beliefs about smoking cigarettes

Referents	Normative Belief	Motivation to Comply	Product
My wife	+1	+3	+3
My mother	-3	+1	-3
My brother	+2	+1	+2
My doctor	-3	+2	-6
Science	-3	0	0
Total			-4

In this case, the person's subjective norm about smoking cigarettes might be considered rather negative. The influence of his wife's attitude is moderately preponderant and the influence of science is irrelevant.[2]

The model should be considered stepwise. Beliefs influence attitudes and subjective norms. Attitudes and subjective norms influence intentions. Intentions influence behaviour. That behaviour is ultimately determined by beliefs does not imply a direct link between beliefs and behaviour. The

Theory of Reasoned Action consists essentially of a series of hypotheses which link beliefs to behaviour and each hypothesis requires empirical verification.

The theory does not refer to factors other than attitudes and subjective norms which often are inserted in order to explain human behaviour. Among these factors are personality characteristics (e.g. altruism, authoritarianism, introversion-extraversion, need for achievement), demographic variables (e.g. sex, age, social class and race) and a variety of person-bounded characteristics (e.g. social role, status, socialisation, intelligence, and kinship patterns). These factors are considered potentially important, but they do not constitute an integral part of the theory. They are considered *external variables*. External factors may influence the behavioural and normative beliefs, a subject's evaluation of the implied consequences, or his or her degree of compliance to important others.

However, it is crucial that - as mentioned earlier - there is no necessary relation between any given external variable and behaviour. An external variable will have an effect on behaviour only to the extent that it influences the factors which comprise the core of the model. According to the theory, the effects of external variables are mediated by beliefs and - therefore - taking external variables into account is not expected to improve prediction of attitudes and subjective norms.

2.4 Key Study: The Theory of Reasoned Action and Recycling Behaviour within Households in The Netherlands

2.4.1 Introduction

For exemplifying the application of the Theory of Reasoned Action we selected a study conducted by Kok and Siero (1985). This study instantiates an early, but well performed application of the Theory of Reasoned Action to recycling behaviour - more particularly tin recycling - within households. In addition, the study incorporates some other independent variables which prefigure to the extension of the Theory of Reasoned Action to the Theory of Planned Behaviour.

Inhabitants of the Dutch municipality of Z. (61.500 inhabitants) had the opportunity to participate in a tin-recycling programme. They were asked to separate tins from their household garbage and to deposit the tins in a container near the centre of the city. Until then, just 10% of the population of Z. had appeared to participate in the programme.

2.4.2 Key Concepts and Research Questions

The main question in the study of Kok and Siero was formulated as follows: 'What are the facilitating or inhibiting factors with respect to participation in the tin-recycling programme?' (p.158). They derived the independent variables from three theoretical points of view: (a) attitude change through communication, (b) the relationship between belief, attitude, intention and behaviour, and (c) acceptance of responsibility.

For reason of shortness and clarity, we will focus on (b), though the authors propose for parts (a) and (c) several concepts - e.g. attention, comprehension, acceptance of responsibility - which later emerge in many other publications on recycling behaviour.

Key concepts were operationalised in the following way: As to *behaviour*, respondents were asked if they had participated in the recycling programme, i.e. had selected tins from their own household garbage and brought them to the container, and how many times (indicating 'maintenance of behaviour'). For assessing *behavioural intention*, respondents were asked if they intended to participate in the programme in the future. In accordance with Ajzen and Fishbein's recommendations, *attitude* was both directly and indirectly measured. Respondents' attitudes were directly measured by their judgements on participation in the tin-recycling programme by means of three five-point scales:

- good - bad
- desirable - undesirable
- acceptable - unacceptable

In addition, attitudes of respondents were indirectly measured by their *evaluation* of twelve possible consequences of participation in the programme, using a 7-point 'good-bad' scale, ranging from -3 to +3. Next, the respondents indicated on a 6-point scale their *behavioural beliefs*: the degree to which they believed selected consequences of recycling behaviour (Table 2.3) to happen ('very likely' to 'very unlikely').

In the same way, people's *subjective norm* was also directly and indirectly measured. Respondents were asked to indicate on a 5-point scale ('probable - improbable') if other people whose opinion they valued wanted them to participate. Next, subjective *normative beliefs* regarding eight reference persons and institutions were measured on a 6-point scale ('probable- improbable'), and their *motivation to comply* was measured on a 6-point scale ranging from much to little compliance. Indexes were constructed according to Ajzen and Fishbein's prescriptions.

Table 2.3 Potential consequences of recycling behaviour

1	is pro-ecology
2	reduces the extent of refuse-dumps
3	reduces wasting of raw materials
4	reduces the number of refuse-bags
5	reduces exhaustion of raw materials
6	favours the children's future
7	reduces the wasting of energy
8	is a drop in the ocean (ineffective)
9	always needs some kind of subsidy
10	gives trouble at home
11	costs time and effort
12	gives trouble at the container

The authors asked their respondents also to assess the influence of seven potential bottle-necks in participating in the programme.

Table 2.4 Potential bottle-necks in participation

1	must keep it in mind all the time
2	sharp brims
3	cleaning the tins
4	occupying space at home
5	distance to the container
6	bring to the container
7	spending time

Interestingly, in addition to questions after age, education, and income, respondents were also asked how they spent their time during the week (housekeeping, work, and leisure).

2.4.3 Data Collection and Analysis

First, questionnaires were mailed to 1508 female inhabitants of the Dutch municipality of Z., who were aged between 20 and 65, comprising a 10 percent sample of the total female population of that age in Z. A majority (56%) returned a filled-in questionnaire. This first questionnaire broached roughly six main issues: awareness of the programme, comprehension of the programme's purpose, attitude toward participation, intention to participate, (participation) behaviour, and behaviour maintenance. On the basis of the answers given, the respondents were divided into three groups: (a) not aware of the existence of the programme; (b) aware, but not participating; and (c) participating. In a second round 715 respondents were willing to answer the questions of a second questionnaire. All in all, 39% of the original sample filled in both questionnaires. The second questionnaire aimed at obtaining more detailed information about the stages just mentioned. Because participants were strongly over-represented in the sample, results had to be interpreted cautiously. Using the direct attitude scores, two subgroups were selected from the whole sample: a 'most positive group' (33%) consisting of the respondents with the highest scores, and a 'least positive group' (also 33%) having the lowest scores. An analysis of variance resulted in a large number of significant differences.

2.4.4 Findings

The largest differences between both groups emerged regarding the assumed positive consequences of programme participation, being the first seven behavioural beliefs mentioned in table 2.3. The 'positives' believed significantly more strongly in these consequences and attributed higher value to most of them. As to the negative consequences, the 'positives' evaluated one consequence ('gives trouble at home') significantly less negatively, while they less strongly believed in other negative consequences ('costs time and effort'; 'gives trouble at the container'). Evidently, there is reason to believe that behavioural beliefs do matter. As to attitude, directly measured attitude and indirectly measured attitude - rather surprisingly - appeared to be significantly but rather weakly correlated, while direct measures of attitude and social norms appeared to be better predictors of intention than both corresponding indirect measures.

Further, the family household - being the immediate social context of the subject - appeared to be relatively important regarding the subjective norm: the respondent's partner and her children were the most important reference persons, while friends were less important and remaining reference persons and institutions appeared to be rather unimportant. Quite in accordance with Ajzen and Fishbein's theory, socio-demographic variables - except age - were indeed unrelated to behavioural intention and even the effect of age disappeared when disconnected from attitude and subjective norm.

But - most interestingly - difficulties, mentioned in table 2.4, appeared to be connected with recycling behaviour and - in contrast to the

Theory of Reasoned Action - their effect remained significant even when attitude and social norm were factored out. In addition, respondents who participated in the programme appeared to have more time available for housekeeping and more leisure time compared to non-participants. The authors conclude that practical difficulties do inhibit participation in the tin-recycling programme, partly independent of attitude and subjective norm. Evidently, the Theory of Reasoned Action as such seemed to fall short.

2.5 The Theory of Planned Behaviour

The conceptual framework of Ajzen's Theory of Planned Behaviour (1988) is an extension of the Theory of Reasoned Action. In contrast to the Theory of Reasoned Action, the Theory of Planned Behaviour explicitly recognises the possibility that many behaviours may not be under complete control. Control over behaviour can best be viewed as a continuum. At one extreme are behaviours that encounter few if any problems of control, such as voting choice: once the voter has entered the voting booth, selection among the candidates can be done at will. At the other extreme are events, such as sneezing or lowering one's blood pressure, over which one has very little or no control. Most behaviours fall somewhere in between these two extremes. The degree of success of their performance will depend not only on a subject's intention, but also on such partly non-motivational factors as availability of opportunities and resources. As to these 'control factors', Ajzen (1988) distinguishes between internal factors (e.g. information, skills and abilities; emotions and compulsions), and external factors (e.g. opportunity; dependence on others). Collectively, these factors represent the actual behavioural control or lack of control people have over their behaviour. However, the Theory of Planned Behaviour does not consider the actual control people have, but the degree of *perceived behaviour control.*

The distinction between people's actual control and their perceived control is crucial. The Theory of Planned Behaviour considers the possible effects of perceived behavioural control on actual behaviour, rather than dealing directly with the amount of actual control a person has in a given situation. Because the Theory assumes behaviour to be a function of salient beliefs, perceptions of behavioural control are considered to be grounded on *control beliefs*. The more resources and opportunities a person thinks he possesses, the fewer the obstacles he expects, the greater should be his perceived control of behaviour. These beliefs may be based on personal experience in the past or be influenced by second-hand information, by observing the experiences of important others, or by other factors that contain relevant information. But if the individual has relatively little information about the situation, if behavioural requirements or available resources have changed, or if new and unfamiliar elements have entered into the situation, a measure of perceived behavioural control may add little to accuracy of prediction (Ajzen, 1987). In short, the model postulates three conceptual determinants of intentions. The first is the attitude toward the behaviour. The second predictor is the subjective norm. The third and novel antecedent of intention is the degree of perceived behavioural control. This factor refers to the perceived ease or difficulty of performing the behaviour (Ajzen, 1988).

Figure 2.2 expresses two important features of the Theory of Planned Behaviour. The first assumption implies that perceived behavioural control has implications for intentions. People who believe that they have neither the resources nor the opportunities to perform a certain behaviour are unlikely to form strong behavioural intentions to engage in it, even if they have a positive attitude toward, or a positive subjective norm regarding, the behaviour. In figure 2.2 this assumption is represented by the arrow linking perceived behavioural control to intention.

The second feature is the possibility of a direct link between perceived behavioural control and behaviour. The performance of a behaviour depends not only on motivational intention, but also on adequate control over the behaviour in question. Perceived behavioural control can, therefore, help predict goal attainment independent of behavioural intentions, as far as it reflects actual control with some degree of accuracy. In that case, it may, according to Ajzen, be considered a partial substitute for a measure of actual control (1988).

The importance of perceived control over a behavioural goal has been demonstrated in several studies on diverging issues, such as the prediction of weight loss intentions and actual weight reduction (Schifter and Ajzen, 1985), on scholastic performance (Ajzen and Madden, 1986), on leisure activities, performance of cognitive tasks and voting behaviour (Ajzen, 1991).

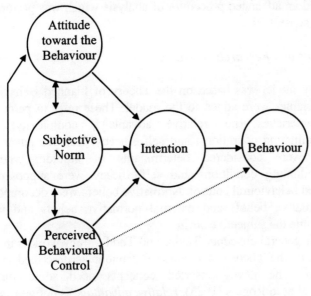

Figure 2.2 Theory of Planned Behaviour
Source: I. Ajzen, 1988, p. 133

2.6 Key Study: The Theory of Planned Behaviour and Recycling Intentions within Households in the U.S.A.

2.6.1 Introduction

Taylor and Todd (1995) intended to develop and test an integrative model in order to explain individual intentions to engage in waste management behaviour, more in particular recycling and composting behaviour. For several reasons, their study fits nicely with this chapter.

First, it is primarily based on the Theory of Planned Behaviour. However, some key variables - in the broader literature known to be determinants of attitude, subjective norm, perceived behavioural control, and behavioural intention - were added to the model. In consequence, the model developed may be considered an important step forward in the development of the Planned Behaviour Theory, while some of the new concepts - in particular 'compatibility' and 'facilitating conditions' seem to be quite significant in relation to the functioning of households. Next, the authors follow the Theory of Planned Behaviour in a highly consistent way with respect to the selection of variables and the wording of the questionnaire. In addition, they used an advanced procedure of analysis which was performed for both activities separately.

2.6.2 Key Concepts and Research Questions

Taylor and Todd's model was based on the Theory of Planned Behaviour, and some key variables were added to the model. These refer to perceived innovation characteristics (i.e. relative advantage, complexity, and compatibility), facilitating conditions, and self-efficacy. Relative advantage and complexity were considered determinants of attitude, whereas compatibility, facilitating conditions and self-efficacy were supposed to influence perceived behavioural control. Normative beliefs were decomposed into internal normative beliefs and external normative beliefs and were assumed to determine the subjective norm.

As to their general concepts, Taylor and Todd's framework is in line with the concepts of the Theory of Planned Behaviour as described in the preceding section. The newly inserted concepts need some further elucidation. According to Rogers (1983), *relative advantage* is defined as the degree to which an innovation provides benefits that supersede those of its precursor, and may include economic benefits, image enhancement, convenience and satisfaction. *Complexity* represents the degree to which an innovation is perceived to be difficult to understand and use. According to Taylor and Todd, more favourable attitudes toward recycling and composting will result when perceived relative advantages are high and perceived complexity is low. Taylor and Todd conceived of *facilitating conditions* as access to resources necessary to perform the behaviour. Key facilitators in their study include access to recycling programmes and access to a composter. The more readily accessible these resources are, the stronger the Perceived Behaviour Control and the subsequent intention to recycle and compost.

Amongst other things, facilitating conditions comprise perceived *compatibility*, which is defined as the degree to which the innovation fits with the potential adopter's values, lifestyle, previous experience, and current needs. According to Taylor and Todd, the more compatible recycling and composting are with an individual's values and daily routine, the stronger the perceived behavioural control and the intention to recycle and compost will be. The same hypothesis applies to accessibility of resources. Finally, *self-efficacy*, generally defined as the perceived ability to carry out a behaviour, refers here to the perceived effectiveness of control variables in waste management. While complexity focuses on attributes of behaviour, efficacy is a characteristic of the subject.

2.6.3 Data and Analysis

The survey was conducted with individuals from a sample of households in a city with 120,000 inhabitants. Questionnaires were delivered to and picked up from households in midsummer 1993. Only one individual within each household (the authors do not mention which one) completed the questionnaire. Respondents were given the opportunity to win a variety of prizes ranging in value from $25 to $300. The response rate was approximately 20%, comprising 761 respondents. At the time of the interview, the local recycling programme had been in effect for 4 years and the composting programme had been in effect for 1 year. In the community the recycling programme was started with the delivery of a free recycling 'blue box' to each household. Composters had to be purchased and picked up, but the price was subsidised. Thus more effort was required to begin composting. The final sample consisted of 700 individuals.

A series of steps resulted in the measuring scales for each of the constructs in the model. Items to measure behavioural intention, attitude, subjective norm and perceived behavioural control were formulated according to Ajzen and Fishbein's suggestions (section 2.3). Salient beliefs about recycling and composting were elicited from a convenience sample, and raters were asked to sort the questionnaire items into categories which represented the constructs of relative advantage, complexity, normative beliefs, compatibility, facilitating conditions, and self-efficacy. Several pilot tests were conducted to assess the validity of the scales. In the analysis all belief items were combined with the evaluative component following the procedure suggested in the Theory of Planned Behaviour for each of the decomposed belief constructs.[3]

2.6.4 Findings and Discussion

Taylor and Todd summarise their findings on recycling in figure 2.3.[4] All coefficients in the model appeared to be significant. Both attitude and perceived behavioural control significantly influence behavioural intention. But strangely, subjective norm is inversely related to behavioural intention, suggesting that the higher the pressure from the reference groups, the lower the subject's intention to recycle. In its turn, attitude appears to be influenced particularly by 'relative advantage', while 'complexity' does not seem to

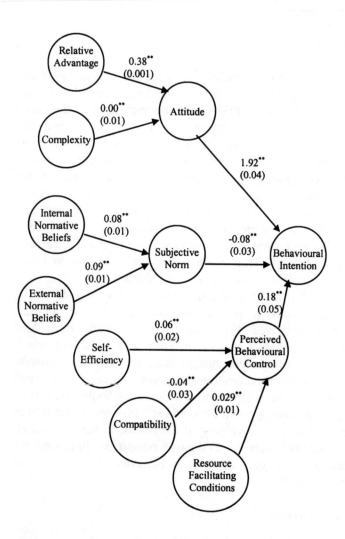

Figure 2.3 Path coefficients for recycling
Note: Standard errors in parentheses.
          *p < .01; ** p < .001.
Source: Taylor, S. and Todd, P. 1995, p.617

matter. 'Internal normative beliefs' and 'external normative beliefs' seem to exert equal influence on the subjective norm in the expected direction. Finally, perceived behavioural control appears to be strongly driven by 'resource facilitating conditions'. 'Self-efficacy' turns out as much less important and 'compatibility' appears to be even slightly negatively related to perceived behavioural control.

Discussion As far as intentions are concerned, Taylor and Todd's integrated management model seems to have a rather high predictive power for the dependent constructs, and the results of the analysis largely support the superiority of the Theory of Planned Behaviour to the Theory of Reasoned Action. In addition, the new constructs the authors inserted appeared to enhance the explanatory value of their model.

However, the study has certain limitations as well. First, and most obvious, it focuses on the explanation of intentions of waste management behaviour, while peoples' behaviour remains unconsidered. Indeed, some other studies confirm a (direct) relationship between recycling intention and behaviour (Jones, 1990; Goldenhar and Connell, 1993; Hamid and Cheng, 1995). Nevertheless, the way intention and behaviour are intertwined is still questioned. are better predictors of behaviour than unstable ones.
For instance, according to Macey and Brown's findings (1983) an important aspect of intentions is their degree of stability: stable intentions.

Second and more generally, recycling behaviour should not be conceived as a static and isolated phenomenon. Schultz et al. (1995) caution against easily generalising research results from studies conducted ten or more years ago. Interest in recycling programmes has increased and the character of the programmes has changed. Early recycling programmes were predominantly voluntary and restricted to the collection of a few specific materials. Modern curbside recycling programmes imply the collection of multiple materials. The proliferation of recycling programmes brought both monetary and social incentives, along with a reduction of effort required to recycle. More people are recycling today and, doing this for a variety of reasons, the relationship between environmental concern and recycling may have diminished or even disappeared. Nevertheless, the key studies we offered imply considerable improvements of the original models and put us on the track of a number of unanswered questions which require new directions for research.

2.7 Conclusions and New Directions for Research

2.7.1 Conclusions

In line with most research on sustainable behaviour, and quite in accordance with both the Theory of Reasoned Action and the Theory of Planned Behaviour, Taylor and Todd's research uses individuals as units of analysis. From a family household's perspective, such an approach is quite inadequate. Kok and Siero inserted at least some aspects of the family household's interior into their model - especially allocation of time - but their approach does not substantially touch the household as a group nor specific group practices.

One further aspect of the household's situation pertains to the material conditions of resources households are dependent on. Ajzen's model as well as the integrated model of Taylor and Todd imply this aspect, but just as far as conditions are *perceived* by their subjects. Both issues call for new directions. We derive further suggestions for 'new directions' partly from critics of both theories, partly from research using different views on sustainable behaviour in a broader sense.

Some factors will be excluded, because - despite their relevance - they are beyond the scope of this book. Such factors refer for instance to 'awareness' of the implementation of a recycling programme (e.g. Lansana, 1992), 'knowledge about' and 'competencies' in recycling practices, or 'specific skills' to perform various tasks (Wilhelm and Keith, 1987; Corral-Verdugo, 1996). We will just indirectly broach the abundant and often contradictory literature on the role of personal values, environmental concern, and feelings of responsibility regarding sustainable behaviour and recycling behaviour in particular (e.g. Vining and Ebreo, 1990; Granzin and Olsen, 1991; Oskamp et al., 1991; Schultz et al., 1995; Stern et al., 1995a; Bagozzi and Dabholkar, 1994).

2.7.2 New Directions for Research

This section offers five suggestions for further research. The first two refer immediately to the household as a context of recycling behaviour. The next concerns the influence of previous behaviour, being an apparently important but rather neglected determinant of recycling behaviour. The role of the life-course is intriguing in a somewhat surprising way and is the subject of a fourth suggestion. Finally, we discuss the question: recycling, a behavioural or a structural matter? The answer may counterbalance the one-sidedness of social psychological approaches.

1 The household situation Ajzen (1988) mentions 'situational factors' as one of the moderators between general attitudes and specific behaviours, which means that attitudes are assumed to interact with situational variables in their effects on behaviours. Such situational characteristics may serve to activate implicit dispositional tendencies. However, according to Ajzen (1988) relatively few studies seem to have submitted this hypothesis to a direct test. Until now, research has touched few issues which may be considered aspects of the household situation, beyond merely adopting demographic household or housing characteristics into the research model.

A first aspect concerns the relative salience of household members as social references regarding recycling behaviour. We already mentioned the findings of Kok and Siero (1985) on the importance of the influence of partner and children rather than the influence of friends, other reference persons and institutions. These findings are supported by research results of Macey and Brown (1983) who for that reason recommend directing promotional strategies to the household as a unit as well as to the individual person. A second aspect pertains to the division of tasks within the household. Which household member manages garbage disposal is a relevant matter. Several studies found no significant differences between men and women (Vining and Ebreo, 1990; Hopper and Nielsen, 1991; Oskamp et al., 1991; Gamba and Oskamp, 1994). However, other studies show differences between the two sexes regarding environmental issues (e.g. Widegren, 1998). For instance, the relationship between norms and intent to recycle appeared to be stronger for females than for males, and past experience with recycling appeared to be directly related to behaviour for males only (Goldenhar and Connell, 1993). Therefore, who performs recycling activities in the household and who co-ordinates and takes responsibility (if anyone), are important but as yet unanswered questions.

Remarkably few studies focus on the way parents and children interact and communicate about matters of sustainability, and on the way households operate as sources of information (e.g. Granzin and Olsen, 1991; Sutherland and Ham, 1992). The importance of this issue is indicated by Kok and Siero's finding (1985) that households having a child at a school where attention has been given to the recycling programme are more aware of a current recycling programme than other households.

Other aspects of a household's situation may also influence its recycling activities: availability of time and synchronising of circuits.

Respondents who participate have more time available for housekeeping and more leisure time than others, even when attitude and social norm are factored out (Kok and Siero, 1985). As to synchronising circuits, the collectors' recycling circuit may or may not be synchronised with the households' recycling circuit. Both issues fit nicely with the concept of *compatibility* as used by Taylor and Todd.

Important questions for further research concern issues just mentioned: the relationship between task division within households and sustainable behaviour (including taking initiative, co-ordinating and controlling recycling and energy saving), patterns of interaction and communication about matters of sustainability, and the meshing of (public or non-public) collecting systems with households' time-scales.

2 Facilitating conditions Soon after the publication of the Theory of Reasoned Action in 1980, Sarver jr. (1983) heavily criticised the theory because it 'could not be seriously regarded as a tool for the prediction and understanding of human behaviour' (p.156). In his view, Ajzen and Fishbein failed to consider the implications of what he called the 'context of opportunity'. This means a situation which provides an opportunity for a person to act in a manner consistent with his beliefs about, attitude toward, 'subjective norm' and intention with respect to, a specific behaviour. We suppose that the insertion of perceived control beliefs into the Theory of Planned Behaviour was Ajzen's answer to Sarver's important objection. But the 'context of opportunity' or - as we will call them - the facilitating conditions imply not only the perceived opportunities or conditions, but also those of which the subjects are hardly or not at all aware (and which they therefore do not mention in interviews).[5]

A household's *facilitating conditions* imply many different components which are relevant to its sustainable practices. For instance, housing characteristics do matter. Recyclers are more likely to live in a single-family house compared to non-recyclers. Houses seem to offer more storage space compared to apartments, condos and mobile homes (Neuman, 1986; Oskamp et al., 1991; Derksen and Gartrell, 1993). However, the significance of having more space may depend on the economic context. In Mexico having storage space appeared to produce a negative influence on recycling. Extra storage space seemed a condition for increasing the consumption of space, furniture, and other belongings rather than as an opportunity for recycling (Corral-Verdugo, 1996).

Facilitating conditions (or barriers) refer also to distance, method of collection and way of sorting. Three studies in the seventies - mentioned by

Schultz et al. (1995) - have examined experimentally the effect of increased bin *accessibility* on recycling participation: the closer participants are to a collection centre the more likely they are to recycle. High-rise government buildings, inoperable elevators, and distance to the place of recycling are probably relevant to recycling practices (Lansana, 1997).

Next, the *method of collection* refers to a 'facilitating condition' or to a 'barrier'. Studies on differences between communities with a curbside collection programme and communities with a drop-off location programme, revealed that the former had a considerably higher rate of participation compared to communities with drop-off collection programmes, or no programmes at all (Folz, 1991; Derksen and Gartrell, 1993). Third, the required *effort of resorting* materials is considered a barrier. Oskamp et al. (1996) - using observational measurements of several aspects of recycling behaviour - found a commingled programme (all recyclables mixed together in a single collection bin) achieving a remarkably higher average weekly participation rate, a much larger volume of recyclables and a significantly higher level of consistency in households' participation across a two-year period, compared to another, separation-based programme in an adjacent city.

The findings of Derksen and Gartrell (1993) show the powerful effect of facilitating conditions. Being in a recycling programme, i.e. having access to 'blue boxes' appeared to have a strong and independent effect on recycling behaviour, while pro-environmental attitudes had no direct effect on recycling behaviour, but simply enhanced the effect of having access to the recycling programme facilities. Other findings demonstrate that having a bin not only increases recycling behaviour but even enhances the awareness of the social and environmental consequences of recycling (Guagagno, et al., 1995).

Many studies emphasise the importance of changing the facilitating conditions for households and - in consequence - of transforming the 'high-cost' into 'low-cost' behaviour. Such behaviours vary from use of public transportation facilities (Diekmann and Preisendörfer, 1992), to household recycling behaviours (Guagagno et al., 1995).

Further research - using interviews as well as observations - should focus on the way housing characteristics and other material conditions, and ways of collecting and sorting waste, facilitate or hinder sustainable behaviour patterns within households. Facilitating conditions will appear to contribute considerably to the critical transformation of attitudes and intentions into behaviour.

3 The role of previous behaviour Bentler and Speckart (1979) proposed and tested an extension of the Fishbein and Ajzen model, regarding three related domains of attitudinal relevance, i.e. alcohol, marihuana, and hard drug use. They supposed previous behaviour to affect both current intentions and future behaviour and they incorporated it into the Theory of Reasoned Action model. Analysis of results supported their hypothesis that incorporation of previous behaviour into the model did indeed more successfully reproduce the data. They showed that a model which includes a direct path from prior behaviour to later behaviour provided a significantly better fit to the data than did a model representing the Theory of Reasoned Action in which the effect of past on later behaviour was assumed to be mediated by intention. A significant portion of behavioural variability appeared predictable from attitude and previous behaviour with the effects of intentions partialled out. Research on class attendance or absence (Frederick and Dossett, 1983) also showed that previous behaviour had direct effects on actual behaviour and intention, unmediated by attitude and subjective norms. To Ajzen the residual effect seemed small enough to be attributable to method variance shared by the measures of prior and later behaviour. However, one case, i.e. searching for a job, showed - even in Ajzen's view - that the introduction of past behaviour produced an improvement in explained behavioural variance that was probably too large to be attributable to method variance.

Does previous behaviour influence actual behaviour in an independent way as far as recycling and - more generally - sustainable behaviour is concerned? Findings from research are somewhat ambiguous. Maccy and Brown (1983) found that with respect to energy conservation in households intention did not add significant explanatory power above and beyond that of past experience. From their research findings among university students Goldenhar and Connell (1993) found out that past experience with recycling added directly and indirectly (via intentions) explanatory power to the original Theory of Reasoned Action and the Theory of Planned Behaviour. Hamid and Cheng (1995) used past behaviour as a predictive variable and found it to contribute significantly to the prediction of behavioural intention after the other variables had been controlled. However, the relationship between past and current behaviour was rather moderate and appeared to be quite ambiguous as to its effects. The authors suggest that intentions are likely to be formed through the occurrence of past behaviour, and that past behaviour predicts best what people intend to do (ibidem, also Bagozzi and Dabholkar, 1994).

The effect of previous behaviour may vary according to the kind of behaviour to be predicted. Past experience may be the best predictor of behaviours which are repeated at a high frequency and which through direct previous experience are familiar to the subject. The more direct the previous experience, the more likely that the subject is to engage in the behaviour again (Macey and Brown, 1983; Neuman, 1986). Recent findings on curbside textile recycling support this supposition (Daneshvary, 1998). In consequence, efforts should be made to make these measures part of an individual's routine.

Perhaps because of operating beyond rational choice, the influence of previous behaviour or habit has been rather neglected. As to sustainable behaviour, we assume it to be a powerful predictor which is tightly interwoven with family households' history, and which therefore should be recommended for advanced research in the field of family households.

4 People's life-history Among the many independent variables used in research models on environmental behaviour, people's age seems to be omnipresent and - compared to many other socio-demographic characteristics - rather relevant (e.g. Lansana, 1997; Widegren, 1998). However, the *way in which* age is related to environmental concern or behaviour most often remains in the dark, but is nicely illustrated by a quite modest but fascinating study by Hallin (1995).

Hallin performed a small-scale, qualitative study in a small town in the U.S.A., involving 10 households with high environmental activity and 10 households with low environmental activity. His analysis resulted in five groups of conserving respondents: 'the Depression generation', 'the children of the Depression generation', 'the Vietnam generation', 'the role model representatives', and 'the gradual evolvers'. The 'Depression generation' consisted of people who grew up during the Great Depression of the 1930s. They emphasised the necessity to pay cash, to not be in debt, to save and to preserve. Distinctly, their behaviour was to a large extent determined by their experiences during the 1930s, and it was only vaguely motivated by concern over environmental problems. Many of them had experienced poverty and their values were shaped by their history. While age appeared to be negatively correlated with environmental concern, the elderly people's behaviour could, quite understandably, appear to be conserving, we might say not on purpose, but consequentially. The second group of conservers were those who had inherited their parents' value systems. They had been raised to be conservative. Some of them, like their parents, did not relate their conserving behaviour to environmental problems. Their behaviour rather seemed to have originated from thrift. A third group also consisted of younger conservers, but they had more particularly changed their value system during adolescence or young adulthood occurring at the time of the Vietnam war. Their shift in consciousness was determined by a crisis in the value system of society, when many people tried to find an alternative to the prevailing system. Like 'the Depression generation', 'the Vietnam generation' kept its new value system through time. A fourth group consisted of younger conservers who changed their behaviour as a result of becoming role models (e.g. teachers) and had to change their behaviour because of occupational status. It was the role of teacher or of environmental specialist that had triggered their changed behaviour. The last group also comprised younger conservers. Their change was not triggered by world-wide events or by specific experiences; rather, their changes had evolved gradually. Their behaviour could be understood as a process in which altruistic social norms were gradually internalised and translated into individual behaviour.

Hallin's study highlights the importance of relating environmental concern and environmental behaviour to peoples' personal history and to the historical context in which their personal history is embedded. As with previous behaviour, people's life history is strongly connected with the history of the household (s)he is a member of, and - in consequence - with the family household's particular culture.

Until now, history had a rather minor role in research on environmental problems and certainly implies a 'new direction' for research in the field. Appropriate research methodology has largely still to be developed. Chapter 7 (The Longitudinal Approach) offers several conceptual frameworks which will be helpful.

5 Recycling: an individual or a structural problem? The larger social context is inevitably related to behavioural practices within households, but is clearly missing in the Theory of Reasoned Action and in the Theory of Planned Behaviour. It would clearly go well beyond the limits of this section to elaborate more or less completely the influence of the larger social context. Suffice it to offer some instances which predominantly serve to bring out the importance of a structural view.

First, instead of using bare demographics as explaining factors, it is important to study environmental concern and behaviour within the context of people's everyday life and of the problems they have to cope with day by day. The issue can be nicely elucidated using the role of household income. In most research models income level is inserted as an individual factor. However, a low level of income may be part of a more structural state of deprivation. For instance, Howenstine (1993) found indifference towards recycling ('I don't care') particularly striking in Chicago's lower-income areas. In his view, drugs, crime, poverty, and unemployment make recycling appear insignificant by comparison.

Second, as we saw in sub-section 2, facilitating conditions are quite important as to stimulating recycling behaviour, and are supposed to be crucial in transforming intentions into actual behaviour. However, as will be further elaborated in chapter 6, facilitating conditions within households - comprising e.g. housing characteristics, accessibility of recycling provisions, methods of recollection - are largely determined by external agencies. Therefore, the way external agencies operate cannot be omitted when seeking a sufficient explanation of households' recycling patterns. Also Schultz et al. (1995) state that individual variables account for the percentage of variance to a rather limited degree, and they consider the incorporation of specific city recycling policies necessary.

Third and most fundamentally, Ungar (1994) argues that the attitude-behaviour model, as represented by for instance the Theory of Reasoned Action and the Theory of Planned Behaviour, misconceives the structural basis of most environmental impacts at a macro-level. He rightly states that the attitude-behaviour model is essentially atomistic and voluntaristic and that individuals only ostensibly make personal choices and exercise their sovereignty in the free market. He refers to Schnaiberg (1980) who developed the idea of 'distorted consumption', implying that consumers make constrained choices in markets where greater power is exercised by producers and government agencies. Most important is his pointing to the commitments that are implied in past decisions made by institutions beyond the level of individual households, commitments that constrain individuals or households to follow set patterns of behaviour. For instance, the building of suburbs and households' decision to live in them create strong dependencies on the automobile, as a result of distances, insufficient public transport facilities, and local life-style patterns (Owens, 1990). Another instance pertains to the field of housing policy, e.g. decisions made on dwelling size, facilities, and housing density (Van Diepen, 1998). At this level, governmental and non-governmental agencies operate through legislation and programmes, standards and regulation processes, social impact assessment, and technological and production innovations. Recent studies generally argue in favour of a macro approach that focuses on collective actions, instead of conceiving macro-social structure as an aggregate of individual attitudes and beliefs. They recommend that recycling programmes be integrated with community organisation programmes, employment programmes and renovation activities or other visible neighbourhood improvement activities (Howenstine, 1993; Ungar, 1994; Lansana, 1997).

Suggestions for advanced research refer to the three just mentioned levels: environmental concern and behaviour within people's everyday life and meaning structure; the role of external agencies as to providing appropriate facilities; and the - often unintended - environmental consequences of large-scale policies of national ministries and international enterprises. We offer a theoretical framework to tackle at least some of these issues in Chapter 6 (The Opportunity Structure Approach and the Housing Market).

Notes

1. In order to be able to compare the beliefs of different individuals or groups of individuals, the authors suggest to identify the set of beliefs that are salient in a given population: the beliefs most frequently elicited from a representative sample of the population constitute the 'modal set' of beliefs for the population in question (Ajzen and Fishbein, 1980, p.68).
2. As with the 'behavioural beliefs', a standard set of modal normative beliefs can be composed by asking a representative sample of the population under study to list the other people who function as referents regarding the specific behaviour (Ajzen, 1988, p.30).
3. Factor analyzes for both the recycling and composting data were conducted to assess construct validity of the scales. Items appeared to adequately measure the hypothesized constructs. The integrated waste management model was tested by performing a so-called structuring equation modeling procedure. In each model, overall fit, variance explained, and the significance of paths were considered.
4. For reason of brevity we omit the findings on composting behaviour; the reader may see Taylor and Todd's article in the Bibliography.
5. We reserve the term 'opportunity structure' for large-scale opportunities offered by social institutions (see Chapter 7). The term 'facilitating condition' is part of a helpful conceptual framework developed by Triandis (1979; Ross and Nisbett, 1991).

3 The Strategy Approach and Temporary Migration

3.1 Introduction

The interest in the strategies of family households clearly developed in close connection with changes in economic welfare. Interest increased in Western Europe and Third World countries during the eighties. In relation to poverty and underdevelopment, it was started in the United Kingdom in the early 1980s as a key concept for addressing questions about the impact of economic change on the functioning of households (Pahl, 1984; Morris, 1994). The increasing pressure on the poor to supplement welfare or to generate income in the absence of welfare made insight into household strategies highly relevant. This research interest has been sustained by the fiscal interest of states throughout the world in the caring capacity of family and community as a supplement to, or replacement of, state-provided welfare (Roberts, 1994).

Certainly, the development and maintenance of a strategy comprises many elements of rational choice. As such, the Strategy Approach directly connects with the Rational Choice Approach as elaborated in the foregoing chapter. But in contrast to processes of rational choice, strategies are *qualitate qua* future-oriented. Hence, strategies imply processes of rational choice and are a first exemplification of the context within which rational choices develop.

We first argue in favour of the relevance of this rather recent Strategy Approach for studying households in Western and non-Western cultures. Next, we will present an overview of the way in which several authors have circumscribed and applied a number of key concepts concerning strategy. Together they comprise the fundamentals of what may be called a 'Strategy Approach'. Third, we will turn to a specific field of household strategy, in particular migration-related strategies. The Strategy Approach is exemplified by the means of two key studies which have been performed in Southern Europe and in Southeastern Asia. These studies also indicate the degree to which the Strategy Approach can be applied to the functioning of households in cultures which strongly differ from cultures in highly industrialized societies. After having formulated several conclusions, we will round off the chapter with suggestions for 'new directions' for future research.

3.2 The Relevance of the Strategy Approach and of Temporary Migration

From a large-scale point of view, knowledge of household strategies is important because insight into the way family households adapt to larger changes in society contributes to an understanding of the variety of models of industrial development (Mingione, 1994). The consideration of social factors and relations within and between family households was previously considered typical only of studies on backward regions, exotic groups, and strictly subsistence economies. But social factors, social relations, and family strategies form part of the picture of modern societies and their varied adaptation to socio-economic change as well. Roberts (1994) further highlights the importance of the informal sector to the study of the strategies of households. The informal economy makes use of non-contractual but binding relationships, while kinship is the basis of many of these. Families often find the flexibility and accessibility in the informal economy that the formal economy does not possess. In addition, and not unimportantly, the informal economy and household strategies are essentially territorial phenomena. Both are embedded in localized sets of understandings, practices, and relationships.

Among sociologists, strategic analysis has become popular because it offers an alternative to the type of neo-positivism which directs its efforts towards discovering universal laws. Strategic analysis can be as revealing about constraints as it is about choices and about the ways in which constraints and opportunities influence individual preferences (Crow, 1989; Crow and Hardey, 1991). It is definitely not confined to the functioning and preferences of individuals, which characterize the majority of economic studies in the field, but can fruitfully be applied to group processes as well.

At last, the Strategy Approach is relevant because it stresses the autonomy of households and their indefeasible purposiveness. Prominent is the idea that households affect economic and social processes as an integral part of economic life rather than the idea that it is households that respond to the economy (Morgan, 1996). As such households are important because they are able to resist what Habermas (1981) calls the 'colonization' by both the economic and the state system. In order to be morally adequate and effective in their own terms, government policies have to respect this very autonomy. We will elaborate upon the issue further in the last chapter.

Migration by family households is an important phenomenon from a macro-social as well as from a micro-social point of view. From a macro-level view, patterns of migration are perceived as the manifestation of processes of unequal development among regions, countries, or social groups. On a global level, capital flows and migrant labour flows are in opposite directions nowadays. Companies in highly developed countries move their activities to countries which have a much lower wage level, while migrant labour enters these countries at the same time (De Swaan, 1994). On a regional level, migration from rural areas to cities is a mechanism for supplying the urban labour market with cheap and skilled workers (De Oliveira, 1991).

In many cases, migration at a micro-level is part of household strategies. It may be resorted to by members of poor and landless households, expecting better chances of survival or some improvement in their level of welfare. However, migration may take many different forms as to its destination, endurance, and their individual or familial character. For example, referring in particular to Third World countries, Gilbert and Gugler (1992) distinguish among circular migration of men, long-term migration of men separated from their families, family migration to urban areas followed by return migration to the community of origin, and permanent urban settlement. But women also appear to participate substantially in streams of migration, due to the quantity of migrating women as well as to its economic and social consequences (Palriwala, 1990; De Oliveira, 1991). At the micro-level, consequences of migration deserve attention from different points of view. On the one hand, migrants are vulnerable in the countries they migrate into. They often have no lawful title to residence, have no legal safeguards, and are exposed to all kinds of exploitation on the labour market and the housing market, while access to health provisions is limited (De Swaan, 1994). On the other hand, the households or household members who stay behind may easily be confronted with irregular payments from the members who emigrated, while the local community will be bereft from its most active labour force.

3.3 The Strategy Approach: The Conceptual Framework

3.3.1 A Strategy's Characteristics

In management sciences, strategy or strategic decisions are attributed several characteristics (Johnson and Scholes, 1989). First, strategic decisions concern the scope of an organization's activities. It implies the number and range of its areas of activity. Second, strategy entails the matching of the organization's activities to the environment in which it operates. Next, strategy has to do with the organization's activities within its own resource capability, implying the countering of environmental threats and taking advantage of the opportunities it offers. Fourth, corporate strategic decisions have major resource implications in terms of its need to obtain properties for development and access to funds with which to do this. Next, strategic decisions are likely to affect operational decisions or to set off waves of lesser decisions. Further, the strategy of an organization is affected by environmental forces and by the values and expectations of those who have power in the organization. Finally, strategic decisions affect the long-term direction of an organization. More briefly, Anderson and his co-authors (1994, p.20) define a strategy as 'the overall way in which individuals, and possibly collectivities, consciously seek to structure, in a coherent way, actions within a relatively long-term perspective'.

Application of the strategy concept to family households certainly requires several modifications of these characteristics. These modifications pertain to the idea of a family household as a unit, the idea of consciously seeking, the idea of coherence of seeking, and prescriptions for action in the long run. Each of these aspects deserve some elaboration.

First, the question arises as to the validity of *household strategy* as a concept which implies the household or family as a group that acts as if it were an individual (Scott Smith, 1987). Some critics stress the primacy of the individual. One or both parents may develop a particular strategy, for instance a financial strategy, more or less independent from his or her partner. Both men and women may develop an employment strategy independently of one another, or may adopt separate family strategies which imply arrangements with kin beyond the household to secure, for instance, child care (Leira, 1987). Obviously, individuals are much more distinctive as units of analysis compared to households. A related problem concerns the fact that the concept of a household strategy may obscure the extent to which there is internal differentiation of interests within the unit. In short, the internal dynamics of the household all remain easily out of focus: the way in which individual members' interests conflict, the way coalitions are developed and maintained, and the way in which conflicts are resolved (Moch, 1987; Folbre, 1987). The concept of household strategy requires at least that members to some degree adopt a comprehensive view of their situation, including taking account of the actions of others with whom they interact. In a most strict sense, it is assumed that in case all the members of a group adopt an identical view of their situation, then there may exist not only individual strategies but also collective strategies such as family strategies (Brenner and Laslett, 1986). However, such an identical view may be considered rather exceptional. The notion of a household strategy does not imply that household decisions can be treated as totally consensual nor that each partner makes an entirely separate decision without any reference to the other's behaviour (Jordan, 1992). If households as collectivities are seen as playing a game of 'getting by' in the economy, then household members cooperate to achieve what is in their collective interests as members of a household.

Other critics of the concept of a household strategy point to the fact that in many societies the role of households or families is insignificant compared to the role kinship or other wider social networks play. They therefore hold that it does not make sense to treat households as social actors (Cornell, 1987).

If asked, household members tend to confirm their pursuing of plans. For instance, large-scale research by Anderson and his team-mates (1994) found out that when asked for the existence of any plans for themselves or their households, a rather high proportion of respondents appeared to think ahead and actually do plan in significant areas of their lives. Nearly half (48%) of all households might be considered 'high-level planners', while very few households (around 4%) were classified as 'chronic non-planners'.[1]

Such results do not directly prove the existence of *household* strategies. Nevertheless, they provide reason to consider a household strategy as an emergent property which may parallel strategies of individual members (cf. Anderson et al., 1994). In our view, to some degree household members generally adopt a comprehensive view of their situation, take account of the actions of others with whom they interact, and share common interests and objectives in the long run. Family households may be viewed as collectivities as far as their members cooperate to achieve what is in their collective interests, be it bare survival or a reasonable level of welfare.

Consciously seeking implies an element of rational choice. Household strategies imply that its members can choose, and that their choices make a difference, despite the economic and social constraints they meet (Scott Smith, 1987; Brannen and Wilson, 1987; Crow, 1989). Evidently, choice alternatives often fall into a fairly limited range of possibilities which strongly vary among the different socio-economic classes. As to households, in most capitalistic countries the most notable distinction derives from the labour and financial resources between the two-earner/no-earner division or the distinction between the long-term unemployed, the insecurely, and the securely employed (Morris, 1994). Some social groups may be forced to accept unemployment rather than being able to choose among job categories (Crow, 1989). However, other authors emphasize that even when the behaviour of people is driven by overwhelming poverty, the poor are able to select among response options (Van Ophem, 1988; González de la Rocha, 1991). These options that remain for the (urban) poor may be few but they do exist. Hardey and Crow (1991) suggest that the situation of many one-parent households might best be described as one of 'constrained choice' in which the strategy devised by those involved has a crucial bearing on the outcome.

Next, strategies provide broad and coherent prescriptions for action rather than comprising neat blueprints. They entail seeking to control and make sense of life's exigencies. Strategies are always being reviewed or amended in the light of unforeseen events. Events may force people to reassess their plans and use short-term devices in the transition from one strategy to another (McCrone, 1994). This does not, however, necessitate abandoning the concepts of strategy. The coherence of strategic activities also deserves some further elaboration. As to household strategies, it is not uncommon to refer to distinctive strategies. Pahl (1985), for instance, uses the term 'household work strategy', which refers to distinctive practices which are adopted by members of a household collectively or individually to get work done, more particularly formal work, informal work, and self-provisioning. Rudolph (1992) distinguishes household composition strategies which are worked out by peasant families as an answer in particular to labour requirements. There is a kind of calculus in such a strategy which implies a necessary balance between the family labour force size and land size at a given level of agricultural technology. Family composition and intrafamilial relationships reflect the way in which people work out solutions for old age throughout their life-course (Hakansson and LeVine, 1997). Importantly, demographic characteristics are not introduced as independent or explaining variables, but rather as issues on which decisions are more or less consciously made as stepping-stones within a long-term strategy.

Strategies need not connect together all aspects of people's lives in an articulated and explicit way. Anderson and his team-mates (Anderson et al., 1994) argue that life is only manageable if large areas are taken-for-granted. Not all aspects of people's lives require a continuously high level of active planning and organization. But, in order to be conceived as strategies, actions should at least to some degree be comprehensive, coherent, and consciously entered into (Crow, 1989).

3.3.2 Characteristics of Coping

In a general sense, definitions of coping are as varied as the disciplines from which coping theories have emerged. The most common distinction is problem-focused versus emotion-focused coping, or coping responses aimed at changing the stressor versus at dealing with one's own emotional reactions to it (Skinner, 1995). Skinner and Wellborn (1994) conceptualize *coping* as 'an organizational construct which describes how people regulate their own behaviour, emotion and orientation under conditions of psychological stress'. Such regulation refers to how people mobilize, guide, manage, energize, and direct their behaviour, emotion, and orientation, or how they fail to do so. Coping is inherent to a stressful situation in a psychological as well as in a physiological sense. It may unfold over time, sometimes over years, dependent on the duration of this situation and the subject's ability to cope with it. Suffering from aids, for instance, results in a long-term situation of stress which burdens the whole household (Barnett, 1992/1993).

Boss (1988) conceives *family coping* in a similar way as the cognitive, affective, and behavioural processes that are used to manage a stressful event or situation. Stressful events ask for short-term reactive responses, as in cases of crisis and in an unpredictable environment. In case of an economic crisis, domestic units, consciously or unconsciously, may put into practice a range of actions in order to protect the standards of living that prevailed before the outbreak of the crisis. Such actions are, for instance, directed towards protecting food consumption by reducing consumption of other goods and services, intensifying the household's burden of work, sending more members to the job market, reducing members' personal income, and generating goods and services (clothing, food items) within the household which were previously purchased in the market place (González de la Rocha, 1991). Several authors (Graham, 1986; Deacon and Firebaugh, 1988) exemplify the issue describing the teenage single parent with major resource constraints in terms of time and money who follows a more 'directional' than a 'goal-oriented' procedure. Behaviour is directed towards both satisfaction of urgent needs and minimizing uncertainties and risks within the actual situation of the household.

While strategy should be restricted to forward-looking approaches, coping is predominantly reactive towards the stressful event or situation. Every household has to use 'coping devices' some of the time, and some households rely on these all of the time, making little or no attempt to plan. *Coping devices* are defined as 'mechanisms for handling the day-to-day problems of life' (Anderson et al., 1994, p.29). The following fragment (McCrone, 1994, p.74) nicely illustrates this concept.

> A couple in their early thirties with two young children. The wife is an assembly operative in a local electronics factory, and the husband is a fireman. While they showed little sign of adopting a long-term strategic perspective, the female partner kept careful and rigorous accounts. She says: 'How I work is... I budget for my mortgage, my house insurance, my electric, my TV license weekly, so I take that all off G.'s pay at the start when he gets it every week, and I put so much in one account, so much in this account, so much in that account, and I pay my TV stamps, and I've got my payment thing, for the electric.

This household clearly does not claim to plan, but has managed succesfully to 'get by'. Both strategies and coping should be considered as actions which require a certain degree of creativity from people in response to a specific situation.

3.3.3 A Household Strategy's Context

As to the context of a household's strategy, a distinction is made between internal frames and external frames. A first *internal frame* pertains to a household's general *orientation to life*. A life orientation refers to the way in which one approaches life and relates to reality. It acts as a blueprint for life, providing a sense of direction. It is an outlook on life or a view of the world consisting of an infinite number of life issues, such as one's attitude towards work, religion, society, the economy, politics and so on (Sullivan Norton, 1989). Such orientations to life imply characteristic beliefs, norms, and implicit principles which, at a higher level, may also mark a specific group such as a household. For instance, such an orientation may concern a present time-orientation rather than a future time-orientation. For some family households the future is more uncertain and insecure than it is for other social groups. This in turn encourages them to 'take things as they come'. Households who have the same economic options but different time perspectives may organize these options quite differently (Askham, 1975; Wallman, 1986). In a similar way, dependent on the life-orientation, unexpected events may be experienced as a challenge, a threat, or a loss of competence (Skinner, 1995).

Life-orientations are part and parcel of a household's *subculture*. Each household has its own subculture which significantly affects the ways in which it will operate. Importantly, a subculture entails a shared set of belief systems comprising both descriptive rules, which refer to what is true, and prescriptive or normative rules, which refer to what is right. Some normative means of controlling behaviour are clearly codified. However, social behaviour is predominantly controlled through norms internalized by an individual member and is reinforced through ongoing interactions (Anderson et al., 1994).

Households' strategies also develop within *external frames*, entailing higher-level structures and rules. Several authors (Jordan et al., 1992; Anderson et al., 1994; Morgan, 1996) mention higher-level frameworks, such as the kin-network frame, the education-system frame, the capital-labour frame, the gender frame, and the state-power frame. Rules of the higher-ordered framework positively or negatively influence, not determine, the degree to which household members have access to resources and their possibility to develop a strategy.

The significance of the *kinship-network frame* strongly varies across cultures and also across different groups within one and the same culture (Harris, 1990; Palriwala, 1990). For specific groups such as teenage mothers, the family of origin may according to some rule be a primary source of assistance for specific groups, such as teenage mothers, for instance. Hence, they may decide to stay with their parents and expect to receive more help than if they leave home for an uncertain marriage (Deacon and Firebaugh, 1988). In case of low income or income instability, extended networks of economically cooperating kin and friends provide a reasonable degree of stability and security (Deacon and Firebaugh, 1988; Harris, 1990; Jordan et al., 1992). However, informal social networks may also function as a kind of a trap, as in the case of Southern Italy where the system of social integration is based on the dominance of patronage redistribution. Such a system diverts individual and family resources away from any of the possible alternatives of rational and professional allocation (Mingione, 1994). According to Mingione, the only realistic opportunities of acceptable employment in this area, alternative to involvement in organized crime, depend on the operations of the patronage hierarchies and on the redistribution of resources from the central state. What in that region really conditions social behaviour is the pervasive monopoly of the clientelistic system.

At the higher level, *gender-related frames* operate in all cultures. As to economic resources, access to land as a means of livelihood in some Third World countries is an important resource for both men and women. Where land is transmitted bilaterally, inheritance may imply access to resources for women. But in the absence of means of production, bilaterial inheritance means transmission of responsibilities to women, but not the yields (Palriwala, 1990). The law often impedes the access of women to resources. After the death of the previous head of the household, their widows are quite likely to become head of the household. But they often begin with an economic handicap, since they may lack control over productive assets. Older widowed women tend to receive houses, while their children may assume control of the productive land or business as their share of inheritance. Although the law prevents eviction of widows, it is much less protective of whether or not they receive such assets as those of rice fields, dry fields, gardens, cattle, and machinery (Hetler, 1990).

Regarding work-related strategies, the *capital-labour frames* are particularly relevant (Pahl, 1985; Wallerstein and Smith, 1991). For instance, access to the labour market is largely influenced by conditions including, for instance, relative amount of payment elsewhere in the labourmarket, rules of employment security, availability of arrangements that support family roles, such as maternity or paternity leave, child care arrangements, the possibility of shorter hours and leaves, and pensions (Tilly, 1987; Deacon and Firebaugh, 1988).

At last, households' potential for strategy development is dependent on the rules of the *state-power framework.* The 'state' has to be conceived of in a very broad sense: as a differentiated set of institutions or organizations, such as central government departments, courts, the police and quasi-autonomous agencies closely linked to it. Each body has its own rules, policies, and practices which are not necessarily consonant with each other, and do not necessarily reflect one ideology, aim, or set of interests (Fox Harding, 1996). The impact of the state-power frame and the way in which households deal with it differs among socio-economic categories of households and among different cultures within the same state. For instance, the way in which poor households make use of and are hampered by the rules and administration of welfare benefits in order to 'get by' is questioned by Morgan (1996) and extensively exemplified by Jordan et al. (1992).

All these frameworks may facilitate or hamper strategies family households develop and maintain in their life-course. Now, the question may arise if these concepts fit the strategic practices of households in different cultures. In order to answer this question, we will present two key studies, one of which was performed in Portugal, the other one in Indonesia. Both studies focus on temporary migration as part of work-related strategies by family households.

3.4 Key Study: Migration by the Male Partner in Portugal

3.4.1 Introduction

We first focus on a study which Bentley (1989) performed in Portugal. This study is intriguing for several reasons, in particular because of the main role cultural values are supposed to play in important decisions the households involved had to make. It is true that a conceptual framework is largely lacking and that the information given on how data are collected and analyzed is quite limited. However, the description of the situation of the households in everyday life is quite extended and Bentley's findings are quite elucidating and very apt for evoking discussion.

Bentley wanted to gain insight into the way cultural values help people to consider or discard certain alternatives for action. More in particular, he intended to highlight the way in which cultural values allow households to opt for long-term separation through the emigration of one household member. In his view, the use of long-term emigration may be considered an economic strategy. Bentley elaborates the point, describing how the values of a very Catholic little community allowed villagers to reach a very big decision: to send the principal wage earner abroad, alone, to earn money for the household.

3.4.2 People's Life Situation and History

His case material comes from fieldwork (1983-1984) in a *freguesia* (a smallest political administrative unit) in the Northwestern Portuguese province of Entre Douro e Minho. The place covers about 10 square kilometers of hilly woods and cropland on the eastern edge of a plateau, 15 kilometers from a regional city. Because Penabranca (fictitious name) is so close to the city, people can live there and commute to work in town, generally by bus or motorcycle. In those days, the village entailed 261 households, comprising a total population of 1109 people. Agriculture made up an important minority fraction of its total economy. Farms were divided into a large number of different parcels and land and cattle were distributed quite unequally. The upper 10% of the households farmed 60% of the farmland. Many people were involved in marginal tasks much of the time which reflected prevailing unemployment, like scouring the forest for acorns to sell to large farmers as hog feed and saving household ashes to sell to farmers as fertilizer. Before emigration, people would have been waiting at the threshing floor every morning at 5 o'clock to try to acquire work. Farmers picked the ones they wanted and sent the rest away. According to informants, there was widespread begging and occasional starvation.

In the mid 1960s, France opened its doors to emigrant workers and men from the village poured across the border, including many share-croppers and day labourers. Traditional patterns of labour use and social relations changed dramatically. Out-migration in the village was very high. Between 1950 and 1980, the population stabilized due to the high amount of out-migration, which reached a peak of 402 net out-migrations in the 1960s. In 1984, half of the people whose parents still lived in the village lived abroad. Between the 1960s and the 1980s, the number of sharecroppers declined from 20 to six, and agricultural labour became scarce. Agricultural work in the village and the region became increasingly feminized. Daily farm chores were performed by women, especially on the smaller farms. The following case of a couple, called Fernando and Maria, was reasonably representative of the local migration pattern:

> Fernando and Maria were - at the time of the study - in their mid 30s, and not from very wealthy families. Maria had inherited a cottage with a tiny garden. The couple moved into Maria's house, with Fernando's father, who died two years later. By the time their second daughter was born in 1959, they could no longer live on the money they made as agricultural day labourers. They decided together that Fernando should emigrate to France, to send money home. Emigration was illegal, so he had to sneak across two borders before he reached France. Fernando was gone for three years without coming back. Finding steady work was hard. He would find a job, at low pay and just be getting ahead when he would lose that job. He wasn't able to send money home during the first three months. However, eventually they saved enough money to buy a big house and about a hectare of land. In 1981, after 22 years abroad, Fernando retired and came home to live the life of a semi-retired, small-scale dairy farmer (Carvalho et al., 1982, mentioned by Bentley, p. 80).

Out-migration has been important in Portugese life for centuries, with a major movement to Brazil in the 1910s and a much larger migration to Western Europe in the 1960s. Next, migration has been predominantly a male activity. Generally, men went to Western Europe (especially France) while women and children stayed in Portugal to work the land. Women who emigrated generally went a few years after their husbands and generally came from households with little or no land to tie them to their home village.

3.4.3 Findings and Discussion

What allowed this long-term emigration of husbands without dissolving their marriages? Bentley distinguishes and describes the following values as significant:

Marital commitment Marriage was generally contracted between people of roughly similar economic status. Courtship often took six or eight years and involved conversation to such degree that courtship itself was called 'talking'. Courting couples met on Sundays after mass. They were generally sitting within sight of the young woman's home, but out of earshot, and they talked for hours. Some of the couples were allowed to spend any time alone together only after a number of years. This lengthy courtship prepared couples for a long-term commitment. Divorce was never an alternative. No divorces occurred in the recorded history of the parish.

Economic marital fidelity People in this region did not have strong romantic notions of marriage. The cozy, sexy part of marriage was generally to last for about a year. While love was supposedly not the tie that bound, shared cultural values did. Sexually, women were expected to remain faithful. While men were away in France they might have visited prostitutes, but not very often because it was considered irresponsible to spend money on personal entertainment. On the other hand, while men sent money home to their wives they expected that the money would be saved for substantial purposes. They also expected that the household members who stayed at home would feed themselves as much as possible with their garden or farm produce. Hence, in an economic sense, husbands and wives expected a strict fidelity from their spouses.

Hard work and deferred gratification Villagers shared the intensive farmer's work ethic; small-scale, peasant farmers clearly dominating numerically. Farmers commonly worked from sunrise to sundown, and although they did not work in the fields on Sundays, they often used Sundays to repair equipment. Women worked all their waking hours. People were experts at not spending money. They virtually never ate in restaurants or went to movies, and rarely bought new clothes. Clothing and equipment were repaired over and over again so money could be saved for major purposes.

Evidently, emigration did reward in many cases. After many years abroad, the migrant often was able to build a new house in the village or to remodel an old one. These houses were often massive, two-story monuments, complete with brass and marble exterior stair-cases and six colours of tile blanketing the outside walls. Inside they were comfortable. The new-built house had an important secondary function: it reflected that the ex-migrant had been succesful. The purchases that these ex-migrants commonly made - new houses, hot and cold running water, and land for growing food - importantly indicated that things bought were to the benefit of all household members more or less equally. According to Bentley, instead of being perceived as a symptom for lack of responsibility, the out-migration of men was perceived as a very responsible act because men did leave to earn money for their families. According to the author, cultural values about marriage and divorce, being part of the village morality, helped some households to decide to send the husband alone to a foreign country. The values of marital commitment, economic fidelity, and deferred gratification guaranteed to both marriage partners that the money earned elsewhere in Europe would be saved for the good of the whole household and that household members in Portugal would be largely self-supporting in the husband's absence.

Discussion The question now is, if the conceptual framework, described in section 3.3, is appropriate, to analyse the information provided. Our interpretation of the information runs as follows. A *household strategy* emerged as far as the first goal of most migrants was to save money to build a house or remodel their existing house. Having a long-term goal in mind, as in a case of building a house over the long term, indicates the existence of a strategy rather than of coping. However, Fernando and Maria's case probably exemplifies a mixed form; they could not longer live on the money they made as agricultural day labourers. In addition, the building of a house after returning to the village might be considered a common goal of both partners, or at least to deliver shared benefits. The existence of a consensus between both partners is further indicated, at least to some degree, because both partners decided together that Fernando should emigrate to France.

More striking however, is the influence of the *cultural context*. Divorce did not occur in the parish and was not considered an alternative. The expectations of wives and husbands regarding strict economic fidelity and the farmer's work ethic may be conceived as further components of the cultural context. Instead of being perceived as a result of a lack of responsibility, out-migration was viewed as a very responsible act. However, it is not the kinship network, as represented in our conceptual framework, but rather the *village network* that predominates in the description. This very network supported the couple's consensus and therefore allowed them to make decisions rapidly and prevented them from having conflicts.

Inserting *tradition* adds an element of historicity and dynamics, and thus enriches the conceptual framework considerably. The existence of a long-standing tradition of out-migration may have enforced feelings of 'rightness' of the inherent decisions. The *gender-related framework* clearly emerged where evidently the rule prevailed, that men go to Western Europe while the women and children should stay at home to work the land. And the *capital-labour framework* becomes apparent, where extreme poverty was a major factor in deciding (on migration) which resulted in the tradition of outmigration and which made Fernando and Maria's decision unavoidable. Its power also becomes apparent in that the amount of resources available to the household is related to the pattern of migration. As Bentley (1989, p.87) mentions in his conclusion:

> Yet the observation that people with much land tend not to emigrate, people with no land tend to emigrate as whole households, and households with some land tend to send off only the husband suggests that material factors strongly influence the decision to emigrate.

3.5 Key Study: Migration by the Female Partner in Indonesia

3.5.1 Introduction

Hetler's study (1990) inquired into the social and economic context of households which were headed by women in an Indonesian area. This area was characterized by a rapid development sponsored by the government and was also characterized by self-help efforts of households through short-term circular migration. In contrast to the foregoing key study, in this region many women, being wives of household heads, migrate independently of their husbands. In general, the contribution that women deliver to the household's income, predominantly within the informal economic sphere, is considerable (also Niehof, 1995). In some households the male head migrates, leaving his wife to remain behind. In other cases both the male head and his wife migrate, leaving someone else in charge, often a daughter or elderly mother of either the husband or his wife. Hetler describes rather extensively the life situation of the people involved, the changes which took place during the last decades, and their patterns of migration behaviour.

3.5.2 People's Life Situation and History

Hetler selected a village, Jaten, in the Regency of Wonogiri in Central Java, which is an area where short-term, circular migration had become increasingly important to the local economy. In those days, the village of Jaten was a community of 6,000 inhabitants, including the people who were present as well as those who were temporarily away. It is located at one hour's drive by bus south of the city of Solo. Programmes subsidized by the government generated many changes over the last decades. These interventions included a family planning programme, maternal-infant health services, a travelling health team that arrived each month, and a hospital located five kilometers away. Since 1976, three primary schools have been built in addition to the one that already existed and virtually all children of primary school age were enrolled. An irrigation canal that would extend from the newly completed dam 10 kilometres upstream on the Solo river to all ricefields in the village was being built and was considered crucial to this farming community. Control of sufficient water would enable triple cropping of rice for the first time in the village.

Village officials reported at that time that about 80 percent of all households had at least one person who was an economically active circular migrant. Many people had migrated for the first time within the past five to eight years. But a number of respondents reported that their first migration took place during the 1950s and 1960s and - in the case of a few of them - even earlier. For many women who migrated, the initial experience of migration occurred years ago when as girls they left in the company of others. Evidently, circular migration had been of long standing. According to Hetler there is a strong tradition among lower class households throughout much of Central Java for both partners to work. Women participate in productive work on par with men and men provide child care and perform other domestic tasks if their wives are busy working. This tradition of sharing work has been incorporated into migration ever since short-term, circular migrants went to earn. Only a few wives accompanied their husbands to urban places while not earning themselves.

3.5.3 Data Collection

Data collection consisted of a five-stage, multi-round survey, consisting of both present and currently absent members of all 903 households. The information was supplemented by individual case studies, interviews with village officials, direct observation of neighbours and of migrants in urban areas with similar occupations. It also included copying records in both the village and at the statistics and family planning offices at the district and regency level. The survey was followed by a selection of a study group of

327 households who participated in a labour force survey and the migration history of individuals and marital histories.

3.5.4 Findings and Discussion

Of all 903 households, 14 per cent were headed by 'de jure' female heads who in most cases had divorced, were widowed, or were permanently separated. The survey further identified a proportion of 21 percent 'de facto' female headed households, comprising for one part women who served as heads of households on a day-to-day basis in the absence of the 'de jure' head, and for another part migrant women who lived on their own for much of the year.

Among wives of household heads, twice as many appeared to be independent, urban-based 'de facto' female heads, as there were rural-based 'de facto' female heads. Among the 312 female heads, some of them (27 percent) had migrated at less than thirty years of age. Also, few female heads (10 percent) had migrated at sixty years and older. In contrast, among the female heads aged thirty to forty-four years, 66 per cent were migrants and among women aged forty-five to fifty-nine years, 59 percent were migrants.

Further, as to the number and age of surviving children, female 'de facto' heads in urban areas indeed tended to have on average less adult children (19+ years) compared to female 'de facto' heads in rural areas. They tended to have on average more children 14-18 years of age, and to have somewhat fewer children 7-13 years of age. Finally, they had a clearly lower average number of children 0-6 years old, albeit their average number (1.4) was still considerable. According to Hetler, the presence of young children to these women did not seem to be sufficient reason to stay home rather than migrate.

In addition to the survey findings, the interviews delivered insight into the relevant options the urban female heads had for child care. If the child was of school age, the most common solution was to leave the children at home in the village. Earning money to keep children in school was one of the primary reasons for migrating. Older children were supposed to take care of themselves as well as to help in the care of younger siblings. Many male heads assumed the responsibilities of cooking, washing clothes, and child-care duties. Some women had an aged mother or a married daughter who stayed at home with the new baby. If they had children or babies less than two years of age, migrant women took this youngest child with them, especially if they were still breastfeeding. Some took a young girl with them to take care of the baby during the time they themselves were absent because of work. Other women who had no family help carried the baby around while they worked. If children were a few years older, three to six years of age, mothers might leave these children alone for most of the time, while they were working. These children were supposed to be able to play on their own.

Regarding the finding that in cases of individual migration a wife of a head appeared to be 2.6 times more likely to migrate alone than her husband, the question arose: why is it they and not their husbands who migrated? This question is particularly interesting while migrant men had the potential to earn more money in the area of migration. According to Hetler, it might be explained by the fact that there were few lucrative income earning occupations available to women in the village in those days and that women could make rather good earnings in the city. For landowning men, there were sufficient economic opportunities in the village in agriculture, in housing construction, or in village politics. Their households were somewhat upwardly mobile and they had the venture capital to send a woman to the city on an independent enterprise. In the urban area, the earning activities of women and men from this village were quite specialized. Women almost always sold traditional herbal tonics kept in bottles and carried in large baskets on their backs. In contrast, men who migrated usually sold soup containing boiled dumplings made of ground meat mixed with flour. According to both men and women interviewed, men made more money than women in their specialized occupations. However, women could start out with very little capital and their daily costs were low. Most of their daily income was therefore profit. By social convention, women were denied access to carts, which were available to men, and thus were restricted from selling soup. Nevertheless, female migrants did contribute significantly to household income. In some cases their earnings amounted to half the total household income.

Interestingly, women who belonged to the local elite kept their distance from these economic practices and their attitude was negative. They strongly supposed that migration of these women, being wives and mothers, had an adverse effect on children and families in general. Migrant women themselves were fully aware of the disapproval by the upper class, but they clearly felt differently. The income they earned outweighed the potential negative aspects of migration. In a similar way, men in households from which women migrated were much less concerned about the absence of their wives because, according to Hetler, such an arrangement made good economic sense. Migrant women preferred to identify with their role as a wife and mother in the village rather than with their role of heading a household in the city. Their role as head of a household in the city had no legal bearing within their village and had little or no status in the city where they remained. Therefore, in urban areas 'de facto' female heads remained invisible.

Discussion The case description contains rather scarce information to decide if a real strategy is apparent here. 'Earning money to keep children in school' is mentioned as one of the primary reasons for migrating. It indicates one rather long-term goal of migration behaviour and it also indicates the existence of parents' aspirations for their children's future. The case description also suggests at least some options as to deciding in favour or against migration because migration behaviour seems to be not strictly bound to certain demographic characteristics of the households involved. Also, the sharing of domestic work by husband and wife refers to the existence of a *common* strategy, but its character as an intentionally inserted behaviour is not clear.

The role of the *cultural and structural frame* becomes more apparent from the description of the case. First, the existence of a tradition of migration, going back to the 1950s and even earlier, may be considered supportive. Also, the fact that many women gained experience when they left their village at young age in the company of others may be relevant. Further, the strong tradition among lower-class households for both partners to work, be it on productive work, child care or domestic tasks, undoubtedly facilitated migration of either partner.

The influence of both the *capital-labour frame* and the *gender frame* appears to be closely intertwined. While landowning men have sufficient economic opportunities in the village, for women income earning occupations are rather scarce. In the urban area women can make good wages, despite social conventions which favour men regarding the kind of selling products and access to carts. At last, a *class-related frame* appears to be active through the disapproval by the upper class of the migration behaviour of lower-class women. Its influence can hardly be empirically assessed, but it is undoubtedly part of what Gramsci (1971) called 'ideological hegemony' (see chapter 5).

3.6 Conclusions and New Directions for Research

3.6.1 Conclusions

From the findings of both key studies as well as from the earlier mentioned research results (Anderson, 1994), we conclude that strategy is a useful concept which will lend itself to further empirical verification. In both key studies, elements of the conceptual framework emerged as relevant and often quite elucidating in regards to the decisions implied in the process of migration, more in particular the concepts implied in the kinship-network frame, the gender-related frame, and the capital-labour frame. The key studies added further specifications to the cultural values, particularly in the case of Portugal, which - being internalized by the family household - were embedded in the village-network frame. Also, the crucial role which history and tradition play in not enforcing but rather conducing to migration by the male or the female partner, became apparent. Both Pahl (1975) and Anderson (1994) found tradition to be relevant to participation by married women in the labour market.

It is true that this conclusion takes us far from the tight definition of strategy and strategic decisions by Johnson and Scholes we referred to in the beginning of section 3.3. Households do more or less define the scope of their activities, they match their activities to the environment, or, as we termed it, the context in which they operate. They tune their intended activities to their resources and access to funds, and lesser decisions are derived from strategic decisions guided by values of those in power. But differences between organizations (within management sciences) and family households are striking as well. In family households, strategies and decisions are incremental rather than pursued in the long run. They are guided both by internal goals and motives and by external forces. Most salient, they are less strictly organized compared to corporate strategies. They arise and develop from people's life world instead of from organizations' objectives. Other theoretical approaches are needed to get a good grasp of these aspects. However, within the frame of the Strategy Approach, several issues remain unanswered and deserve further investigation.

3.6.2 New Directions for Research

Reflecting on the conceptual framework described in section 3.3 and our conclusions, we derive several new directions for further research. A first proposal refers to the relationship between household strategies and a changing cultural context. A second one concerns the relationship between poverty and the ability households have to develop a strategy. A next proposal focuses on the relationship between life-cycle and strategies. Finally, an important issue concerns the relationship between 'strategies' and 'ways of being'.

1 Culture and household strategies Both key studies underline the importance of the cultural framework within which strategies of households develop. Cultural frameworks are important because they may facilitate the achievement of consensus among both partners of a household and therefore, as a latent function, prevent conflicts. The migration of one of the partners is an example of a far-reaching decision that requires consensus to a certain degree. The key study in Indonesia underlined the relevance of consensus on the importance of children's education, the sharing of domestic work, or on the appropriateness of household members to take care of the young children. Consensus is undoubtedly also important regarding the sharing of benefits, as the Portugal key study showed. More in general, consensus is quite crucial to the allocation of financial resources within family households. The issue will be further elaborated in the next chapter. Processes of modernization, however, may deeply affect the degree of consensus within family households. As a consequence of modernization, prevailing cultural norms and rules will be less taken-for-granted. Hence, consensus between partners within households will be less obvious and many practices which are taken-for-granted as yet will require increasingly negotiation. Future research should, therefore, focus on household strategies in relation to changing cultural patterns within which households operate. Both chapters 4 and 5 offer conceptual frameworks to tackle these delicate issues.

2 Poverty and the strategy of households Pursuing work-related strategies appeared to be strongly related to respondents' employment status. Those with the lowest employment status showed the lowest proportion of respondents who 'had thoughts about jobs in five years' or 'did believe to have a career'. Unemployed men and women attained the lowest proportion as 'to knowing what they want to do in their work lives over the next five years' (Anderson et al., 1994b). Jordan and his team-mates (1992) found very few signs of strategies among poor households and they connected this absence with the fact that employment was too irregular and unpredictable to allow planning, in particular regarding the labour career. If these couples followed an implicit strategy, it was an income strategy rather than an employment strategy. Each partner appeared to be free to get the income as he or she chose once they had agreed about the item of expenditure and how it would be paid for. Hence, when studying household strategies, it is important to consider the (un)predictability of the social context, as well as to discover the real issues around which strategies actually evolve. Such issues may differ from what the researcher (as an outsider) has in mind beforehand. Among very poor households, one particular strategy emerges saliently.

Jordan (1992) found that households do tend to 'bend the rules', i.e. the rules of the benefits system, in order to 'get by'. Hence, the question is important: How do households 'get by' in a situation of extreme poverty and in what way do they interact with the rules and the rulers which determine economic opportunities?

3 Strategy and the life-cycle According to the findings of Anderson (1994), the young are more likely to think about a job or believe they have a career than the old. A more intriguing finding is that respondents in their late thirties or early forties seem to form some kind of 'watershed'. A significant proportion of the respondents appear to begin to view life in a less proactive and more defensive kind of way. While four-fifths of the men in their twenties and three-quarters of the women in the same age class indicate they are thinking ahead, they appear to change very slightly in their thirties. Then comes a significant fall among those in their forties, especially for women. Hence, as far as paid work is concerned, strategies appear to be gender-related and deserve further research from that point of view.

González de la Rocha (1994) highlights another aspect of the life-cycle which is closely associated with poverty. She distinguishes among several stages in the life-cycle of (urban) households: expansion (the domestic unit grows and increases its number of members through birth), consolidation or equilibrium (children are ready to work and participate in the domestic economy), and dispersion (members separate in order to form and organize their own units). She distinctly formulates:

> ....a household in expansion is an 'unbalanced' unit, in economic terms measured by the workers-consumers ratio, in the sense that there are many more mouths to be fed than arms to work. The consolidated household, whose principal characteristic is precisely the equilibrium between earners and consumers. A household in its dispersion phase is, in theory, subject again to economic unbalance, since it is generally adult and economically active members who move from the household of origin to form and organize separate households, leaving aged parents who are economically inactive or who earn lower wages (1994, p.25).

González de la Rocha's research extensively demonstrates the many ways in which poor households can also maintain survival strategies. The way in which the ability of family households to pursue certain strategies in interaction with their life-cycle stage is an important issue for both researchers and policy-makers.

4 *'Means-end'* or *'way of being'* The concept of 'strategy' implies the presence of goals, which in its turn implies that activities are directed towards these goals. Activities are therefore assumed to be means-end motivated within rational frameworks (Edwards and Ribbens, 1991). In much thinking about strategies, intellectual cognition, rational choice and purposive action are emphasized, while the relevance of complex emotions to social life and variable qualities of *being* are suppressed. Edwards and Ribbens elaborate the issue as to women's activities. Their family-based understandings are rooted in a concern with processes rather than goals, with activities and ways of being which are regarded as valuable in their own right rather than as means to ends. In a research project on women combining family and education, these women were concerned to *be* a mother/partner and student in the ways they thought and felt fit to the best of their abilities. For the women themselves, the effects of the different ways in which they moved between family and education upon their relationships with their partners was an unintended 'outcome' rather than a goal they worked towards.

The issue of the relationship between people's orientation towards 'means-end' and their orientation towards 'way of being' is crucial and certainly deserves further investigation. We will return to the issue in chapter 8 (The Morality Approach and the Issue of Care) and in the final chapter.

Note

1. It should be mentioned that cross-tabulation of the four variables used in the index did not indicate a single underlying dimension. For most couples more than one single dimension of planning/not planning became apparent

4 The Organisation Approach and Resource Allocation within Households

4.1 Introduction

The Organisation Approach is intended to bring out what in many studies on family households has been stored in 'the black box'. Barlett (1989) mentions several reasons for this seemingly curious tactic. First, in many studies a Western bias predominated which considered all important cultural activity as taking place in the public sphere and, in consequence, neglected all that happened in the private sphere of the home (also Niehof, 1994). In addition, research on this topic is methodologically very difficult: access to many households is necessary, a representative sample of the kinds of processes occurring within the psychosocial interior of the family has to be assured, the measuring of such processes is difficult, and data have to be gathered over a sufficiently long period.

The Organisation Approach also challenges the idea of the family household as a unit. Considering the household as a unit implies a community of interests among members and their mutual agreement to share resources. However, as Scanzoni (1979) states, the assumption of communal interest reflects the ideology of the times, in particular the 'sixties'. In those days a perspective dominated that assumed egalitarianism as a given and strived to promote an ideal of mutuality which was never clearly defined. It seemed to reject the assumption that power is an inevitable element in any social structure, including marriage, and that as such it ought to be systematically investigated for theoretical and policy reasons.

Since then, however, many scholars have endeavoured to open this black box within divergent disciplines and have investigated social processes which are involved in the flows of scarce resources within households. For instance, empirical evidence indicates that in many cases male and female members do not pool their resources, or pool them incompletely (Brannen and Wilson, 1987; Bruce and Dwyer, 1988; Pahl, 1989; Jelin, 1990; Engle,

1990). The Organisation Approach digs into the ways in which members of the organization collect and allocate resources in order to achieve collective or individual goals. In everyday reality the picture is usually still more complex. If internal segmentation within the family household is admitted, the lower-level units or subjects need in fact not be considered as entirely enclosed within the larger unit. They may be linked to external units, e.g. kinship networks, as well (Guyer, 1988).

As in other chapters, we will first clarify the relevance of the Organisation Approach, particularly as applied to processes of resource allocation within households. Next, while borrowing concepts from several basic studies, we will propose a conceptual framework on processes of allocation of resources and specify it to allocation of financial resources. Some key studies are used to illuminate the way in which these and other concepts can be operationalized for research. We derive some findings concerning the prevalence of different allocative systems, the background of financial allocation patterns, and some characteristics of earning and spending behaviour within households. A number of conclusions and some 'new directions' for further research will finish the chapter.

4.2 Relevance of the Organisation Approach and of Allocation of Resources

In Organisation Theory, the very structure of an organisation is increasingly viewed as being central to its performance (Butler, 1991). Within Home Economics and some related fields, the so-called 'Open Systems Model' predominates. This model implies that an organisation exists in an environment, that its survival rests upon its ability to make exchanges with the environment, and that it has to adapt to environmental changes. Each sub-system is assumed to fulfill its functions as the various organs of a biological system do (Paolucci et al., 1977; Deacon and Firebaugh, 1988; Key and Firebaugh, 1989; Goldsmith, 1996). However, as Butler (1991) importantly argues, Systems Models disregard the potential for conflict and goal disparities in organisations. Hence, he proposes a political model for studying organisations that contain the crucial notion that the activities of participants may be political and that they may use power to further their interests rather than the interests of the total system. Obviously, to some degree the interests of the total system have to be served by its members and there has to be sufficient agreement over goals within the system in order to survive.

Among the many different processes within the organization of family households, processes of resource allocation, or the assignment of resources to specific goals or subjects, are crucial (Hardon-Baars, 1994). If the family household is not just a community of interests and of mutual agreement to share resources, then immediately unequal power relationships and unequal distribution of benefits may come to the fore. Much depends on who in the household determines the way in which resources are allocated and who has access to which resources. Patterns of resource allocation within households may change according to changes in the wider society and with changing involvements by its members in external networks. For instance, at least in Western countries, women's participation in the labour market has increased strikingly during the last decades. While the increase in women's employment has mostly been in part-time work, women are nevertheless coming to spend an increasing proportion of their lives in employment. These changes give rise to questions about the possible impact on intra-household relations (Brannen and Wilson, 1987; Vogler and Pahl, 1993). One might suppose that increased participation in the labour market leads to increased power in the decision-making of households. But changes in labour market participation might reinforce rather than reduce inequalities in access to power and financial resources within the home (Brannen and Wilson, 1987; Morris, 1987; Vogler and Pahl, 1993).

Furthermore, as Pahl (1983) and other authors (Zimmerman, 1995; Presvelou, 1996) importantly point out, policy-makers' hidden assumptions about flows of resources within the household should be checked because such assumptions lie at the root of policy decisions regarding, for instance, the measurement of poverty, taxation, and social security policy. The idea that the household is a unit and that those who bring money into the unit will share it with other members has had the effect of creating the ideal of the single breadwinner who brings home and shares the 'family wage'. It also provided few remedies for dependents who do not receive their share of the household income. An assessment of income on a household basis means the concealment of much hidden poverty in cases of an inequitable allocation of money within the household. Reducing the amount of benefit by the government going to wives will mean a disproportionate cut in the standard of living of women and children in the poorest families (Brannen and Wilson, 1987).

We will focus on money because in many societies it is a source of power, and income and wealth are central expressions of advantage (Pahl, 1983). Deacon and Firebaugh (1988) call money 'the avenue by which increasing interdependence with the general economy has occurred'. Other resources will be dealt with in the next section but omitted in the other sections, although relevant research findings have rapidly increased, for instance, on the allocation of time (Mauldin and Meeks, 1990; Horrell, 1994; Horrell, Rubery, and Burchell, 1994) and the use of energy implied in the allocation of domestic work (Gershuny, Godwin, and Jones, 1994).

4.3 A Conceptual Framework of Resource Allocation

As to allocation of resources within family households, we derive a conceptual framework primarily from the writings of Pahl (1983; 1989). However, research in non-Western countries offers some additional concepts which broaden the reach of Pahl's original framework. Successively, we will deal shortly with the concepts of control, management, budgeting, control points, rules of allocation, normative expectations, and resources.

First, as to allocation of financial resources, Pahl (1983) distinguishes between control, management, and budgeting. *Control* is mainly exercised at the point where money enters the household, or, more precisely, the household economy. It concerns decisions such as which allocative system should be adopted within the household, which spouse should have the final say on major financial decisions, and which spouses have control over personal spending money and have access to joint money. *Management* concerns putting into operation the particular allocative system which the couple have adopted. Household expenditure takes place within a number of different categories, such as food, fuel, clothing, rent or mortgage, insurance, transport, leisure activities, and so on. *Budgeting* is concerned with spending within expenditure categories. Deciding between food and insurance is management, while deciding between steak and mince is designated as budgeting. Control is a pivotal concept which should be distinguished from responsibility. Being responsible for food purchases does not necessarily imply control of the flow of food into the family household.

Roldan (1988) distinguishes - presumably following Pahl's main lines - several *control points* exercised at the entry stage of money. A first control point concerns the sharing or withholding of information about the real amount of a partner's earnings. A second control point refers to a partner's decision-making power over the proportion of his or her earnings (s)he keeps as personal spending money. A next control point relates to the form in which the allowance is given to the housekeeper, whether as a lump sum or in installments. A fourth control point concerns the decision whether to pool one's earnings or to keep them apart for special expenditures. A fifth control point relates to several mechanisms of (re-)control, culminating in an ultimate veto power on types of expenditure, for instance major expenditures such as buying land or new furniture. A last control point (distinguished within allowance patterned management) pertains to the dominating definition of what is necessary, basic, and the minimum acceptable standard, for instance regarding children's clothing, schooling, and outings.

The control points determine the internal access the different members of a household have to its resources. The ways in which men and women come to a division of resources constitute a 'subtle and opaque process in which the actors themselves construct their negotiation and produce their own rationales and interpretations' (Brannen and Wilson, 1987). Processes of allocation finally result in an equal or unequal distribution of resources, and eventually in a degree of deprivation for one or more members.

The next elements which operate within family households concern normative expectations and rules of allocation. Relevant *normative expectations* regulate interaction and exchanges between members of family households. Distribution of resources and consumption goods appears to follow gender and age lines (Pahl, 1983; González de la Rocha, 1994). Many wives perceive their husbands as being 'rightfully' in control of family household's finances (Pahl, 1983). Roldan (1988, p. 238) mentions several such normative expectations that women most commonly hold as an initial conjugal expectation. For example:

> Husbands should provide a housekeeping allowance sufficient to support the family if possible, given the low or very low level of men's earnings.The housekeeping allowance should be as high as possible, and should cover most basic expenditures.

Normative expectations may also regulate exchanges between members of different households. For instance, they concern the choice of the main persons who give practical assistance to elderly relatives (Qureshi and Simons, 1987), or norms which otherwise stress the reciprocity of kinship ties (McKee, 1987).

Engle (1990) derived a number of *allocation rules* from social psychological theory which informally govern exchanges between partners in social relationships. The first one relates to 'equity theory', according to which human beings believe that rewards and punishments should be distributed in accordance with recipients' inputs or contributions, or, in short, 'equal pay for equal work'. According to this rule, for instance, differences between sexes in nutritional status and supposed inequalities in food distribution may be attributed to the perceived utility of the children. A second allocation rule is designated a 'needs rule', which implies that a scarce resource is allocated to the family member who is most in need of it. For instance, 'a mother would give her last bit of tortilla to a sickly infant rather than to a hungry older child' (Engle, 1990). From research in Guatemala, Engle and Nieves (1988, mentioned in Engle, 1990, p.71) derived an 'equality rule' as a third rule of distribution: 'that each person should receive an equal share of the available food'. Following this rule, younger and smaller children would receive relatively *more* than older and taller family members. According to Engle, which rule is applied will depend on many factors, including the characteristics or values of the distributor, the type of resource, and the resource constraints. For instance, in India, particularly in the lean season when food supplies are relatively limited, the most vulnerable, being the least well-endowed, the younger, the girls, and the motherless appear to receive systematically fewer nutrients (Behrman, 1990).

Normative expectations only gradually differ from the more abstract rules of allocation. Normative expectations refer more directly to prevailing norms in the social network of the family household, and hence are clearly related to the normative beliefs we met in chapter 2. Allocation rules are more abstract and are rather related to the general values family households hold.

Resources comprise human resources as well as material resources. Human resources are all the means that are vested in people that can be used to meet demands, such as cognitive insights, information, psychomotor skills, affective attributes, health, energy, and time. Material resources are nonhuman means for meeting goals and events. They entail natural and processed consumption goods, housing, household capital, physical energy, money, investments, land, cattle, and access to technology (Paolucci et al., 1977; Deacon and Firebaugh, 1988; Hardon-Baars, 1994; Goldsmith, 1996; Ssennyonga, 1997). According to Wallman (1986), together they make up the objective structure of livelihood. Their form and scarcity provide the framework for action and determine the options available in a given situation at a given time. In addition to human resources and material resources, some authors further distinguish a third kind of resource which they designate as 'social capital', consisting of a network of kinship and friendship relations which households can resort to and provide services and information in exchange for others (Bourdieu, 1986; Jelin, 1991; González de la Rocha, 1994).

As for *financial resources*, it is important to distinguish among different forms of income. Wallerstein and Smith (1991) classify forms of income into five major varieties:

1. 'wages' or 'the receipt of income (usually cash, but often partially in kind) from someone or some entity outside the household for work performed';
2. 'market (or profit) income', or 'the net income resulting from making something in the household and sell it in the local market';
3. 'rental income', or 'income derived from the remunerated use by someone outside the household of some entity to which the household (member) has (legal) property rights', for instance renting space, tools or facilities to neighbours;
4. 'transfers', or 'receipts of income for which there is no immediate work-input counterpart, in many cases representing deferred compensations, but often rather obscure, particularly in case of private transfers';
5. 'subsistence income', or 'what the household itself produces, being (in almost all cases) part of what it requires to reproduce itself', for instance through hunting, gathering or agriculture.

According to the authors, the real income of households is normally made up of all these components. All forms of income should be kept in mind. As the authors put it (p.231):

> ...two things at least seem clear. First, few households in the modern world, anywhere, can afford over a lifetime to ignore any of these sources of income. Second, wage-income, even for households that are thought of as fully dependent on it, remains only *one of five* components, and as a percentage probably rarely approaches, even today, a massive proportion of the total.

Regarding income, Morris' distinction (1990) between household income and domestic income may be useful. *Household income* refers to the total amount of money received by the various members of the household from whatever source. *Domestic income* refers to the total income available for spending on the collective needs of the household.

4.4 Key Study: Systems of Money Management, a Small Scale Study in Britain

4.4.1 Introduction

We selected Pahl's study because it has unmistakably initiated an important tradition in the field of studies on family households. It comprises a coherent body of theoretical concepts, representing an important step forward in research methodology on a complicated issue, and delivers many interesting research findings.[1]

4.4.2 Key Concepts and Research Questions

The main aim of Pahl's study (1989) was to gain better knowledge of patterns of financial management within households and to investigate the significance of different allocative systems for individual members of households. More in particular, the study aimed at investigating some main hypotheses. The first and most fundamental hypothesis was 'that couples do organize their money in significantly different ways, and that thus it is possible to devise a typology - or typologies - of allocative systems'. A second set of hypotheses was derived from the argument 'that the allocative systems adopted by couples are related to other aspects of their lives, such as the level of income of the household, whether both, or one or neither partner is in paid employment, and so on'. A third set of hypotheses was concerned with 'the ways in which financial arrangements within a marriage can serve as evidence of more fundamental processes', more in particular that financial inequality might reflect other sorts of inequality (Pahl, 1989, p.47).

Pahl distinguished among different ways of organizing money, which were mainly based on the three elements mentioned in section 4.3: *control, management,* and *budgeting.* However, the primary concern was management. She used two main criteria for identifying systems of money allocation. The first criterion concerned the extent to which each partner had access to the main source of money coming into the household. The second criterion related to the extent to which (s)he had responsibility for managing household expenditure. However, as was evident from case studies and further analysis, the four different allocative systems 'shaded into each other'. The four systems can be summarized as follows:

1. *The (male or female) whole wage* In this system, one partner, usually the wife, is responsible for managing all the finances of the household and is also responsible for all expenditure, except for the personal spending money of the other partner. This personal spending money is either taken out by him (her) before the pay packet is handed over, or is returned to him (her) from collective funds. If both partners earn, both pay packets are received and administered by the partner who manages the money. Where a whole wage system is managed by a husband, his wife may have no personal spending money of her own and no access to household funds.

2. *The allowance system* Partners who maintain this system see themselves as having separate spheres of responsibility in financial matters. In the most common form of this system, the husband gives his wife a set amount

and she is responsible for paying for specific items of household expenditure. The rest of the money remains in the control of the husband and he pays for other specific items. Thus, each partner has a sphere of responsibility in terms of household expenditure. If a wife does not earn, she only has access to the 'housekeeping' allowance and, since this is allocated for household expenditure, she may feel that she has no personal spending money of her own. The allowance system has many variations, mainly because of the varying patterns of responsibility.

3. *The pooling system or shared management* The essential characteristic of this system is that both partners have access to all the household money and both have responsibility for management of the common pool and responsibility for expenditure is more or less shared. The partners may take their personal spending money out of the pool. On the other hand, one or both may retain a sum for personal spending. When this sum becomes substantial the system begins to acquire some characteristics of the independent management system.

4. *The independent management system* The essential characteristic of this system is that both partners have an income and that neither has access to all the household funds. Each partner is responsible for specific items of expenditure. Though these responsibilities may change over time, the principle of separate control over income and separate responsibility for expenditure is maintained.

Pahl distinguished between collective expenditure and individual expenditure. Most households buy some items, such as housing, fuel, and basic food stuffs, collectively. As to these items, there can be little or no variation between the standards of living of different members of the household. At the other extreme, there are items which are typically bought on an individual basis, such as cigarettes, clothes, and entertainment. The standards of living of different members of the same household may considerably vary as to these items. These variations may reflect individual tastes, but they can also reflect differences in access to income, whether earned or shared within the household.

4.4.3 Data Collection and Analysis

Pahl's research focused on married couples with at least one child under 16 and was carried out in three different parts of Kent (U.K.). A random sample was selected from the age-sex registers in three different health centres and approached for an interview. Husband and wife were interviewed first together and then separately, and interviews were completed with 102 couples. The respondents could not be considered as representative of a wider population of family households, but the households selected appeared to be reasonably similar to the larger population of married couples with dependent children in Britain. In the interviews, the criteria appropriate for distinguishing one pattern of money management from another were approached in different ways. In joint interviews questions regarding *control* were formulated as follows: 'In very general terms, how do you organise the money that comes into the house?' In separate interviews, Pahl (1989, p.67) asked a number of different questions: 'So who would you say really controls the money which comes into the household?', 'Do you feel you have to justify to your husband/wife spending money on some of the things you buy?'

Regarding the *organization of money*, she asked: 'Why did you decide to arrange your finances in the way you have described?', 'What are the major disadvantages for you?' To assess the jointness or separateness of control in a more objective way, the existence of a joint and separate bank account was taken as a first indication. Having a joint bank account supposedly indicated some degree of sharing. In addition, the wife's answer to the question: 'Who really controls money', was also used as an indicator.

As for *individual responsibility*, couples were asked in the joint interviews which partner was responsible for spending on a range of items which most couples have to purchase (rent or mortgage, fuel, house insurance and consumer goods). Another question was asked as follows: 'Would you say that in general you have separated spheres of responsibility or does it not matter which one of you pays for what?' (Pahl, 1989, p.67).

4.4.4 Findings and Discussion

Among the abundance of findings, we select those which concern the prevalence of the four allocation systems and the reasons given by the respondent for keeping their system. For brevity's sake, we have to omit other findings, particularly results on the meaning of money, the negotiation of money, and spending patterns.

The prevalence of the systems of money management Among the family households in the sample, the system of 'shared management' seemed to prevail (56%). The 'allowance system' followed rather distantly (22%), and was in its turn followed by the 'wife management (whole wage) system'

(14%), and the 'independent management system' (9%). A parallel category of the 'husband management (whole wage) system' appeared to be not represented among the sample. The results do agree quite well with the findings of some other investigations which have been performed in the same years.[2] Most of the couples pooling their money claimed that they shared responsibility for financial management. Each of them pretended to have equal access to the couple's financial resources. Findings showed that pooling couples did indeed have a greater degree of jointness (a joint bank account, a joint building society account, joint savings) in the way they organized their finances. But still more intriguing was the finding that among pooling couples there was a division of labour, so that financial management lay in the hands of one partner or the other. Few of them had an equal share in money management. Among many couples with a shared management system, either husband or wife was responsible for paying bills. Hence, Pahl distinguished between 'wife-controlled pooling' and 'husband-controlled pooling'. The results also suggested that wives were more likely than husbands to feel they had to justify spending to their partners. The difference was particularly marked among couples who managed their money jointly.

Table 4.1   Reasons given by wives and husbands for their system of money management

	Wives	Husbands
Ideological reasons		
System seemed natural/right/fair	41	53
Practical reasons		
Seemed more efficient/ 'it just works for us'	27	22
Response to way in which wages/ salaries paid	22	19
More convenient/ one partner able to get to bank	19	15
Psychological reasons		
Wife 'better manager', so she manages money	23	15
Husband 'better manager', so he manages money	10	9
Generational reasons		
Tried to avoid parents' mistakes	5	2
Money management similar to parents' system	4	1

Note: Numbers mentioning each reason. Numbers add up to more than 102 because some individuals gave more than one reason.
Source: Pahl, J. (1989), *Money and Marriage*, p.95

Explaining patterns of financial allocation Pahl grouped the reasons for holding the management system under four headings: practical explanations, psychological explanations, socio-economic explanations, and ideological explanations. These findings also deserve more explicit discussion.

Practical reasons were those which attributed causes to such things as the opening hours of banks, or the form in which wages were paid. For instance, a wife managed the money because she was able to go to the bank when it was open, because she knew what the children needed, or because she was responsible for food and, therefore, for shopping. Arguments were mentioned such as 'seemed more efficient/it just works for us', 'response to way in which wages/salaries are paid', and 'more convenient'/'one partner able to go to bank'. The practicalities of everyday life evidently shape the way in which couples organize their money.

Differences in personality and temperament Some people viewed themselves as careful, level-headed financial managers, or as people who 'let money flow through their fingers like water'. Reasons implied that: 'Wife is a "better manager" so she manages money', and 'husband is a "better manager", so he manages money'. The following example elucidates this kind of explanation:

> A school cleaner and a miner explain why she manages the money: 'When we first married, Bill wasn't good with money - it burnt a hole in his pocket. So we talked it over and now we have this. The advantages? I don't have to worry when the bills come in. It gives me the heebie jeebies, if I don't have the money to pay the bills'. Husband: 'I think she's the better manager than what I am and she has the time to pick the prices and knows the need of the house. The advantages? I don't have to worry about the money, where it goes and how it goes (Pahl, 1989, p.101).

Carefulness with money appeared to be shaped both by income and by gender. In general, wives were more likely to be viewed as careful than husbands, both by themselves and by their partners. This difference appeared to be especially marked among low income couples, where more wives than husbands were described as 'very careful' and fewer as 'not very careful' or 'not at all careful'.

Differences in social and economic structures include the level of household income, the employment pattern of husband and wife, their life cycle stage, and their reponsibility for their children or elderly relatives.[3]

As to the management of finances, wife management was more common in case the household income was relatively low. The allowance system comparatively prevailed where household income was relatively high. Shared management was found at all income levels, while the independent system was most common among couples where partners were employed and earned relatively large amounts of money. As to the control of finances, particular differences were salient between wife-controlled pooling and husband-controlled pooling. Wife-controlled pooling was found most often among households with a medium-level income, among couples where both partners were employed, where wife's earnings amounted to over 30% of husband's earnings, and where both partners were middle class or where the wife was middle class and her partner lower class. On the other hand, husband-controlled pooling was associated with a relatively high household income, with a husband being the only one in employment, with a wife having no earnings, and with both partners belonging to the working class or the middle class. In cases where the husband was middle class and the wife working class, the husband always controlled the pool or the joint account.

Ideological influences concerned belief in the 'naturalness' of inequality within marriage, and were mentioned in the interviews as, for instance, 'system seems natural/right/fair'. Reasons categorised as 'ideological' were given more frequently than any other particular category of reasons, particularly by men. Studies of couples where the woman rather than the man was the chief earner showed the force of ideologies as to the conjugal contract. The following fragments (Pahl, 1989) nicely illustrate the issue:

> He does: he has all the money. I come home and hand him my pay pocket - like a fool! Then he hands me back money for food for the weekend and bits for myself. I don't think people believe I hand my pay pocket over. Most of the time it's the woman what controls the money, but in our position with him not working it's been reversed. With him being at home all day he has to do most of the shopping. The husband's comment on the situation is as follows: 'It's done me good, to be honest - it's taken a lot of responsibility off the wife and drawn me more into the family and the running of the family (p.113).

According to Pahl, female breadwinners have somehow to compensate their husbands for the loss of breadwinner status. Breadwinning wives hold back from exercising as much power as they might, given their financial contribution, and tend to involve their husbands in financial responsibility. We return to the issue in the next chapter.

Discussion   Pahl's findings definitely open the black box of family households as far as the allocation of financial resources is concerned. Her findings defy the idea of the family household as a unit of members who have common interests or who share equally in common benefits or burdens. Certainly, the sample she chose is quite restricted. Conclusions can hardly be generalized and ask for research on a much larger scale. Nevertheless, issues that immediately draw attention concern the relationships between the type of financial management system households employ and their social economic characteristics, more in particular the relationship between a low level of income and a female-controlled management system (Wilson, 1987). Morris (1990) supposes there is a greater need for the close surveillance of spending where income is low and, as a result, there is a high probability of unitary control. As to the association between shared management and higher income, she argues that the higher the income is, the less need there is for tight control of spending and the more viable a joint system. Such an explanation does make sense, but as Pahl herself comments, in cases of low income, being in control means to bear a burden rather than to have power. Thus, the question remains to be answered: why is it predominantly the wives who have to bear it?

Inequality of power between husbands and wives is reflected in Pahl's findings on expenditure, particularly in the large proportion of earnings women make available for household consumption, such as food, rent, child care, and other necessities. This finding is corroborated by results from many other studies (Morris, 1990; Jordan et al., 1992; McCrone, 1994; Chen, 1996). We will return to the issue in the next section. Also intriguing is Pahl's finding that, among the few self-employed people in her sample, the necessity to have a separate account for the business emerges. This could have the effect of keeping the financial arrangements of husband and wife separate. The same pattern emerged from studies in Indonesia (Van Velzen, 1994; Niehof, 1995). If self-employed people are conduced to have a separate account, the question arises after being employed and earning an income oneself influences the degree of control in financial matters. A second key study further illuminates these issues.

4.5 Key Study: Systems of Money Management, a Large Scale Study in Britain

4.5.1 Introduction

Vogler's study (1994a, 1994b, 1994c) is quite in line with the foregoing key study, but it also broadens its scope and deepens several intriguing findings. Vogler started with the same classification of financial management systems and continued Pahl's distinction between the several pooling systems. She also introduced several new concepts, operationalized them as questions, and performed some additional statistical analyses.[4]

4.5.2 Key Concepts and Research Questions

Vogler's objective was to show how allocative systems are related to gender inequalities between spouses in control over financial decision making and to gender inequality in access to money. In addition, she wanted to find the main determinants of different allocative systems and the extent to which they change over time. Ultimately, her aim was to assess the plausibility of arguments in favour of the family becoming a more egalitarian unit or the arguments in favour of a reinforcement of existing inequalities in access to power and to household resources, both in relation to the increasing participation by women in the labour market.

First, Vogler distinguished between strategic control over household finances and financial management as an executive function, because both functions might be fulfilled by different persons. *Strategic control* referred to control over infrequent but important decisions such as which allocative system should be used and how much should be spent on collective domestic expenditure, as opposed to the amount of personal spending money. *Executive management* implied ultimate responsibility for organizing household money and paying bills. These concepts were used for further determining the differentiation in financial management among the pooling households, as had resulted from Pahl's study. Vogler defined three different analytical forms of pooling based on the responses of both partners to the management indicator: 'real joint pooling', 'male-managed pooling' and 'female-managed pooling'. Those couples in which one or both partners claimed husbands were responsible for management were classified as using a *male-managed pool*; those in which one or both partners claimed wives were responsible for management were considered as using a *female-managed pool*; while those couples in which both partners agreed that both were equally responsible for money management were denotated as using a (real) *joint pool*.

Further important concepts concerned inequalities in access to money as a resource. Regarding this, Vogler distinguished between *financial deprivation* and *access to personal spending money*. Both concepts remain undefined, but were operationalized into interview questions.

Finally, Vogler tried to measure what Pahl termed 'ideology' by means of several attitude scales. She supposed that *self-identity as a breadwinner* might be a key factor underlying access to household resources. A distinction was made between normative attitudes towards gender roles inside and outside the home. Normative attitudes inside the home referred to which members *should* have ultimate responsibility for ensuring an adequate household income and that housework was done properly. Normative attitudes outside the home concerned gender roles as to participation in the labour market.

4.5.3 Data Collection and Analysis

Vogler's analysis is based on data from 1,211 couples who participated in the Social Change and Economic Life Initiative, a British study funded by the Economic and Social Research Council. These couples appeared to broadly correspond to a national sample in terms of their economic and demographic characteristics (Vogler and Pahl, 1993). Interviews were conducted jointly with both partners. In order to reduce the risk of consensus answers, a large proportion of questions were answered by means of self-completion booklets. Each partner was given a self-completion booklet in which they ticked their own answers without conferring with each other. Whenever possible, analysis was based on both husbands' and wives' answers. To assess the *strategic control* and to get a more general indicator of control over the most important decisions, Vogler (1994, p.232) used the questions: 'Who has the final say in big financial decisions?' and 'Who in the household has the most say over the most important decisions?'

As to *executive management*, Vogler asked both respondents who in the household had ultimate responsibility for organizing household money and paying the bills. Each couple's responses were combined into a single five-point scale showing both partners' perception of money management, as well as the extent of agreement or disagreement between them.

As to *financial deprivation* of individual members of households, Vogler (1994) used a list of items and asked her respondents: 'please tick *any* of the following that you *yourself* have had to do *over the last two years* to make ends meet when your household was short of money'. The list included the following items:

- missed a meal
- reduced meals spending
- turned down heat
- cut down on social life
- given up holiday
- cut back on clothes
- reduced savings
- got into debt
- financial help/others
- borrowed money
- other (for example, hire purchase goods repossessed)

To provide a rough summary index of the experience of financial deprivation, people received a score of one for each action that they had taken to cope with financial difficulty in order to detect differences in the level of deprivation by husbands and wives.

Normative attitudes to gender roles within the home were measured by asking both respondents and partners whether they thought the husband, the wife, or both equally *should* have ultimate responsibility for ensuring the family to have an adequate income and ensuring the housework to be done properly. *Normative attitudes to gender roles outside the home* were measured by a series of Likert scales relating to men's and women's labour market participation. Individuals were asked to say how much they agreed or disagreed with the following three statements:

1. Men are more suitable than women for positions of responsibility at work;
2. I'm not against women working but men should still be the main breadwinner in the family;
3. In times of high unemployment married women should stay at home.

Individuals' responses to each of the three items were aggregated into an index of sexist attitudes.

4.5.4 Findings and Discussion

Space again permits just a selection of findings. We will centre on the results regarding the relatedness between the constituting variables of the financial management system, the results of the regression analyses - which imply all the variables mentioned above - and at last some findings on financial deprivation and access to money.

As to the financial management systems, Vogler's findings prove that the pooling system was indeed very heterogeneous. In short, in 61% of pooling households, at least one and often both partners nominated one or the other of them as ultimately responsible for management. Distinguishing between the three different forms of pooling based on 'ultimate responsibility', the 'real joint pool' appeared to account for only 20% of the overall sample. The male- and female-managed pools accounted for a further 15% each.

Strategic control ('Who has the final say in big financial decisions?') varied markedly with the type of allocative system used in the household. Saliently, the joint or female-managed systems seemed much more likely to be equally controlled than the male-managed systems. As to general control over the most important decisions ('Who in the household has the most say over the most important decisions?'), couples using the female-managed or joint systems were much more likely to have an equal say over the most important decisions than those using the male-managed system or the housekeeping allowance system. The first mentioned systems were also markedly more egalitarian and were associated with lower levels of disagreement between partners over who exercised control compared to male-managed systems. They were also more likely to be subject to joint control. The distinction between 'male pool', 'joint pool', and 'female pool' appeared also to be relevant in relation to power, measured by combining the answers to the questions on the financial and general sphere. Couples using the joint or female-managed systems were markedly more egalitarian than those using the male-managed systems. Furthermore, the 'joint poolers' and the 'female poolers' were somewhat more egalitarian in power sharing compared to the 'male poolers'. As to the determinants of the systems of allocation, Vogler carried out a series of logistic regressions on the two allocation systems which seemed to be at opposite extremes: the joint pool system and the housekeeping allowance system. These analyses included, amongst others, labour-market factors and variables which concerned socialization, education, generation, and attitudes. The analysis showed that the four strongest influences on the 'joint pool' were both spouses' socialization, the husband's educational qualifications, the husband's attitudes to the domestic division of labour, and the wife's employment status. Husbands having been brought up in pooling households, having a high level of education, having a non-traditional attitude toward the domestic division of labour, and wives having been brought up in pooling households, were considerably more likely to use the joint pool than the opposite categories.

The four strongest influences on the housekeeping allowance system were husbands' attitudes to women's labour market participation, husbands' attitudes to the domestic division of labour, spouses' joint class position, and the husband's class position. Husbands having negative attitudes towards women's labour market participation and traditional attitudes towards the domestic division of labour showed to be over three times more likely to use the allowance system than husbands with less traditional attitudes. Intermediate class couples and service-class husbands were found to be considerably more likely to use the allowance system than husbands or couples in the other categories. Again, after controlling for other factors, systems of allocation appeared more strongly related to the husbands' characteristics than to the wives' characteristics. Wives' normative attitudes evidently were found to be even insignificant.

However, introducing the husband's status as breadwinner into the analysis had a clear impact on the several associations. In households which had the allowance system, the addition of the male breadwinner variable reduced the coefficients for wives' non-employment and part-time employment, as well as for husbands' attitudes to the domestic division of labour. In joint pooling households, the same variable reduced the coefficient for wives' full-time employment to insignificance and lowered that for the husbands' attitudes toward domestic division of labour somewhat. Vogler concludes that the husbands' status as breadwinner was clearly the most important variable in predicting the housekeeping allowance system and the third most important variable (after husbands' socialization and education) in predicting the joint pool.

Regarding *financial deprivation and access to money*, results showed that the most common things which people had to cut back on were social activities, clothing, holidays, and, somewhat less, heat and savings. Wives generally had to cut back more than husbands, but the difference between them clearly varied with the system of allocation. The largest differences between husbands and wives emerged among couples who used the female pool, the female whole wage system, and the housekeeping allowance system. Differences were smallest among couples who used the jointly managed pool. These differences between spouses persisted within income groups and within social classes, but inequalities were larger when income was lower. As to access to money, Vogler had asked both partners who in their household had the most personal spending money. Her findings showed that with just over half of all couples, both perceived personal spending money as equally distributed. A further 12% agreed that the husband had the most personal spending money, while 4% assessed that the wife had the largest amount to spend for herself. Across all management systems, male partners appeared to have access to more personal spending money than female partners. But inequalities in personal spending money also varied markedly with the type of financial management system. In particular, in households practicing the housekeeping allowance system and, curiously, also in households which used the female whole wage system, husbands clearly disposed of a relatively large amount of personal spending money. In contrast, relatively many households which had a joint pool system and households which maintained a male pool system agreed as to having equal access to personal spending money.

Vogler perceives a growing polarization between the female-managed systems (which imply more inequality) on the one hand, and the joint pool systems (implying more equal sharing) on the other hand. The justification of such a view may be questioned. Her findings evoke other questions as well. For instance, why is it that female-managed systems are associated with considerable gender inequalities in favour of husbands regarding the amount of personal spending money and financial deprivation, particularly in low income households? Female control of finances, though being associated with greater decision-making power for women, does not prevent them from being financially deprived (Vogler and Pahl, 1994). Evidently, the way in which concepts such as power, decision-making, and deprivation are interrelated needs further clarification. Further clarification is needed even more because allocation systems were more strongly related to the characteristics of husbands than to the characteristics of wives, such as regarding their normative attitudes, for instance. Such a finding may reflect the existence of latent kinds of power, related to unequal interdependence between partners.

4.6 Conclusions and New Directions for Research

4.6.1 Conclusions

Reflection on Pahl's original hypotheses and Vogler's main objectives leads to several main conclusions. Their findings clearly support the existence of different allocative systems among family households. Their findings also show predominantly consistent relationships between the type of allocation system and social class. Female dominated systems prevail among households with lower incomes, while allowance management (which is in fact a male-dominated system) prevails in household with a higher income. Pahl's hypothesis that the management system should be associated with paid employment of the female partner also received empirical support, and was further refined by Vogler's results which indicated that it is fulltime employment rather than part-time employment which is decisive in a change in a household's financial management system. Both projects focus on the question whether financial arrangements refer to other sorts of inequality between husbands and wives. Such inequalities emerged in relation to personal deprivation and access to personal spending money. Comparisons between the allocative systems of the parents of the couples studied and the study couples themselves showed a large decline in the housekeeping allowance system and a large increase in some form of pooling.

Nevertheless, Pahl and Vogler are rather pessimistic about the actual state of affairs regarding equality in households. They mistrust pooling management because this implies both joint pooling and the practically inegalitarian practises of male and female pooling. Only a modest part of households (about one-fifth) use the egalitarian joint pool. In terms of ultimate responsibility, the joint or female-managed systems are much more likely to be equally controlled than the male-managed systems (Dobbelsteen, 1996; Vogler and Pahl, 1994). Additionally, according to Pahl's findings, husbands appear more likely to have more money for personal spending and for leisure compared to wives. Husbands are also more likely than wives to take their personal spending money from their earnings while wives are likely to use housekeeping money for their personal needs. Besides this, even when wives exert female strategic control over finances, they experience significantly higher levels of financial deprivation than husbands and they have less access than husbands to personal spending money. These findings raise many questions for further research.

4.6.2 New Directions for Research

We derive suggestions for future research partly from the conceptual framework and the findings from both key studies, and partly from other research in the field. These suggestions refer to the impact of normative expectations, already incorporated into Pahl's framework regarding the influence of parental socialization, the relevance of 'situational factors', and the concept of a 'general fund' within households.

1 The operation of normative expectations Pahl (1983) considered normative expectations as one of the main variables which determine the allocation system. Their operation became apparent from her findings which suggested a discrepancy between theory and practice in the attitude of husband and wife toward earned income. Both partners were likely to define the husband's income as earmarked for collective consumption. Actually, many husbands did not make all their income available to the family, especially in households where wives were given an allowance for housekeeping. In addition, their earnings from 'second jobs' were more likely to be kept secret than earnings from 'main jobs' to be kept secret. In contrast, wives' incomes tended to be earmarked for individual expenditure. In practice, however, most wives used their income to buy things for the family or added their earnings to the housekeeping money (Pahl, 1989; Morris, 1990). Such a paradoxic between theory and practice deserves further investigation. Vogler's results do not support the resource theory that changes in labour market participation are leading to greater equality in household financial arrangements in any deterministic way (Vogler and Pahl, 1993). She found full-time employment as more decisive compared to part-time employment. But her findings strongly suggested that changes toward greater equality will depend substantially on effective challenges to the husband's traditional status as the main breadwinner in the household. Traditional statuses are related to normative expectations and these are implied in ostensibly propositional definitions. Such definitions are part of ideologies, which may change in response to changes in, for instance, the employment status of people. But such change may occur quite slowly, and may appear as a process of 'lagged adaptation' (Gershuny, 1996; Gershuny and Brice, 1996).

The way in which normative expectations impede equality deserves further investigation. In particular, two interrelated normative expectations came to the fore: the definition of one's earnings as earmarked for collective or individual consumption and the definition of the roles of husbands and wives as primary or secondary earners of the family household.

2 The influence of parental socialization Vogler's comparison between respondents' allocation systems and the systems used by their parents indicates a large decline in the housekeeping allowance system, a marginal decline in the female whole wage system, and a marked increase in some form of pooling. A moderate increase in the use of the joint pool and moderate increases in the male and female pools emerged. At the same time, a considerable intergenerational continuity among couples' households and their parents' households was evident in the findings. Parents' allocation systems emerged with the highest percentage in the household allocation system held now. Nearly half of those using the female whole wage system and housekeeping allowance systems had been brought up in households using these systems when they were young. However, the influence of socialization appeared to vary across social classes. It appeared to be weakest in the service class, where respondents were more likely than those in other classes to shift to the joint or male pool, regardless of the management system their parents held. The influence was most strong in the working class, where the female whole wage system exercised much greater holding than in other classes.

Parental socialization profoundly impinges on children's behaviour in most divergent fields such as young adults' leaving the parental home (Baanders, 1998) and food preparing practices (Menell et al., 1992). Systems of financial management may be considered part of rather inflexible gender ideologies, which are also acquired in childhood (Hochschild, 1989). Such acquisition may develop less by instruction than by imitation. Other studies (e.g. Brannen and Moss, 1987) suggest that the gendering of breadwinning occurs very early on in marriage. This then plays a fundamental role in structuring both partners' future behaviour both in the labour market and in the house. It plays a crucial role in the reproduction of gender inequality as well. Research findings are scarce on when and how children acquire knowledge of money and the economic system in general (Hira, 1997). Hence, further research should focus on the way parental norms and practices influence actual patterns of management within their children's households. Such research should imply longitudinal studies particularly.

3 Situational factors Pahl refers to a study by Todd and Jones (1972) which suggested that the form in which the husband was paid was closely associated with which spouse payed the bills for fuel and rates, rent or mortgage. Where the husband was paid in cash, the wife was likely to carry out these duties. Where he was not paid in cash he was likely to have responsibility for the main bills. Pahl herself found striking differences between the household where the husband was paid weekly and those where he was paid monthly. When the employed men were paid weekly, the wife was likely to manage the money and to be responsible for the rent or mortgage, the rates and the insurance. When the husband was paid monthly he was likely to manage the money and to be responsible for these items. Weekly payment of male wages appeared to be even more closely associated with female responsibility for financial management than did low income. The impact of the way in which wages are paid appeared also in Brannen and Wilson's research (1987). Their results showed that in households where the wife was paid monthly and the husband weekly, the women's monthly earnings would often go towards the monthly or quarterly bills, such as housing or fuel, while the husband's weekly earnings were used for weekly items like food.

Another situational factor that emerged from Pahl's research was that her respondents explained their financial management practices by referring to, for example, the opening hours of banks or their personal working hours. She rightly comments that time-schedules and location characteristics themselves reflect economic forces and ideological assumptions about which household member(s) will make use of the provisions and services of economic agencies and who will supply the biggest profits (Pahl, 1989). Situational factors thus can operate as facilitating conditions and can be used as instruments for change at the same time. Hence, research should also centre on practical opportunities and constraints regarding changes in financial management. We will return to the role opportunities and constraints may play in chapter 6.

4 The concept of a general fund As to households in non-Western countries, anthropologists find the idea of a single household fund a highly difficult concept. In many cases, funds appear to be pooled individually, as well as familially, and also communally. A pool of land, money, food and goods may belong to an entire multiple-family household, then each nuclear family unit within the extended household has its own pool while, finally, each adult controls personal property and funds (Wilk, 1989). As a focus of study, inequality in access to resources and negotiations between partners may be particularly difficult in polygynous units, which thus far have been paid hardly attention to (Ssennyonga, 1997). Additionally, financial resources other than those from wages in non-Western countries are relatively important compared to their role in family households in most Western countries. Thus, these also deserve special attention.

Apart from the gender inequality implied in some management systems, the consequences of these systems regarding the welfare of family households deserve further study. For instance, Wilk (1989) compares a patriarchical system with a democratically managed system. In the first, the male head of the household controls a single central fund which includes most agricultural products, cash from selling crops, and the cash earnings from all the members. In the second system, management is not patriarchally controlled and all members contribute to the single fund and share rights to its use. Each decision is conceived as a group decision over common resources. According to Wilk, the patriarchal household budget in the short run can motivate and concentrate its resources for particular goals, like buying young hogs to feed. But in the long run, the system gets in trouble when help and labour of all members are required, but hesitantly given. The second kind of management system appeared to be the most succesful in the long run. When its members had agreed to pursue a strategy, they acted together and were willing to invest extra work time, extra effort, and extra attention to the project.

The issue offers many interrelated suggestions for further research. Gender inequality may be one good reason for investigations on existing systems of financial management and on how to achieve some change. However, no less important are the benefits which result from one system compared to the other, and the opportunities which result to household members for acquiring an equal share.

Notes

1. The information on this key study is mainly derived from Pahl's book *Money and Marriage*. Other sources will be explicitly mentioned when used.
2. Pahl mentions *Marriages and Money* of the 'Family Finances Group' (1983), *The two-Paycheck Marriage* of the 'Bird's Eye' group (1983), and studies by Graham (1985) and by Homer, Leonard and Taylor (1985). As in Pahl's study, the first two studies may be biased as the couples involved knew they were taking part in a study of financial matters and were willing to discuss this very sensitive aspect of marriage with an interviewer. Pahl supposed it to be likely that these samples were biased towards couples who were reasonably happily married and for whom money was not particularly problematic. The third study mentioned may have included more couples for whom money was a problem, while the fourth study was performed among battered women.
3. Socio-economic explanations are not mentioned by respondents themselves (table 4.1). Pahl explains that it is hard for a respondent to see oneself as part of a social category and harder still to recognize the extent to which membership of a given category makes it likely that one will behave in a particular way. However, many other studies also show the relevance of social and economic factors (Graham, 1987; Wilson, 1987).
4. For this key study we derived the information predominantly from Vogler's contribution 'Money in the Household', in Anderson, M. et al. (1994), pp. 225-266.

5 The Power Approach and the Division of Household Production Tasks

5.1 Introduction

According to the Power Approach, behaviour within family households is explained by power relationships between household members. Power is associated with processes of decision-making, and decision-making undoubtedly reflects power relations. However, power and decision-making do not necessarily go together. For instance, Bankart and Bankart (1985) found, that despite many decisions Japanese mothers make at home, only 11% of the children said that their mother was the boss in their family. In Soviet society, it has been suggested that wives dominate virtually all areas of family life, but it is unclear how much power women actually have in their marriages (Boss and Gurko, 1994).

Power encompasses decision-making, but decision-making is just one level at which power operates. Decision-making is a way of acting which more or less consciously develops at a specific time and place. Decision-making can be studied apart from power as a frame of reference. For instance, many consumer studies have focused on household decision-making in order to be able to predict purchases of all kinds of commodities, such as cars, clothes, cleaning utensils, etc. Other studies do not have decision-making as their main focus, but contain important information on such power-related aspects as, for instance, spouses' influence strategies in purchase decisions (Davis, 1981; Spiro, 1983; Kirchler, 1990; 1993; 1995).

Thinking about power within family households underwent radical changes during the last decades. These changes reflect different approaches varying from individual and voluntary views to culture-bound and ideological points of departure. In our view, power is a phenomenon which develops through behavioural practices, social positions, relationships, institutions and larger societal processes. It is rooted partly in individual resources, partly in structural conditions, and in rules which determine access to scarce resources and opportunities.

While power within the family household encompasses all relationships between household members, such as those between parents and children, grand-parents and parents, or between children within one and the same household, an overwhelming majority of research has focused on power relations between husbands and wives and, particularly, on gender. This chapter focuses on the gender issue.

First, we will elucidate the relevance of the power approach to the study of family households and the relevance of the issue to which some theoretical frameworks will be applied, i.e. the division of household production. Next, we will examine two conceptual frameworks which embrace power as their key concept. The first one emerged from the field of family studies, the second one has been derived from the field of political sociology. Two key studies will be described to demonstrate ways in which these frameworks can be translated into a research design and research methodology. Finally, we formulate a number of 'new directions' which are beyond the reach of the frameworks offered and require other, and perhaps new, conceptual frameworks.

5.2 The Relevance of the Power Approach and of the Division of Household Production Tasks

Not only did thinking about power undergo radical changes, interactions within family households themselves changed as well, reflecting a change - at least in many Western countries - from a 'command household' towards a 'negotiating household'. Negotiation requires discussion, arrangement, consent, compliance, and accomodation of wishes. Members also have to recognize their personal desires, make them explicit, and bring them to the fore in an assertive way. Compared to traditional marital patterns, relations have become more diversified and more difficult to predict. In short, rules have given way to negotiations (De Swaan, 1983). By consequence, the issue of power may have changed radically and will remain in a continuous 'state of change'.

The private world of family households, the world of economic institutions, and the world of public policy operate in continuous interaction. The way in which people (learn to) socialize in the private world inevitably influences the way they will act and think in both other systems, and vice versa. Similarly, changes in the division of power occurring within family households will be crucial to changes occurring in the larger society, and changing power relations in the larger society will throughly influence changes in family households. Therefore, understanding changes in internal power relationships will enlarge our understanding of societal changes, while the reverse also holds true.

Power is concerned in most other theoretical approaches described in the chapters of this book. For instance, it is substantially implied in processes of resource allocation, as well as in the development of family household strategies and, at a different level, in the way households react to their opportunity structure. Thus, power operates as a pivot on which many other approaches and issues hinge.

In order to exemplify the usefulness of theories on power in the functioning of family households, we decided to focus on the issue of *the division of household production tasks.*

Some key concepts need preliminary clarification. In our view, *household production* implies activities performed on behalf of the welfare of household members or the functioning of the family household as a group, entailing economic as well as non-economic activities. As for non-economic activities, most research further distinguishes between domestic work in a comprehensive and in a strict sense. Domestic work in a strict sense implies just housework, for instance preparing meals, cleaning the house, and shopping. Domestic work in a comprehensive sense also implies child care and child guidance (Coltrane, 1996). Accordingly, we will use *housework* to denote domestic work in a strict sense and *domestic work* to denote the more comprehensive assembly of tasks.

Studying the division of household production is important for several reasons. First, as argued earlier, changes that occur within family households may influence the meaning of phenomena at a collective level. For instance, gender (and its inherent connotations of power inequality) is produced and reproduced through the division of household labour (Greenstein, 1996). If sharing household tasks indeed carries the potential for transforming the meaning of gender in this and the next generations, as Coltrane (1996) states, then the observation of slowing and accelerating changes in sharing or non-sharing within households is of utmost importance. Additionally, large-scale social changes may require changes in the division of domestic work. For example, recent social and demographic changes in Japan require men to make a transition from 'workaholic fathers' to 'nurturant fathers'. Multigenerational co-residence in Japan is expected to decline, and, as a consequence, the presence of older female family members who can ease the burdens of housework will decrease as well. Women's increasing participation in the labour force will result in more demands on Japanese husbands to take a greater share in household responsibilities (Ishii-Kuntz, 1993). Further, findings from research in different countries and cultures strongly indicate that many women are overburdened as a consequence of combining paid work and family life (Danes et al., 1994). In case of wife's employment, the division of household work remains strongly unequal. The proportion of total hours spent on domestic work of employed wives tends to differ only slightly when compared to the proportion of time spent on domestic work of non-employed wives (Demo and Acock, 1993, in Greenstein, 1996a, 1996b; Van der Lippe, 1993). Evidence indicates that the division of domestic work influences the health of people. Gottman (1991) found in a longitudinal study that men in the United States who did housework were far more healthy four years later than those who did not. They appeared to be less overwhelmed by their wives' emotions, less avoidant of conflict, and had lower heart rates during marital conflict than men who did no housework. On the other hand, it was discovered that wives whose husbands hardly contributed to housework suffered more from psychological distress (Coltrane, 1996).

In the next paragraphs we present two conceptual frameworks and key studies which represent basically different views on the phenomenon of power. Each one represents a main stream in the theory on power and catches different and important aspects of the phenomenon.

5.3 A First Conceptual Framework: Power as an Outcome

According to Blood and Wolfe (1960), within the context of marriage and family living, power is manifested in the ability to make decisions affecting the life of the family. The power to make decisions is influenced by the prescribed authority pattern. For instance, in a patriarchical system both the husband and the wife will ordinarily take for granted that the husband should make most of the decisions. He derives some assertiveness from the social norm, and she derives a measure of deference from it. According to Blood and Wolfe, however, considering the large variations even within a traditional society, there must exist other sources of marital power apart from authority. These sources must be sought in the comparative resources which the husband and the wife bring with them to marriage, a resource being anything that one partner may make available to the other, helping the latter satisfy his needs or attain his goals. In addition, Blood and Wolfe introduced a second factor which is closely related to resources. This factor refers to a person's competence, i.e. his or her possession of special skills, including skills to make decisions or knowledge about decision-making in the public area. Balancing both partners' contributions and competencies is rarely a conscious process. It is an 'automatic readjustment' which occurs as the contributing partner discovers that he or she has or has not a lot to offer to the marriage. Power accrues spontaneously to the partner who has the greater resources at his disposal, placing him or her in a strategic position.

Both authority patterns and personal resources were originally thought to be interdependent and influential in the balance of power between husband and wife. However, Blood and Wolfe questioned whether they were equally important. According to one theory, authority or ideology prevails: families do what the culture tells them to do. According to the alternative theory, pragmatism predominates: families do what their own 'characteristics' (i.e. their comparative resources) dictate. Blood and Wolfe tested both theories in an extensive study among families in the Detroit area in the United States.

In order to measure the precise balance of power between husbands and wives, Blood and Wolfe assessed both partners' influence in all the decisions which had ever been made. Obviously, a complete record of decisions would be unobtainable and unworkable. Therefore, they relied on a sample of decisions to represent the larger whole. To estimate the relative power between husbands and wives, eight decisions were selected:[1]

1. what job the husband should take;
2. what car to get;
3. whether or not to buy life insurance;
4. where to go on vacation;
5. what house or apartment to take;
6. whether or not the wife should go to work or quit work;
7. what doctor to have when someone is sick;
8. how much money the family can afford to spend per week on food.

Results of the analysis lead the authors to the conclusion that, although families could be found varying from one extreme to the other, most families 'bunched together' around the mean score, indicating families were slightly skewed to the husband's side in absolute terms. In more general terms, Detroit families apparently were, on the whole, extraordinarily alike as far as the balance of decision-making was concerned.

Blood and Wolfe's crucial question concerned the prevalence of either the ideological theory or the comparative theory about the sources of power. To test the power of the first theory, they searched for the segments of the population in which the patriarchical tradition supposedly still survived. They assumed this tradition would be intact among those families which had been exposed less to urban, industrial, and educational influences: families now or formerly living on farms, immigrant families, old couples, uneducated couples, and Catholic marriages.

The results were rather surprising. None of these expectations were confirmed. No differences emerged between the families living on farms and those living in the city. Immigrants turned out to be even less patriarchical than native Americans. Husbands of active white Protestants had just as much power as husbands of active, white Catholics. The highest power scores were not reached by the older generation but by the young post-World War II marriages. Not without pathos, the authors (1960, p.44) stated that 'the contemporary married couples are freed from the "dead hand" of patriarchical tradition'. They implied that wherever husbands had a great deal of power at that time, it was not because they and their wives held a patriarchical belief system. In their view the role of culture had shifted from sanctioning a competent sex over an incompetent sex to sanctioning a competent marriage partner over an incompetent one, regardless of sex.

In addition to answering the question of whether the American family had changed its authority pattern, Blood and Wolfe tried to answer the question of whether the division of labour had changed too. Their findings indicated that the division of labour could also be declared equalitarian in the sense that both husbands and wives participated in it. But whereas the pattern of decision-making appeared to be flexible and shared, the division of labour was found to be highly specialized and more stereotyped. Nevertheless, to a certain degree, power and the division of labour appeared to be connected. Couples who shared more than half their decisions did more housework together. At the other extreme, couples who made few joint decisions did correspondingly little work together. More generally, power and the household's division of labour appeared to coexist in almost any combination. According to the authors, they could best be considered separately rather than welded into artificial combinations.

Further analysis of possible determinants of the division of labour between husbands and wives proved - as Blood and Wolfe (1960, p.57) formulated - that the 'sheer availability of one partner to do the household tasks appeared to be the prime determinant of the division of labor'. They added, more or less emphatically: 'Nothing could be more pragmatic and non-ideological'.

In general, the authors concluded that the division of labour in the modern family did not differ from the division of labour in the traditional family. What did change was the shift of the pattern of decision-making towards sharing. Therefore, contemporary American families could not be considered conservative. What did not change were the 'bio-social reasons' which formerly shaped the traditional family and which, at that time, implied the differential resources which men and women brought to their marriage.

Many critical remarks unavoidably came and continue to come to the fore (Komarovsky, 1967; Cromwell and Olson, 1975; Olson and Cromwell, 1975; Safilios-Rothschild, 1976). Questions which arose included: are the decisions Blood and Wolfe submitted equally important and do they indeed represent the most important ones within family households (e.g. Blood and Wolfe consciously omitted decisions on children)? Is power implied in just making the final decision, or is it already implied in precurring discussions or even in the prevailing, cultural patterns of the division of labour? If competencies do indeed differ between men and women, is this for 'bio-social reasons' or 'by culture'? If an unequal division of labour results from 'sheer availability', from where does this unequal availability arise and is it indeed just a 'non-ideological matter'? A recent key study nicely exemplifies several weak points of the framework.

5.4 Key Study: Power and Households' Agricultural Production in China

5.4.1 Introduction

This project is quite appropriate for the elucidation of the preceding framework. It is clearly designed, consistently follows the conceptual framework, and considers in particular the relative resources both partners possess. Both wife and husband of each household are involved as sources of information, and the household is explicitly the locus of information.

In addition, its results refer to a large population within a cultural context which strongly differs from culture in Western countries. By consequence, it shows the relevance of a comparative perspective in the sociology of decision-making. While the study focuses on decision-making regarding agricultural issues in farming households, it highlights an important, but rather neglected aspect of household production.

Finally, the author Chen (1996) assumes decision-making to be gender-specific, which makes gender a key variable in this study. Gender is assumed to influence decision-making both directly and indirectly: in a direct way because gender is related to specific household tasks; indirectly because gender is related to the unequal power between men and women.[2]

5.4.2 Key Concepts and Research Questions

The study's specific objective is to identify women farmers' participation in agricultural decision-making in Southern China. It intends to identify the actors in agricultural decision-making as well as the factors that determine the extent and nature of their decision-making power. However, it does not dig into the decision-making process itself. The main research question concerns the role of gender in farming household decision-making. The decisions on which the study focuses are limited to those which concern farm management and agricultural production. In short: agricultural decisions. Decisions about family issues are not included in the framework. The folllowing research questions elaborate Chen's main research question:
1. Is there gender specificity in agricultural decision-making? What types of decisions are usually made by male and female farmers respectively?
2. What factors determine the role of gender in agricultural decision-making by farming households? What factors are positively or negatively related to the husbands' decision-making power and negatively or positively to that of the wives? What factors are positively or negatively related to both husbands' and wives' decision-making?
3. Does the type of farming household influence the role of gender in farming household agricultural decision-making?

According to resource theory, the relative power of husbands and wives is assumed to depend on the relative resources (such as education, social status, family wealth, employment, occupational status) which each partner brings into marriage. The husband's and wife's power in decision-making will increase as his or her resources increase and the balance of power will be on the side of the partner who contributes the most to the marriage. Personal characteristics such as age, sex, and stage in the life-cycle may also be important in power and bargaining. However, the degree to which such characteristics are related to power is fundamentally dependent on the structural context, i.e. the way age and sex norms dictate specific social positions, roles, and level of prestige.

Gender is operationalised as the differential positions and roles of husbands and wives. According to Giddens (1994), it is assumed to not refer to the differing physical attributes of men and women, but to socially formed traits of masculinity and femininity. It serves to distinguish the social character and responsibilities of both sexes in a particular social and cultural setting.

A farming household (FHH) was operationally defined (for the Chinese context) as 'a contract unit to which land is allotted by the state, in which a group of people, usually a nuclear family, individually or jointly provide management, labour, capital and other necessary inputs for the production of crops and livestock, and who consume at least part of the farm produce' (Chen, 1996, p.11). The term refers to the agrifamily system in which the subsystems of nuclear family, household and farm are merged. According to Chen, small farms make many decisions based on the circumstances. Long term decisions in Chinese agriculture are often still made by the government, local organizations or institutions. Short-term decisions are made and implemented by the core person who takes care of the farm's daily activities.

Using earlier exploratory studies, available conceptual frameworks, agricultural practices in the province of Sichuan, and the gender pattern of farm management, the following five *types of farm management* were distinguished:

1. Male managed FHH, in which the wife lives away from the farm most of the time and is mainly involved in non-agricultural work while the husband mainly farms;
2. Female managed FHH: same as the first type but with the roles of husband and wife reversed;
3. Mainly female managed FHH, in which both spouses live on the farm, but the husband is mainly engaged in non-agricultural activities while the wife mainly farms;
4. Mainly male managed FHH: same as type three, but with roles of husband and wife reversed;
5. Jointly managed FHH, in which both spouses live on the farm and both mainly farm, usually managing the farm together.

Decision-making was narrowed down to the outcomes of the decision-making process: agricultural decisions (see above) and gender of the decision-maker (husband or wife). The process of decision-making itself was not investigated. *Power* and gender were linked in the operational concept of husband's and wife's decision-making power, measured by identifying the decision-maker (husband or wife) for thirteen agricultural decisions:

- The purchase of agricultural equipment
- The pest control
- The purchase of fertiliser

- The selection of seed
- The adoption of cultivation techniques
- The use of external labour
- The marketing of the crop
- The selection of the type of livestock
- The selection of the type of poultry
- Animal feed
- The sale of animal and animal products
- The sale of poultry and poultry products
- The health care of animals

5.4.3 Data Collection and Analysis

A random sample (1018 farming households) was selected in the 22 townships of Yaan county (population of 49,330 farming households) in the Sichuan province, one of China's South Western provinces and chosen because of its large population and strategic importance to China's rural development. Agriculture is the foundation of the region's economy with approximately 80% of the population rural-registered. The sample was stratified according to type of farming household, yielding five strata. Both men and women were interviewed by the researcher and 40 students from the Yaan professional agricultural school. Every interviewer randomly selected six households of each farming household type. Households not headed by married couples were left out of the analysis.

A wife and husband's decision-making index (DMI) was calculated from the answers given to each of the questions on the thirteen agricultural decisions.[3] The relation between gender and type of decision was tested for all types of farming households.

5.4.4 Findings and Discussion

As to the first and third question, which refer to gender-specific decisions and the role of the farming household type, the finding is most intriguing that none of the decision issues appeared to be dominated by either partner across all types of farming households. In fact, the type of farming household appeared to be a decisive factor in decision-making by husbands or wives. However, decisions which involved a relatively large amount of capital, e.g. sale of animals and animal products, were relatively often shared. The purchase of agricultural equipment, measures for pest control, purchase of fertiliser, selection of seeds, adoption of specific cultivation practices, use of external labour, crop marketing, animal feed, and health care of animals were significantly more often decided upon by women in (mainly) female managed FHHs and by men in (mainly) male managed FHH. Other decisions were to a large extent shared. Gender specificity in the types of decisions emerged most clearly in type five of FHH, the jointly managed one. Table 5.1 represents the way in which issues of decision-making were divided among husbands and wives in the jointly managed type of households.

Table 5.1 Issues more often decided on by husbands and wives

husbands	wives
purchase of agricultural equipment	selection of seeds
pest control	crop marketing
purchase of fertilizer	selection of type of animal
adoption of specific cultivation practices	selection of poultry
use of external labor	animal feed
	sale of poultry and poultry products
	health care of animals

Women generally appeared to dominate when animals were involved, while men were more involved when the decision concerned crops or equipment. According to the author, the results show a gender specificity which indicates tradition or culture as explaining variables, rather than differences in access to resources.

The decision-making index (DMI) of men and women also followed a pattern which reflects the importance of type of FHH as the explaining variable. The average indexes of men and women approached the maximum or minimum according to the gender type of farm management. For the jointly managed FHH, the decision-making index of husbands equalled that of wives (6.5 both). Interestingly, the overall index of wives was even higher than that of husbands: 7.3 and 5.7, respectively. For all farming households taken together, irrespective of type of FHH and type of decision, women seemed to dominate agricultural decision-making. But the question is: do they have more power?

This question has been answered by some other findings which concern the determinants of decision-making (question 2). No single variable explained unequivocally differences in decision-making between husbands and wives across all types of FHH. For instance, education correlated positively with the wife's score on the Decision-Making Index (DMI), but it was negatively related to husband's DMI. Income and contribution of labour showed a similar pattern. The largest overall positive effect on wives' DMI was exerted by the variable which was not hypothesized as an independent variable on the basis of the literature, but which is typical of the Chinese context: sex of children. In four out of five types of FHH, having sons contributed significantly to women's decision-making power. In the remaining type of FHH (the male managed FHH) having children, sons or daughters, did.

The author explains the unequivocal findings concerning education, contribution to labour and other variables by referring to the low status of farming in this part of China. Men have better opportunities for finding off-farm income generating activities than women. In Yaan, only 2.5% of the FHHs are male managed with the wife working and living away from the farm, while 35.2% are female managed with an absent husband. The same pattern prevails with regard to type three and four FHHs: both spouses living on the farm, but only one of them working in agriculture. Husbands who do not work in agriculture have a low DMI. Their education is relatively high, their income contribution is high (because off-farm employment pays better), and their labour contribution is low. However, their low DMI and, correspondingly, their wives' high DMI do not reflect a lack of access to the assumed resources of power, but reflect their marginal participation in agriculture, including agricultural decision-making. Women's overall higher DMI, therefore, reflects their relatively intensive involvement with agriculture rather than having more power.

Discussion The study reveals the highly contextual and gender-specific nature of decision-making and its questionable relationship with power. In the micro-context of the household, type of farming household turned out to be a decisive explaining variable (also Zwart, 1990). Type of farming, however, just reflects the unequal division of (job) status among husbands and wives and the unequal opportunities for finding off-farm earnings. Therefore, in the meso-context of agricultural and non-agricultural labour, who makes agricultural decisions is inversely related to actual power. Chen's findings agree with findings from research on similar issues in the United States (Lyson, 1985; Danes and Rettig, 1993). Evidently, the relationship between decision-making and power depends on the benefits and status of the specific area of decision-making. Next, the significance of culture as an explaining variable comes to the fore. Having sons enhanced women's power, considered typical to the Chinese context. Culture also emerged as a significant factor: decisions on animal-related versus crop-related or equipment-related appeared to be gender-specific.

5.5 A Second Conceptual Framework: The Three-Dimensionality of Power

Sometimes a conceptual framework from a different domain appears to be quite fruitful. Komter (1989) delivered a substantial contribution to the study on power in marriages by proposing and applying a conceptual framework which Lukes (1974) developed within the field of political sociology. In his book *Power*, Lukes offers a conceptual framework on power and argues for a view of power which is radical, in both a theoretical and a political sense. He distinguishes three views on power: a 'one-dimensional view' (the view of the pluralists); a 'two-dimensional view' (the view of their critics); and a 'three-dimensional view'.

Within the *one-dimensional view* (based on Dahl, 1958), the study of concrete, observable behaviour is emphasized. The researcher should study actual behaviour, stress operational definitions, and deliver evidence. As in Blood and Wolfe's approach, the focus on observable behaviour in identifying power involves these researchers in studying decision-making as their central task. Power can be analysed only after careful examination of a series of concrete decisions. Assessing who prevails in decision-making is the best way to determine which individuals and groups have more power in social life because direct conflict between actors presents a situation which most closely approximates an experimental test of their capacities to affect outcomes. Decisions are assumed to involve direct, i.e. actual and observable, conflict. Thus, it is considered necessary (but possibly not a sufficient condition) that the key issue involves actual disagreement in preferences among two or more subjects. Conflict is assumed to be crucial in providing an experimental test of power attribution. Without it, the exercise of power will fail to be in evidence. Conflicts exist between preferences that are assumed to be made explicit, exhibited in actions, and thus are discoverable by observing people's behaviour. Interests should be understood as policy preferences and, by consequence, a conflict of interests is equivalent to a conflict of preferences. Any suggestions that interests might be unarticulated or unobservable are discarded. Similarly, perceptions that people might actually be mistaken about or unaware of their actual preferences, are rejected as well.

Lukes (1994) derives *the two-dimensional view* on power from the writings of Bachrach and Baratz (1970). Bachrach and Baratz' line of thought distinguishes itself sharply from the one-dimensional view on power. First, they take into account that power may be and often is exercised by confining the scope of decision-making to relatively 'safe issues', which goes beyond initiating, deciding, and vetoing. Second, power involves both decision-making and nondecision-making. A decision is a choice among alternative modes of action, while a non-decision is a decision that results in a suppression or thwarting of a latent or manifest challenge to the values or interests of the decision-maker. Nondecisions may not be overt or specific to a given issue, or may not even be consciously made to exclude eventual challengers. They are means by which demands for change in the existing pattern of allocation of benefits can be suffocated before they are even expressed. Third, in contrast to the one-dimensional view, it is considered crucially important not only to identify issues of actual conflict, but also to identify potential issues which nondecision-making prevents from becoming actual.

Common to both the one-dimensional and the two-dimensional view is the stress on conflict, be it overt or covert. If there is no conflict, then a consensus is presumed to exist on the prevailing allocation of values. A conflict concerns the interests of those engaged in nondecision-making and the interests of those who are excluded from the prevailing political system. The observer must determine, if those persons and groups who are apparently disfavoured by the mobilization of bias do have grievances, overt or covert. Overt grievances are those that have already been expressed and have generated an issue within the political system. Covert grievances are still outside the system. They have not been recognized as worthy of public attention and controversy, but are observable to the investigator in their 'aborted' form. Interests are considered to be embodied in expressed policy preferences and sub-political grievances. According to Lukes (1974), however, the two-dimensional view also fails as an adequate representation of power.

The *three-dimensional view* sees the two-dimensional view as being too committed to behaviourism, i.e. to the study of overt behaviour, wherein concrete decisions in situations of conflict are seen as paradigmatic. The two-dimensional view tries to link all ways of excluding potential issues from the political agenda to the paradigm of a decision and, by consequence, it gives a misleading picture of the ways in which individuals, and groups, or institutions succeed in keeping issues out of the political debate. The bias of the system is not only sustained by a series of individual acts, but also, and most importantly, by the socially structured and culturally patterned behaviour of groups and practices of institutions. A second point of critique concerns the association within the two-dimensional view of power with actual observable conflict. According to Lukes, it is highly unsatisfactory to suppose that power is only exercised in case of such conflict. He (1974, p.23) puts the matter sharply as follows:

> A may exercise power over B by getting him to do what he does not want to do, but he also exercises power over him by influencing, shaping or determining his very wants. Only considering actual conflict, is to ignore the crucial point that the most effective and insidious use of power is to prevent such conflict from arising.

A third point of critique refers to the two-dimensional's insistence that nondecision-making power only exists where there are grievances which are denied entry into the political agenda in the form of issues. If people feel no grievances, then they are supposed to have no interests that are harmed by the use of power. But, as Lukes rightly states, this is really unsatisfactory. Characteristic to the three-dimensional view is the presence of a 'latent conflict', which consists in a contradiction between the interests of those exercising power and the 'real interests' of those they exclude. They possibly do not express or are even conscious of their real interests. As Lukes argues later on, the identification of those interests ultimately always rests on empirically supportable and refutable hypotheses.

However, the question unavoidably arises: how is the existence of nondecision-making, of potential issues, of covert and latent conflict, and of the people's 'real' interests proven?

5.6 Key Study: Invisible Power and the Division of Domestic Work in The Netherlands

5.6.1 Introduction

Komter (1985; 1989) performed a study which showed a way to answer such questions and delivered intriguing insights into what she calls 'invisible power', regarding amongst others the division of domestic work. The study consistently used Lukes' theoretical framework, focused on the third dimension of power, and added some important additional concepts (i.e. ideological hegemony). Contrary to our first key study, the project followed a scheme which represented processes (changes and strategies) rather than static features such as bases of power and power outcomes. In addition, the study demonstrated the usefulness of semi-structured interviews (conducted with both wives and husbands), which evoked spontaneous comments rather than pre-structured answers, and a way of analyzing the information collected.

5.6.2 Key Concepts and Research Questions

Komter's study focuses on the less visible, informal operation of power processes and mechanisms in marriage. The study's main question (1989) is twofold:
1. What is the nature of power in marital relationships?
2. What is the connection between marital power, class, and the employment status of the wife?

The study is explicitly based on Lukes' three-dimensional framework of power and on Gramsci's concept of *ideological hegemony* as well (Gramsci, 1971). This concept views ideological control as being achieved by the generation of representations in people's common sense, where contradictions are represented as a unitary whole. Common sense conceptions of the world are to some degree always fragmentary, incoherent, and often inconsistent. Nevertheless, these conceptions are crucial because through these very contradictions and inconsistencies, the differing values of the dominant group and the subordinate group may become apparent. The interests of dominant groups are represented and experienced as general interests and will, by consequence, be experienced by both groups as having been accepted in freedom.

Komter's basic assumption implies that, within marriage, the partners' reasons and motivations for both the presence and absence of desires for change or attempts at change can shed light on marital power. Inconsistencies, ambiguities or contradictions in a respondent's statements are assumed to be part of the mechanisms of marital power.

Komter distinguishes three kinds or levels of power: manifest power, latent power and invisible power. *Manifest power* surfaces in visible outcomes such as attempts to change, conflicts, and strategies. *Latent power* occurs when no changes or conflicts are reported. Latent power encompasses situations in which the needs and wishes of the more powerful person are anticipated, or when resignation results from anticipating a partner's negative reaction or results from fear of jeopardizing the marital relationship. *Invisible power* results from social or psychological mechanisms that do not necessarily emerge into overt behaviour or into latent grievances. They supposedly become manifest in systematic gender differences regarding mutual and self-esteem, and in differences in perceptions of and legitimations concerning everyday reality. The effects of invisible power generally occur beyond the awareness of the people involved.

5.6.3 Data Collection and Analysis

Respondents were selected in and around an average-sized university city in the eastern part of The Netherlands. Two registers of employed women were used. One consisted of female cleaning personnel employed at the university, the other was made available by the Association of Academically Trained Women. Because of insufficient response, couples who had already agreed on participation in the project were asked to suggest other couples who might be inclined to participate in the study, a procedure which delivered by far the majority of respondents. All in all, sixty couples, aged 20-55 with children living at home, participated in the project. Half of the women in both the lower-class and the higher-class group had a paid job. Semi-structured interviews were conducted with wives and husbands separately. Questions focused on:

1. The extent to which women and men have desires for change in several areas of living (i.e. domestic labour, child rearing, sexuality, leisure activities, and finances). For instance, questions were: 'Do you ever have daydreams or fantasies about what you would preferably do? If so, what are these dreams about?'; 'If you could decide completely for yourself, how would you prefer to spend your days?'; 'What change would be necessary in order to reach this?'

2. The extent to which conflicts emerge in these areas. Questions were formulated such as: 'Do you ever disagree (tensions, irritations, quarrels, etc.) with your husband/wife about the way household tasks are performed?'; 'What happens if you disagree?'; 'Can you give an example?'; 'How does it end in most cases?'

3. The strategies women and men employ in their attempts at effecting or preventing change. Questions were asked such as: 'Did you ever try to change somewhat the way in which the work is divided between you and your husband/wife (for instance, offer some help)? If so, what?'; 'How did you handle this?'; 'What happened?'; 'Did it succeed?'; If not, 'Why not?'; 'How did your husband/wife react?'; If not, 'Would you change something?'; 'What?' (way in which the actual regulation arised); 'What would your husband/wife think of that?'; 'What does impede you to change things in this area?'

4. Possible gender differences in mutual and self-esteem, in perceptions of and legitimations concerning everyday reality. These were considered

invisible power mechanisms because they confirm and justify power inequality in an ideological, unintentional, and often unconscious way. Questions, for instance, were: 'What do you value most of your husband/wife?'; 'What do you value most or yourself?'; 'What does your husband/wife value most of you?'; 'Does your husband/wife possess qualities you would like to possess yourself?'[4]

5.6.4 Findings and Discussion

As to the results of the study, we will focus largely on Komter's fourth and last indicator of power concerning gender differences in mutual and self-esteem and in the perception of everyday reality. Invisible power is first and foremost at stake in the information inherent to this indicator. Three invisible power mechanisms were apparent in the analysis: inequality regarding esteem for women and men, perceptual bias, and apparent consensus.

Inequality of esteem Answers to the question of what they liked most about themselves and about their partners were analysed. The number of positive and negative characteristics (which were mentioned spontaneously) were used as an indicator to the degree of self-esteem and esteem for one's partner. Women expressed less self-esteem compared to men. They described themselves as less cognitively competent, while husbands tended to value their personal competence higher than their wives did. Women also mentioned significantly more often negative personal qualities compared to men and had higher esteem for their husbands than their husbands had for them, regarding cognitive competence and personal competence. Both wives and husbands described themselves and each other in terms of classical gender-role stereotypes. The husbands' greater self-esteem supposedly gave them more bargaining power. In addition, every man benefitted from the culturally determined differences between men and women. Komter (1989) considers the power effect invisible because 'the apparent naturalness of the assumed differences in personality traits prevents wives and husbands from acknowledging it'.

Perceptual bias emerged as another invisible power mechanism. Key questions were: 'Who has the greatest responsibility for domestic labour?', and 'Who does in fact perform most of the domestic labour?'. Self-reports on these questions were compared to data regarding amount of time respondents had actually spent on different activities during one week. The analysis delivered several interesting findings. Husbands appeared to underestimate their wives' share in household tasks. They also underestimated their wives' responsibilities and actual share in child care. They overestimated their own contribution correspondingly. According to Komter, this perceptual bias offers husbands the obvious psychological benefit that they have no reason to feel obliged to meet their wives' request to take a greater share in household tasks.

Apparent consensus Husbands and wives seemingly agreed as to the reasons for their task division. Common legitimations included, for instance: 'She has more time available', 'He has no feeling for it', 'He is not born to it', or 'She has more talent for it'. More importantly, Komter found inconsistencies between these legitimations and respondents' personal experiences. For instance, both wives and husbands claimed that 'women enjoy parenting more than men'. When asked directly about their experience of parenthood, however, women appeared to enjoy it somewhat less than men did. Further, men's feelings toward domestic labour were more positive than women's feelings about domestic work. Their positive feelings about domestic tasks were not reflected in legitimations of the division of labour, however. On the contrary, reasons such as 'he dislikes it', or 'she has more pleasure in doing it' *were* in fact frequently mentioned. Finally, wives were less content in all areas studied, as their greater desire for change on almost all domains indicated. Husbands legitimized the existing situation more frequently and were more inclined to emphasize the inevitability of the actual state of affairs by perceiving and presenting it as natural, necessary, and unchangeable. According to Komter (1989), such legitimations - largely taken for granted - contribute forcefully to the perception of daily reality as unchangeable and inevitable and so become part of invisible power.

Komter's findings exemplify important mechanisms which operate in the production and reproduction of power within family households. Many other studies corroborated her findings and deepened similar insights (Hochschild, 1989; Thompson, 1991; Ferree, 1991; Blain, 1994; Boss and Gurko, 1994; Coltrane, 1996; Zvonkovic et al., 1996).

Discussion One might object against considering 'inequality of esteem', 'perceptual bias' and 'apparent consensus' mechanisms of power reproduction. Instead, one might maintain that 'self-esteem' or 'estimation of one's share' should be viewed rather as individual resources and hold 'apparent consensus' to be one among a couple's common resources. However, it is of crucial importance that such mechanisms or resources are generated on the level of collectivity and that they usually operate beyond awareness of the subjects involved. They are used when people explain actual practices within their households and draw on more or less 'free-floating' discourses which have been created collectively elsewhere and act to maintain gendered social structures of inequality (Blain, 1994).

While Komter focuses on ideologically determined mechanisms of power production or reproduction, structural mechanisms, of no less importance, remained largely out of sight. As we mentioned earlier, Gramsci (1971) viewed social institutions as maintaining the existing power hierarchies. In a more general sense, such institutions imply the market system and the public system. The market system contains a specific division of employment, the supply and demand of commodities and services. The public system comprises amongst others: the fiscal sub-system, collective provisions, and social security regulations (Van Dongen, 1992). As to the division of domestic work between husbands and wives, prevailing labour-market regulations result in the exclusion of women from certain jobs which provide higher salary and more security. Such an exclusion results in wives' accepting responsibility for low status work in the home and entering a state of dependence on men to support them. It is not their position in the family, but rather it is the labour market which confines women to a subordinate position in the household. Downskilling of some jobs and the reduction of pay and prestige result from women's entering certain occupations in large numbers or from working arrangements made to accomodate women's household commitments. Worktime flexibility, job sharing, and teleworking attract less attention from employers or from politicians as far as yet (Walby, 1986; Vogler, 1994; Hantrais and Letablier, 1996). These mechanisms are not reserved to capitalist countries. They still operate in Eastern Europe as well (Boss and Gurko, 1994).

5.7 Conclusions and New Directions for Research

5.7.1 Conclusions

When comparing the two conceptual frameworks on power with one another, both similarities and dissimilarities clearly emerge. Lukes' (1974) 'one dimensional view' corresponds with processes of decision-making as a matter of overt behaviour by individual subjects, comprising exercises of power (such as initiating, vetoing, and proposing alternatives) as mentioned by Dahl (1958), and with decision outcomes as measured by Blood and Wolfe (1960). Also the work of Scanzoni and Szinovacz (1980) and of Kingsbury and

Scanzoni (1989) as far as it is concerned with discussions, problem-solving, conflict resolution, overt grievances and explicit preferences, being put on a par with interests, is in line with this view.

The 'two-dimensional view' can in particular be characterized by a mobilization of bias (Bachrach and Baratz, 1970), implying a confinement of the scope of decision-making by the power-exercising Other, the process of nondecision-making, and the recognition of the existence of potential instead of overt conflict issues. Covert grievances, being outside the system, can also be considered inherent to this kind of power. Additionally, Scanzoni and Szinovacz's (1980) concept of 'tacit understandings' neatly fits with this 'two-dimensional view'.

The structure of Lukes' and Komter's 'three dimensional view' is more complicated. In these views, power is not bound to specific actors or couples as units, but is considered a property of a patterned behaviour of groups or of institutional practices. It particularly operates through institutions, practices and social arrangements (cf. Foucault, 1986). Preferences or wants are considered to be shaped by those who exercise power and prevent conflicts to emerge, while the absence of grievances does not refer to the absence of interests being endangered. Crucial is the presence of a 'latent conflict' in which the existing division of resources, competencies and 'sheer availabilities' among different social groups are fundamentally questioned.

5.7.2 New Directions for Research

Our conclusions leave a number of questions unanswered. Together with issues in recent literature, these questions can be transformed into several 'new directions' for research.

A first suggestion concerns the relevance of culture and ideology as to resource theory. Next, the interwoveness of feelings and ideology appears to be rather neglected and deserves further attention. Decrease of gender inequality may be clarified through insights into both resistance and proneness to change, to be addressed in sections 3 and 4. Finally, among many other options, we argue for elucidating the influence of the life course on gender equality as to the division of household production.

Resource theory and culture Time availability is one of the main approaches to explain divisions of domestic work. Indeed, according to people's personal experiences among already sharing couples, time availability seems to be the most important factor in the division of domestic work. Among these couples, the spouse with the fewest employment hours as well as the spouse with the most flexible hours tends to do more of the housework and child care (Coltrane, 1996). Expressions such as 'Who gets to it first' or 'who can work it into his schedule' indicate the importance of the ability to schedule one's employment hours around sharing of both child care and housework.

Two amendments have to be made, however. First, time availability can be hardly considered an explaining variable. It is highly dependent on the structural opportunities offered by the labour market, as delineated above. Second, time availability interacts with culture, as is evidenced by research findings from Kamo (1994). Kamo tested a theoretical model which was based on time availability, resource exchange, and gender perspectives for the United States and for Japan. One intriguing finding of the study concerns the amount of explained variance in both countries. The model's predictors explained 44% of the variance of the husband's relative share of household work in the United States, while it explained only 14% of the variance for Japanese couples. According to Kamo, this difference may result from the fact that economic exchange between household work and resource contribution is more relevant in the United States (where individualism is stressed) than it is in Japan (where collectivistic orientations are equally important). However, a rigid gender stratification, as existing in Japan (also Ishii-Kuntz, 1993), might also explain this difference: in highly traditional societies or families, traditional gender roles between breadwinner and homemaker are so distinctive that individual attitudes and interpersonal dynamics do not matter much. For instance, in the United States, each spouse's earnings affect the husband's relative share of housework while in Japan, husband's earnings do, but wife's earnings do not affect his share of work. This might be explained by the relatively low level of the Japanese wife's income or by her less 'demanding' attitude for an adjustment in the division of household tasks. Furthermore, years of education appeared to be positively related to the husband's share of domestic work in the United States. In Japan, neither spouses' years of education had any effect on his share. Kamo points out that as far as American husbands are concerned, education seems to work as a proxy for gender-role attitude rather than as a proxy for the relative resources (also Shukla, 1987; Hardesty and Bokemeier, 1989; Sanchez and Kane, 1996).

These findings do not deny the relevance of relative resources and time availability, but also indicate that, when these factors are controlled, gender-role beliefs about the division of domestic work remain related to who actually performs it (Ferree, 1991; DeMaris and Longmore, 1996).

Therefore, future studies should focus on the way structural opportunities resulting from the labour market and governmental policy are conducive to a more equal division of domestic work, considering prevailing gender ideologies. The conceptual framework which is offered in chapter 6 (The Opportunity Structure Approach and the Housing Market) may be helpful to these studies.

2 Feelings and ideology Considering that the division of domestic work is largely divided unequally between husbands and wives, the question of 'why most wives see the "lopsided" division of domestic work in their households as fair?' emerged (Ferree, 1991; Thompson, 1991). As for time spent doing stereotypic-female housework, proportionate time rather than absolute time in housework seems decisive to fairness perceptions among women as well as men: the greater the woman's proportion of the couple's total time spent in stereotypic-female housework, the greater the perceived unfairness to her is (Blair and Johnson, 1992; Sanchez and Kane, 1996). Ideologies may fulfill a crucial role as to this relationship. For example, Greenstein (1996b) found that gender ideology interacts with the actual division of domestic work in relation to the experience of fairness. Inequalities in the division of household tasks were related to the likelihood that an egalitarian wife perceived the division of housework as unfair, while the division of tasks was not related to perceptions of injustice among traditional wives. The author considers the role of gender ideology a moderator variable. But as to this issue, research findings are still rather inconsistent (cf. Blair and Johnson, 1992).

The degree to which the husband's or wife's social and emotional (in)dependence is related to perceived fairness is particularly intriguing (DeMaris and Longmore, 1996). Sanchez and Kane (1996) proved that if men feel they would be better off without the relationship with their partner, they are less likely to perceive the actual division of housework as being unfair to their female partners. On the contrary, if women feel they would be better off without the relationship, they are more likely to perceive unfairness to themselves. These findings are corroborated by Lennon and Rosenfield (1994), who show that women who feel they have fewer alternatives to marriage and whose earnings would put them below the poverty line if divorced were more likely to perceive an unequal division of domestic work as fair. These findings indicate that the perception of fairness and similar feelings are strongly related to (unequal) social position and the need for security and, by consequence, susceptible to ideological hegemony. Despite this susceptibility, feelings of 'fairness' and 'entitlement' are important issues, because they are linked to many other perceptions such as of marital quality and may play a crucial role in subjects withdrawing from prevailing ideologies (Blair, 1993; Perry-Jenkins and Folk, 1994).

Handbooks of psychology offer amazingly scant information on emotions and feelings in relation to the issues we have discussed in the context of family households. For instance, Oatley and Jenkins (1996) devote just a few pages to gratitude as a component in the biological evolution of emotions. 'Feelings of fairness' is conspicuously absent in their subject index. Frijda (1986) extensively treats feelings of guilt and shame, but one searches in vain for information on sense of fairness.

We propose the relationship between feelings and actual patterns of domestic work division as a subject for discussion and further research. Prevailing ideologies and dependencies between partners should be considered as intervening variables.

3 Resistance to change Resistance to change is most often ascribed to men's unwillingness to share household work (Willinger, 1993). However, women may actually not want to share the houseworker role and the inherent responsibility with their husbands. Wives may have to cope with feelings of guilt about abandoning their traditional role and have mixed feelings about their husbands doing nontraditional tasks (Tavecchio et al., 1984). Not only do they not pressure on their husbands to share the tasks, but they do not even make 'room' for their husbands' participation. Hochschild (1989) describes several ways in which such an obstruction is performed. Women may play the expert role in baby care, dinner preparation, etc. The tone of their voices may say: 'This is my domain' in order to gain credit for 'doing it all'. A husband's newly acquired skill may threaten the wife's previous monopoly over the attentive and intuitive parts of parenting (Thompson and Walker, 1989; Coltrane, 1996). Distinguishing between task performance and task responsibility is also relevant here. Responsibility implies both noticing the need for the performance of tasks and control in the quality of the task performance (Blain, 1994). It is an invisible burden as well as an invisible power base. By consequence, renouncing responsibility implies renouncing power, even in a relatively low-valued domain.

A curious process called 'balancing the scales' of power may also operate against changes in the division of household production. Both husbands and wives may practice such 'balancing'. For instance, Hochschild (1989) found that, among dual-earning couples, none of the men who earned less than their wives, shared domestic work, while 21 percent of the men who earned more than their wives and 30 percent of the men who earned about the same, shared the housework. Interestingly, if wives earned more than their husbands, both of them emphasized traditional wifehood. Men who were less succesful at work were likely to refuse to participate in domestic work, supposedly to compensate for the success of their wives who were rather more succesful in their career, and as a consequence, were gaining too much power. Women who were primary providers underlined their femininity by controlling housework and thus compensated for their nontraditional behaviour outside the home (cf. Brines, 1994; Bolak, 1997).

Generally, 'fractures' in gender ideology may operate both in resisting and in promoting change. Hochschild conceives such 'fractures' as internal conflicts between what a person feels and what the person thinks he or she ought to feel about marital roles. Some men and women seem to be egalitarian 'on top', but traditional 'underneath', or the other way around. Ideological beliefs may be contradicted by a person's deeper feelings. Such beliefs may also emerge in accordance with his or her deeper feelings and, as a consequence, are reinforced. Hochschild (1989) also discovered that not only do individual partners cherish ideological beliefs, but couples also develop 'family myths' or versions of reality that obscure a core truth in order to manage a family tension. Equally shared work at home when it was evidently not the case, is one example of this. Both 'shifting the balance' and 'fractures' are definitely contradictory to rational behaviour in any strict sense. They should therefore not be skipped in scientific research. On the contrary, they both may imply real 'breakpoints' in a turn towards new patterns or towards the maintenance of existing patterns of task division.

Further research should focus on the question of why husbands and wives resist change in the division of household production, in cases in which rationality would operate in favour of change.

4 Proneness to change Some wives do not resist their husbands' participation in domestic tasks. They tacitly invite their husbands to share work, offer suggestions for doing activities together, or even accept their husband's standards on house cleaning. Apart from the willingness or unwillingness of husbands and wives to accept and to give up task responsibilities and performances, some processes may develop 'underneath', i.e. beyond the level of awareness of one or both partners. They may nonetheless be highly relevant, particularly to gain deeper insight into processes of change. Evidence thus far is, however, predominantly anecdotal.

Hochschild (1989) describes an interesting couple in which the husband shares the second shift because 'he loved his wife and knew how terribly important it was to her to apply to a university's graduate program'. Then, what started as a concession from his side turned out to become a matter of fun for him. He felt amazed about his changed feelings on nurturing and began to feel proud.

'To do it' may thus turn into 'to like it'. Such turnabouts may appear to be primitive, but they are powerful mechanisms which people are barely aware of. Coltrane (1996) lively describes marriages which men entered with very limited knowledge of child development and without any expertise as a caregiver. However, as a result of being with children on a regular basis, they began to notice subtle cues from the children and share the nurturing role. Evidently, sharing childcare does not imply sharing domestic work. Nevertheless, Coltrane also found that by doing child care, men were encouraged to do more domestic work as well. Fathers themselves told that performance of direct child care tended to increase their commitment to doing more of the indirect childcare and housework, to spend more time in the house alone with their children, and to become more aware of household tasks and slowly more willing to perform them. Statistical analyses indicated that the sharing of housework and the sharing of child care were the strongest predictors for each other compared to the predicting power of many other variables. He concludes that when men get more involved in caring for their young children they also get more involved in doing housework.

Such processes imply what in social psychology is termed a 'channel factor', defined as a stimulus or a response pathway that serves to elicit or sustain behavioural intentions with particular intensity or stability (Ross and Nisbett, 1991).

'Proneness to change' seems a promising new direction for research. It might in particular focus on the way in which general attitudes or vague intentions are transformed into a changing division of domestic work and more in general household production, and how channel factors operate within such transformations.

5 The role of the life course Changes in the life-course may, intentionally or unintentionally, lead to changes in the division of household production. Timing of the transition to parenthood exemplifies such a change. Demographic research has underlined its relevance and there has been a sharp increase in delayed childbearing during the last two decades. Coltrane and Ishii-Kuntz (1992) explored how timing of the transition to parenthood is associated with later divisions of traditionally female-dominated housework. They focused on variation among couples with children living in the household. In general, men appeared to contribute proportionately more to housework if the couple had younger children and had delayed childbearing until their late 20s. More intriguing are additional differences they found between early-birth families and late-birth families. Among early-birth families, the *wives'* characteristics seemed to prevail: the wives' larger contribution to the household income and the wives' less traditional values accounted for a more equal division of household labour. Among late-birth families, the *husbands'* characteristics, such as his less traditional gender/family ideology and his fewer employment hours, accounted for differences in the division of domestic tasks. In these households wives' earnings appeared to hardly matter. According to Coltrane and Ishii-Kuntz, wives contributed more substantially to total household incomes among early-birth families, and their less traditional values might encourage them to negotiate for more participation by their husbands. These factors may actually facilitate the abandoning of the homemaker role. The authors assume several life-course factors to be important among late-birth couples. In short, those who have children later have a longer history of negotiating division of household tasks and may have accumulated experiences and observations of other couples they compare with. Delaying child-birth enables couples to develop patterns of sharing early in their relationship and solidify it even before having thought of childbearing (Coltrane, 1996). Next, the better overall economic conditions of couples who delay childbearing may make the wives' financial contribution somewhat less influential. Moreover, the transition to parenthood might offer more opportunities for women who delay childbearing to establish independent identities and develop a sense of self-esteem in their work role (Coltrane and Ishii-Kuntz, 1992).

Life-course characteristics evidently do matter in the division of household production. Further research should also include conceptual frameworks and data on changes in marital interaction, such as Scanzoni and Szinovacz provided (see also Kluwer, 1998). More specifically, we propose the way in which life course characteristics exert influence on the division of household production as a subject for further research, considering both partners' resources and ideologies, and their changing patterns of interaction.

Notes

1. In answering the related question, respondents in the Detroit study were given a choice ranging from 'husbands always' to 'wife always'.
2. The study concerns a PhD-research project which was carried out in rural Yaan, South-Western China under the supervision of the Department of Household Studies at Wageningen Agricultural University, during 1992-1996.

3. All decisions were equally weighted in the analysis. When a decision was usually made by the wife, she was scored 1 and her husband scored 0. When it was usually made by the husband, he was scored 1 and his wife scored 0. When decisions were usually shared, each spouse was attributed 0.5. A wife and husband's decision-making index (DMI) is calculated as the actual number of decision values multiplied by 13, and then divided by the total number of decisions made.

4. These questions were preceded by several questions which referred more specifically to present and past employment behaviour, to perceptions and motivations of non-participation in the labour-market, and were specifically directed to each distinguished group. All interviews were recorded, transcribed verbatim, and recoded twice, reaching an agreement level of about 90%. Responses were analyzed in a qualitative way, searching for common sense notions about gender, motivations for having no desires for change, or for having no conflicts, the nature of impediments, and strategies for change. In addition, if there were a sufficient number of responses available, comparisons were made as to class, gender, and the employment status of the wife.

6 The Opportunity Structure Approach and the Housing Market

6.1 Introduction

The Opportunity Structure Approach widens the scope of rational choice theory through introducing external social institutions: social agencies, their rules and regulations. Social institutions operate beyond the level of individual households. They largely determine the supply of provisions, entailing processes of producing, managing and distributing. In consequence, social institutions and agencies substantially define the opportunities available to family households and may thus influence their choices, and possibly their preferences as well. Opportunities are - like 'extrafamilial constraints' (Morris and Winter, 1978) - beyond the direct control of the family household. Nevertheless, to omit the influence of these institutions would certainly preclude a comprehensive view of behaviour and welfare within households (cf. Drèze and Sen, 1995).

However, supply does not determine behaviour in any strict sense. Behaviour within households depends on the degree to which households have access to provisions and on the degree to which they recognize these provisions as relevant, according to their values and priorities. In addition, behaviour also depends on the preparedness of households to take advantage from certain opportunities, as showed by McCrone (1994) in his qualitative study on the strategy of households. In consequence, in order to be effective, opportunities have to be recognized as such, and hence require a certain knowledge and alertness from the households involved. This stand implies that within the Opportunity Structure Approach households are considered as active agents rather than passive recipients.

However, a ready-made theoretical framework is not available. We shall therefore bring together several conceptual frameworks and integrate them into a more encompassing and coherent framework. There are some necessary constraints. First, in order to avoid vagueness, we have to select a specific area of provisions. We decided in favour of *housing*, because housing is one of the basic needs of households and its provision lends itself quite well to elucidating the complexity of the Opportunity Structure Approach, in particular regarding the ambiguity of the role of family households. Second, we decided in favour of less-industrialized countries. The ambiguity just mentioned comes most clearly to the fore in these countries, where family households often act both as suppliers and demanders. In addition, confining ourselves to housing provision in less-industrialized countries offers the advantage of a rather unusual view on the competence of households which is often unjustly depreciated in highly industrialized countries.

After having elucidated somewhat further the relevance of the Opportunity Structure Approach, we will present a first conceptual framework, i.e. an 'inter-organizational model', which describes the interactions between supplying agencies. Then we outline a framework concerning the roles of three main actors in the field of housing supply, regarding the goals they pursue, the policies they develop, and the resources they dispose of. As to the demand for housing - or what may be called the 'consumption of housing' - we will elaborate several issues regarding the needs of households and the effects of housing, and a necessary differentiation of households. These frameworks having been presented, some key studies will focus on housing provision and housing problems of women-headed households, and will exemplify appropriate methods of research and results which are important to housing policy. As in the other chapters, several 'new directions' will be introduced and elaborated at the end of the chapter.

6.2 The Relevance of the Opportunity Structure Approach and of the Housing of Family Households

Housing is a crucial provision insofar as the characteristics of a dwelling imply opportunities or constraints for the functioning of family households in a strict sense. Its location implies the accessibility of most other facilities which are important to family households, such as the access to an appropriate part of the job market, the access to preferred school types, health care provisions, kinship and other informal social networks, etc. Therefore, as Pahl (1975) pointed out, decisions made on housing have a crucial effect on the life chances of the members of a household. However, in many less-industrialized countries, housing is considered predominantly as an item of consumption, and therefore has a low priority in development plans and aid. Investments in housing have to compete with more 'productive' investments, or with other social provisions (food, health, and education), and often gets the worst part (Schlyter, 1988). An additional reason concerns the fact that in the field of housing the consumer as resident can intriguingly be considered an expert *par excellence* (Van Leeuwen, 1980; Clapham and Kintrea, 1986). His or her expertise challenges existing - often unequal - power relations between 'the suppliers' and 'the demanders' of provisions. But the position of the resident as an expert on housing and urban planning is certainly not uncontested: architects, urban planners, and some housing officials may claim the expert role, albeit in the name of the resident's well-being. Their views on housing and housing quality largely differ from those of the lay expert (Gans, 1972; Pennartz and Elsinga, 1990). Our reasons for selecting women-headed households are manifold.

Despite the fact that women-headed households are a minority among all households, their proportion is substantial and in most parts of the world it is expected to increase (Chant, 1997). Moser (1987) mentions an estimate that one-third of the world's households are being headed by women. Among highly industrialized countries the proportion of single-parent families as a percentage of all families with dependent children varies markedly: from about 7% (1985) in Japan to 27% (1993) in the United States (Firebaugh, 1995).

Next, the housing conditions of women-headed households in squatter settlements or in self-help housing projects are found to be amongst the worst, or at a comparatively low standard (Moser, 1987; Chant, 1987, 1997). They appear to be disadvantaged in several aspects of housing tenure or housing quality. For instance, with regard to home-ownership in Nigeria women-headed households appear to be underrepresented (Arimah, 1997).

Third, within many prevailing cultural frameworks, housing and infrastructural services are more important to women than to men. In addition, it is women who are the experts on the ways in which housing can be improved to increase efficiency (Moser, 1987; Chant, 1987; Smith, 1988). But these facts tend to be ignored by settlement planners.

Further, women often fulfil triple roles: as reproducer (the childbearing and rearing responsibilities), as producer (as primary or secondary income-earners) , and as community manager (as organizers at the community level) aiming at the provision of collective consumption

(Moser, 1987; cf. Schlyter, 1988). Sometimes mothers also have to care for small animals and the cultivation of garden crops. Little time is left for building or improving their own houses or taking part in collective work.

The two key studies we selected focus on different issues. The first - in Kenya - points to the criteria of selection and the degree to which these are detrimental to women-headed households. The second turns toward differences, resulting from different demands, in housing between women-headed households and other households.

6.3 The Opportunity Structure Approach: Conceptual Frameworks

As a first step, we present an 'inter-organizational model' which Burie (1982) developed in order to explain the results of the development of new housing projects. Its importance derives from the way it offers insight into the game-like interaction between actors, an interaction that by no means necessarily has optimal results, at least as viewed from a user's perspective. As to the supply side, we focus in particular on the production of housing (including the provision of land and basic services), and the obstacles thereto, and we largely neglect - for brevity's sake - the distribution of housing. Next, we turn to the demand side of the housing market and take up matters concerned with the needs of households and their criteria for housing quality. A housing market may be defined as 'the totality of supply and demand relations that occur between (aspiring) owners and (aspiring) occupants of dwellings once completed whereby housing services and/or dwellings are supplied and demanded' (Priemus, 1998).

6.3.1 An 'Inter-Organizational Model'

The inter-organizational model is intended to reveal incompatible goals and interests, and unequal power relationships, among competing agencies in a certain field of provisioning, and to illuminate the way in which public authorities intervene between supplying agencies or actors. As a first step, Burie distinguishes between several actors who each try to reach specific goals and who dispose of one or more resources which are needed for the production of dwellings. An actor may himself possess a resource or can acquire resources through market transactions. For instance, a local housing authority itself possesses the resource 'assignment' (because it has been constituted to build dwellings), and acquires the needed financial capital through transactions on the financial market. In highly-industrialized countries, other main actors are institutional investors, architectural companies, building contractors, building enterprises, governmental and municipal authorities, and incidental assignors. Each actor has his specific goals, interests, and specific resources. Burie (1982) mentions a number of such resources without which building is highly improbable. Land is a first resource. An assignment to build, given by an actor who needs the product and who can afford it, is a second one. Third, consent by a number of public authorities regarding the building plans is needed. Building capacity - encompassing building materials, manpower, equipment, and know-how - is necessary. A design is a fifth resource. Finally, financial capital is needed. Importantly, no one actor possesses all the resources needed. For instance, public authorities possess the resource of consent, but they do not by themselves have building capacity. A housing association can issue an assignment to build houses, but does not generally produce a design by itself. Because no one actor can acquire all the resources, actors have to form coalitions which together can pool all the resources that are needed. Being involved in a coalition is rather ambiguous. On the one hand, it implies being able to exert potential influence on the decision-making process. On the other hand, it implies being more or less under the control of the other actors who participate in the coalition (Klijn and Koolma, 1987).

The process of coalition formation is of primary importance to the realization of new housing projects. It is of primary importance because the form of the resulting coalition mainly determines which actors can achieve their goals, and at which cost, and also - and most important - because it determines the resulting housing project. In consequence, the housing project as realized is not the result of carefully performed studies on the best possible solution, but is rather the result of a trial of strength by the participating organizations which each try to maximize their own benefits.

In order to be appropriate to an analysis of housing production in less-industrialized countries, the model needs some substantial changes. For instance, in highly-industrialized countries, households are supposed to participate only indirectly in housing production, e.g. by participating in program or plan development. But in less-industrialized countries households are productive in a much more direct way. Consequently, households as actively involved in the production of housing have to be introduced into the model as actors (cf. Hardon-Baars, 1996).

Burie's model needs further adjustments. As to the resources needed, in Western countries dwelling design is in most cases a resource which only professional experts provide. However, in less-industrialized countries, for instance in squatter settlements, shelters are mostly not designed by professional experts, and high quality according to architectural standards is not at issue. The housing design just arises from the practical knowledge, ingenuity, and imagination of households themselves (cf. Turner, 1976; Gilbert and Gugler, 1992). Hence the skills and ingenuity of both professionals and lay people have to be considered and represented in the model of production. Further, housing production implies not only the realization of dwellings, but also the construction and provision of basic services, such as sewerage, sanitation, water, and electricity. Basic services may often be provided by governmental agencies, but in less-industrialized countries the people may themselves exercise considerable ingenuity to make them available.

6.3.2 The Supply Side: Public Authorities, Building Industry, and Households

It would take too long to describe extensively the roles and resources of each actor involved in most building processes. Instead, we will focus on the roles the three main actors in this field play: public authorities, the building industry, and households. Each actor has its distinct goals, policies and resources. The main question is: why does housing supply fail?

Public authorities: goals and goal-setting Housing policy develops through various stages. In a first stage, public authorities have to be at least aware of the emergence or existence of a serious housing problem. Drastic changes or events often evoke such an awareness. To mention one example: in Kenya, attaining independence caused the government to realize that, among other things, there was a serious housing problem (Obudho and Aduwo, 1989).

In a second stage, governments have to take responsibility for solving the housing problem, in particular that of low-income households. Hardoy and Satterthwaite (1981) found a noticeable increase since 1970 in government support for housing programmes and - partly - a broader provision of basic services. Since then, in many countries National Housing Corporations or National Housing Authorities have expanded their activities in the development of 4- or 6-years building programmes, and in the construction of 'low-cost units'.

In a third stage, governments have to give a certain priority to the resolution of the housing problem. In competition with economic and other social items, housing often ranks low. For instance, in many socialist countries, housing was - especially in the years of new state formation - considered a 'social service' or 'social wage' at no cost to residents, as for instance in Cuba and in China (Darke, 1989; Wang, 1995). However, these policy characteristics did not imply that housing acquired or continued to have top priority. In Cuba, from 1961 on, priority was given to the building of factories and schools. During a next stage, housing production was further subordinated to industrial production. State-built housing tended to be targeted on housing for industrial workers in key economic branches (e.g. Nicaragua, China, Mozambique), or in some countries in agricultural production (e.g. Vietnam).

However, more recently in both less-industrialized and highly-industrialized countries, awareness is growing that housing is not something residual in national development planning, but has to be considered as an integral part of a balanced development process (Obudho and Aduwo, 1989; Darke, 1989).

Public authorities: housing policies Given a certain awareness of the housing problem, a responsibility taken for its resolution, and a priority granted to it, public authorities - at state, federal, and municipal levels - have followed several paths for providing housing and basic services.

1. Public housing programmes: Public housing programmes refer to publicly financed housing, or public loans to cover the production costs of housing. In the mid-'70s housing policies in many countries were dominated by public housing programmes, or such programmes were a major part of housing policies. However, in most cases the product fell far short of the annual increase in demand. Hardoy and Satterthwaite (1981) found that publicly provided housing could only provide for a small fraction of the real need in all seventeen countries involved in their investigation, except in Singapore.

2. Serviced-site schemes: Serviced-site schemes are intended to provide low-income families with a serviced plot of land, with access to credit and technical and financial assistance to build a house on that plot by self-help, or through building groups or a small contractor, all at a price which would

not be beyond the household budget. They are based on the concept of resident control: residents should acquire the freedom to build according to their own resources and priorities (Turner, 1968; Sheng, 1989; Gilbert and Gugler, 1992).

Serviced-site schemes were considered an advance towards providing shelter for a larger part of the population, and to imply more opportunities for informal housing construction. They brought down unit costs since no house was constructed before the lot was sold or leased (Hardoy and Satterthwaite, 1981). However, in the long run some disadvantages became apparent. For instance, even within these programmes, the poorest households were being excluded by specific scheme requirements and the eligibility criteria for building society loans (Rakodi, 1995a; 1995b).

3. Slum and squatter upgrading: In projects of regularization and upgrading, the authorities legalize land tenure and provide or improve basic infrastructure in squatter settlements (cf. Sheng, 1989). Both activities are supposed to stimulate residents to improve housing conditions on a self-help basis. Residents' control is the basic concept also in slum- and squatter-upgrading projects.

Compared to the production of complete housing units by state intervention, slum and squatter upgrading programmes had some advantages. They minimized the need to relocate families and offered large opportunities for informal production activities and for lowering housing costs. They were supposed to reach large portions of urban households which were normally bypassed by public housing programmes. According to Gilbert and Gugler (1992), in order to be successful, sites-and-services schemes as well as upgrading programmes should be accompanied by structural reforms of the land market, taxation and zoning, and urban planning policies.

4. Providing basic services: Basic services concern safe water and hygienic waste disposal, and in a wider sense educational provisions and health care provisions. As far as the informal sector is concerned, the provision of basic services is considered a responsibility of the government (Gilbert, 1981; Soliman, 1989).

According to findings from a World Health Organization survey, for 1975 only two people in five in the Third World had access to safe drinking water, and only one in three had any kind of sanitary facility. Hardoy and Satterthwaite (1981) estimated - on the basis of their findings -

that no significant improvement had occurred by 1980. However, for the late '70s and early '80s, they found 'more serious attempts' to spread basic services such as potable water, hygienic waste disposal, primary education, and basic health care in many of the countries concerned in their investigation.

Public authorities: resources and resource-related obstacles These entail e.g. legislation, finances, and knowledge and apparatus.

1. Legislation: The formulation and implementation of effective legislation which allowed public authorities to acquire land for low-income housing projects or service-site projects was difficult to achieve. In particular, the definition of 'public interest' and the formulation of guidelines for assessing compensation have appeared to be obstacles (Hardoy and Satterthwaite, 1981). Controls on land speculation seemed to be usually ineffective, the area over which the municipality had jurisdiction often did not expand with the city itself, and public authorities were not seriously committed to recapturing much of the unearned increments.

2. Finances: In the case of non-public landownership, the acquisition of land by public authorities was hampered by the level of compensation demanded by private landlords. Authorities simply did not have the financial resources to purchase needed land from private owners at market prices, and then to supply plots at prices which low-income households could afford (Hardoy and Satterthwaite, 1981). Another problem derived from the high land prices in city centres, leaving the government the option of buying land on the periphery of the urban agglomerations (Obudho and Aduwo, 1989). According to Rakodi (1995), for the supply of houses to meet demand an adequate housing finance system is essential, which must include the availability of funding for public sector programmes or serviced-plot programmes, the availability of mortgage finances, and the lending practices of financial institutions.

3. Knowledge and Apparatus: In many non-Western countries, municipal governments lack the political power, the appropriate administrative machinery, and the trained personnel which is needed to guide the development of areas. Some few examples may elucidate the issue. Even if there is an existing demand by more affluent settlers for serviced plots, all too often bad administration causes an unduly long waiting time. Relatively simple programmes - such as service-site schemes - require a

minimum of administration competence in order to maintain their main virtue: relative freedom from bureaucracy (Gilbert and Gugler, 1992). Further, because of a lack of knowledge, central organizations are rather hesitant in applying alternative technologies to lower the costs of housing programmes (Obudho and Aduwo, 1989).

The building industry: goals and goal-setting In less-industrialized countries the building industry comprises two sectors operating more or less separately: the formal building sector and the informal building sector (Soliman, 1989). In the formal sector housing is built by affluent groups and organized institutions, making use of a capitalist mode of production. As far as industrial companies on a private basis are concerned, making a profit is a first, obvious goal. A second important goal is the continuation of the existence of the company. The informal sector comprises semi-informal housing and squatter housing. Semi-informal housing does not utilise the recognized housing institutions and does not follow established regulations. But it has legality of tenure and formal occupation rights. Squatter housing is illegal occupation of mostly publicly-owned shelter and is often obtained by using the squatters' own resources. In contrast to formal housing, informal housing is at least in its origin directed towards realizing use value rather than exchange value.

The building industry: policies and practices Within the building industry several actors operate, each conducting its particular policy and practices. Burie (1982) distinguishes between building contractors and building enterprises. Building contractors usually dispose of just one resource: building capacity comprising building materials, building equipment and labour. Building enterprises bring in all the resources needed, except for formal assent which is reserved to the public authorities. However, in less-industrialized countries distinctions are more refined. Hardoy and Satterthwaite (1981) distinguish:
1. the large construction company, which is in many cases part of a multinational company, has large capital assets, and uses industrialized building techniques;
2. the smaller national firm, which has lower labour productivity and smaller capital assets, and utilizes industrial building materials;
3. the small building firm, which uses mostly traditional craft techniques and often traditional building materials. Its scale of operation involves the construction of just one or two houses at a time;

4. self-help, in which case the household itself - maybe with the help of friends or skilled artisans - builds the house. We return to this actor in the next subsection. In socialist non-western countries the support of self-help building activities was and still is more or less guided by the state and actually performed by different local organizations, such as 'local committees' (Vietnam), neighbourhood committees (Mozambique) and 'mobile State construction teams' (Tanzania) which give technical assistance and training for village communities (Darke, 1989).

The building industry: resources and resource-related obstacles As to their resources, the formal and the informal sector differ in a number of significant ways (Hardoy and Satterthwaite, 1981; Schlyter, 1989; Soliman, 1989):

1. Assignments and support: In the formal sector, the two first-mentioned building actors are the principal operators and they tend to get public housing contracts; it is the formal sector which almost exclusively receives government support for housing production (cf. Van Der Erve, 1989). In the informal sector, the 'self-help' building actor predominates; the small building firm is active in this sector, particularly when no formal work assignments are available to them.

2. Finance: Housing production in the formal sector, including the purchase of land and materials, is largely financed by the government, international institutions, banks, and other private sector institutions. To housing projects in the informal sector, at least until the early eighties, these institutions provided very limited funds, predominantly for the production of cheaper building materials.

3. Legislation: In the formal sector houses are built according to official standards and with official permission; such standards are usually developed for building in industrialized countries and are not matched with the characteristics of locally produced building materials. The informal sector's buildings in most cases deviate from official standards.

4. Building capacity: In the formal sector, large building companies commonly use prefabricated building systems, while building materials have for a large part to be imported. Both public and private enterprises may cooperate with foreign investors using modern equipment and modern construction methods. It may be assumed that this affects both building

and housing costs because of dependence on foreign purveyors, and influences the continuity of the building process.

The informal sector is dependent on the use of cheap building materials. Habitat Recommendations still extensively emphasize the need to develop and use local building materials and local skills (United Nations,1997). Building standards should conserve scarce resources and reduce dependence on foreign technologies, resources, and materials. Further, in order to support informal sector activities, purchase in small quantities, at irregular intervals, and under easy credit terms should be facilitated.

Family households: goals and goal-setting Households may follow several strategies at a time and a housing strategy may be one of these. In the short term, a housing strategy will aim at improving the actual housing situation. In the long run, the ultimate aim of a housing strategy is the continued well-being of the family household (cf. Schlyter,1988). As with the other actors, a second aim concerns the continuation of its existence as a household. As Friedmann (1989) formulated it: 'Within civil society households are the basic decision units for the self-production of life'.

Family households: building policies and practices Households may operate individually, or they may participate in housing cooperatives or locally bound social movements and thus bring also collective and more specific resources into a collective form of housing production (Schlyter, 1989). In Friedmann's view (1989), benefits are mutual: households contribute to the power of collective movements, but on the other hand such movements defend the rights of households in the face of the superior powers of 'organized capital' and 'the state'.

Family households: resources and resource-related obstacles While in less-industrialized countries state intervention is generally less far-reaching than in highly-industrialized countries, the productive role of households and of their informal networks in the field of housing is much more pronounced. Their resources are manifold and elaborated by many authors (cf. Turner, 1976; Friedmann, 1989; Hardon-Baars, 1996). The resources of family households are both physical and non-physical.
1. Physical resources: Physical resources comprise amongst others time available, physical power and skills, and financial resources.
2. Psychological resources: Psychological resources include cognitive resources, such as knowledge and experience, but also - as Turner (1976)

remarked - motivating resources, such as imagination, initiative, commitment, and responsibility, which are in many cases attached to 'irregular' areas of land, and to the use of locally available tools and materials.

3. Social resources: Social resources refer to household members' abilities to organize, to cooperate, to compete, and also to what Turner calls the 'lateral information and decision networks' in which households participate and which have disappeared in large parts of industrialized countries. In so doing, households - particularly those with lower standards of living and those headed by women (Morris, 1991) - call in networks of kin, friends, or work colleagues in order to make use of their knowledge and expertise in housing construction and financing. They also may - whether or not from sheer necessity - turn to informal savings and loans or rotating credit associations to meet mortgage payments for land costs, development charges, loans for building material, or loans for the construction and maintenance of the dwelling (Chant, 1987; Rakodi, 1995b; Kumar, 1996).

4. Political resources: Finally, households dispose of political resources, exemplified in the votes they cast in elections of representatives, at least in democratic societies. On a more collective level, they may thus mobilize political pressure to advocate their interests in exchange for political support.

6.3.3. The Demand Side: The Macro-Scale and the Micro-Scale

The macro-scale: housing need and housing quality On a macro-scale, housing need first implies the current housing shortage. Next, it implies the need for replacement and renewal units up to a certain year. And third, housing shortage entails the need generated by the expected increase in population during a given period. In many less-industrialized countries the housing shortage is enormous and the expected number of dwellings needed far exceeds the total of current housing shortage and of replacement units. For instance, in Egypt - according to a housing programme developed in 1979 to overcome the housing shortage till the year 2000 - the current housing shortage was estimated to amount to 831,000 units, replacement and renewal units needed amounted to 589,999, and the expected increase in population would require 2,180,000 units (Soliman, 1989).

On a micro-scale effective housing demand depends largely on the felt needs of the participants and the means they possess and are willing to invest. In this connection, some preliminary statements which emerged from both The Ecology of Habitat and from the Tenants Movement's representatives are important. The Ecology of Habitat aimed at enhancing people's awareness of being both subject and responsible for their home environment. People's self-esteem and belief in own creativity rank higher than architectural or governmental standards of housing quality. It also offered methods and equipment for achieving these goals (Van Leeuwen, 1980; Van Dam, 1988; Van Wezel, 1993; 1994). The Tenants Movement held similar views. According to Turner (1968; 1972), a household's satisfaction is not necessarily related to official and prevailing standards. Deficiencies in one's housing are assumed to be 'infinitely' more tolerable, if they are the subject's own responsibility than if they are somebody else's. Essential to a full dedication of their resources is that households have to be *in control*. Ward (1976, p.6) pointed out most clearly:

> When dwellers control the major decisions and are free to make their own contribution to the design, construction, or management of their housing, both the process and the environment produced stimulate individual and social well-being.

Turner's stance further - and no less important - implies that a resident has to have the freedom to pursue his priorities according to his values and resources, instead of considering the standards and priorities of housing authorities or of architects. In addition, a household should be able to build according to its wider needs and priorities, even when these are not related to housing improvement, as - for instance - being able to send children to school (Turner, 1968).

Turner's ideas evoked much criticism regarding both of the manner of housing construction and of the licence it would offer to public authorities not to intervene (Moser and Peake, 1987; Hall, 1989; Rakodi, 1995b). But Turner did not suggest that the poor people of the world should become do-it-yourself builders, nor that governments should refrain from intervention in the building production processes. He was quite aware of the fact that people's autonomy depends on the availability of tools and materials, land, and finances, which in their turn depend on the central authorities (Turner, 1976).

As to *housing quality*, his view implies that the important thing is that housing is not what it *is*, but what it *does* in the life of people (Turner, 1972; Ward, 1976; Tosi, 1995). His stance is fully in line with the theorem of Pragmatism: 'real is what is real in its effects'. Therefore, housing quality should be defined and measured according to the effects it has on people's lives and on the functioning of their households. Obviously the question arises: which effects are important? Turner (1976) himself first distinguishes between monetary and non-monetary factors in housing situations. Two monetary factors are important.

1. The first factor concerns 'the dwelling cost ratio', being the price (for rent or amortization and other running costs) paid in relation to the household's income.

2. The second factor comprises the assets, being the 'assets owned by the occupants' which - in case of a market economy - equals the value accruing to the owner-occupier after paying-off mortgages or other liens. Non-monetary factors imply social and economic access, security of tenure, and physical standards.

3. Social access refers to the relative proximity of a dwelling to people on whom the household is dependent for social support and may vary from 'next door' to 'over 1 day's return journey'.

4. Economic access concerns the proximity of a dwelling to the sources of the household's income, affecting time costs and transport costs for commuting.

5. Security of tenure is a further important factor which implies the duration of the household's option for residence, which affects both the continuity of the family household's life, their willingness to invest in housing, and the transferability of the dwelling as an asset. For that matter, perceived security may differ from legality *per se* and may be more highly valued by the household, depending on both the government's attitudes towards informal housing and the amount of political pressure that can be maintained (also Gilbert and Gugler, 1992; Rakodi, 1995).

6. Next, the physical features of the dwelling and its surroundings imply characteristics of space, construction, and equipment. As Turner importantly points out, the physical standards which often most attract the attention of social policy agencies are only one of many factors. It must be emphasized that physical standards as such are meaningless. They too derive their meaning from the effects they have. These effects relate - in Turner's view (1968) - to the function of the dwelling to provide shelter from climatic and social elements.

However, some other factors should be added.

7. The physical standards of the dwelling and its surroundings also define the functional quality of the dwelling, i.e. the degree to which the dwelling facilitates the activities households prefer to perform in their home environment (Van Dam, 1988). Such preferences vary across stages in the life-cycle of households and the culture in which they live.

8. Finally, housing as a source of income is only obliquely mentioned by Turner, but its importance is emphasized by many other authors (e.g. Sheng, 1989; Obudho and Aduwo, 1989; Rakodi, 1995). In their view, as a possible source of income, the type of housing is important. Multi-storey public or private housing projects are often not only too expensive for low-income households, but also unsuitable for 'home-based income generation' resulting from the participation of the household in the informal economy or from (sub)letting of rooms or houses. As to service-site schemes, plot owners may gain additional income by building additional rooms and subletting them to the very poor - the majority of urban dwellers - who cannot afford a plot themselves.

The micro-scale: household priorities and differentiation among family households As to *household priorities* - generally speaking - the housing effects mentioned are important, but their importance may vary between several types of households or between types of settlement. For instance, the priorities of housing factors are quite different between urban and rural households. According to Hardey and Satterthwaite (1981), among low-income households in urban areas access to income earning opportunities may be the primary need. The next most important needs may be access to the informal social network of family and friends, and a short distance to basic services such as water. In contrast, the site of the house in rural areas is usually close to the area in which income earning takes place. The cost of the site itself is only rarely a major household expense.

In addition to the rural-urban dimension, many other dimensions can exemplify the way in which households' priorities depend on the situational requirements households have to cope with. For brevity's sake, we centre on the effect of the stage in a household's trajectory towards settlement. This issue also clearly elucidates the alternating priorities of housing and other provisions.

As to *differentiation among households* we consider the trajectory from immigrant to resident. Turner (1968) distinguishes three stages in a household's trajectory towards settlement: bridge-header, consolidator, and status-seeker. At each of these stages housing priorities differ radically.

For the (very poor) bridge-headers, proximity to income-generating opportunities has the highest priority. Permanent home-ownership, residence (tenure) and modern standards (amenity) have no priority.

For the (poor) consolidator, permanent home-ownership gets priority, access to income-generating sources has lower priority, but amenities become more important.

The (higher-income) status-seeker attaches highest priority to modern amenities rather than to location or tenure.

Sheng (1989) makes the important distinction between 'lowest-income bridge-headers' and 'low-income bridge-headers'. The 'lowest-income bridge-header' will search primarily for three basic functions: (a) a place to live. A particular part of the pavement on a street, a bench in the park, a place under a bridge or a plot of land which is illegally or informally occupied; implicitly, there is also a need for a certain security of tenure; (b) a suitable location. It must be near centres of formal or informal employment, water supply and sanitary facilities; (c) a shelter. Some privacy and protection is needed against hurtful physical and social influences.

Many 'low-income bridge-headers' do not prioritize investment of their income in housing, but rather in food, clothing, employment and informal income-generating activities, education for their children and better access to basic services. Additional income will be used for better or more food and clothes, or for non-essential commodities, for saving money or for saving in properties, and for investments: the education of children, supplies for a store, bribes to authorities to obtain licenses, while anticipating the future generation of income. Investments in housing may in many cases be aimed rather at enhancing income level than improving living conditions: to be able to build more rooms for rent or to use part of the house as a shop or for a workshop. Sheng therefore proposes differentiating 'the consolidators' into four sub-categories:

1. Families who invest their savings in a plot of land in a serviced-site scheme or a regularized squatter settlement, but do not consolidate their house;
2. Families who invest their savings in the consolidation of the house in such a scheme or settlement, but do not pay-off the land;
3. Families who use their additional money for other purposes than to buy land and to improve their houses;
4. Families who spend 20-25% of their income over 15 years or more to become owner of a plot of land and to consolidate their house.

So far, the conceptual framework we have offered is still rather abstract and has to prove its value. We select two key studies from different cultures, aiming at a further instantiation and at offering a provisional check on its value. For several reasons we will focus on just one type of household: women-headed households.

6.4 Key Study: Access to the Housing Market and Women-Headed Households in Kenya

6.4.1 Introduction

Reasons for selecting Nimpuno-Parente's study (1987) were the following: In African cities, planning specific to the needs of women has not been undertaken for a long time. This is the more remarkable, because women usually constituted more than half of the applicants in low-income housing projects and their contribution to the labour input into self-help projects has been estimated at 80 per cent (CBS/UNCF 1984, in Nimpuno-Parente). According to an estimate in 1984, of 1.7 million households in Kenya 29 per cent were women-headed households.

Further, the study is illuminating in that it explicitly mentions the assumptions on which the project policy is based, in particular the criteria of selection and the implementation procedure. Thus, adverse effects come to the fore which may be at least partly considered to be unintended consequences of the authorities' policy.

6.4.2 The Project

The current population was expected to increase very rapidly in urban areas, about 7 per cent per annum, and in the early 70s the demands on housing and infrastructure became urgent. Squatter settlements were erected by low-income households. In response, Nairobi City Council (NCC) abandoned its policy of constructing conventional low-cost houses for rent and focused instead on a more cost-effective site-and-services approach. The World Bank was willing to give financial support, and the Urban Study Group proposed Dandora (an area 10 kilometres east of Nairobi) to become a model for urban development of a community of 60,000 people. The area was selected mainly because it was the only substantial and uncommitted parcel of land owned by either the government or the NCC. The site was adjacent to existing housing areas and within easy reach of the city centre and two industrial areas. The NCC established a Housing Development Department (HDD) to oversee the project. One of its divisions was the Community Development Division responsible for the selection of beneficiaries and for extending social support to lowest-income households. The HDD was to confine itself to the provision of infrastructural services and sanitary facilities. Housing construction should be carried out by those to whom plots would be allocated. The HDD also had to administer materials and loans, and to provide technical guidance and supervision during the period of construction. Finally, it was required to specify criteria for the selection of project participants. Infrastructural facilities were built by contractors and were to be operated and maintained by the NCC: sewerage, access and circulation roads, domestic plumbing, street lights, municipal refuse collection, and storm-water drainage. Plot beneficiaries could choose between three plot types, varying as to the plot size, the content of the 'wet core', the amount of loans for materials, and the lease agreements concerning number of rooms to be built and the term of repayment.

The Dandora project was to achieve two different goals. First, it had to benefit those households whose limited earning capacities precluded access to conventional housing. Its second aim was to recover a substantial proportion of the project's costs. In particular this aim influenced the criteria for selection.
Applicants:

- had to have a monthly income in the range of Ksh. 280-560 ($15-30);
- had to pay a down payment of Ksh. 600;
- had to be heads of household;
- could not own other property in Nairobi;
- had to have lived for more than two years in Nairobi;
- needed supporting employment documents.

6.4.3 Data and Analysis

The Site and Services Project was initiated in the 1970s, funded by the Nairobi City Council (NCC), the Kenyan Government, and the World Bank. The scheme was planned to be implemented in five phases, and when completed 6,000 serviced plots would have been provided. Nimpuno-Parente's study focused on phase I in which 1,029 serviced plots were to be completed for a population of 6,000-10,000.

A large majority (89 per cent) of the women who applied to the project were heads of households and had on average five dependants. They originally had come to Nairobi as migrants from rural areas, looking for jobs in the city, following their husbands, or escaping failed marriages. When applying, they lived in different areas in Nairobi, most of them living in rented rooms or shacks. Their housing conditions had often been precarious, illegal and shifting from place to place. Housing insecurity and job insecurity often reinforced one another. For them, the Dandora settlement appeared to offer security of tenure, legality, improved housing conditions and title to land. It was thus in striking contrast to traditional practices in which women could not inherit land.

The study aimed at examining the difficulties that women faced both in fulfilling the criteria for selection and as project beneficiaries. Findings also show how project assumptions about both self-help and finance could be detrimental to women.

The research was carried out in 1984, six years after the first phase of plot allocation. Beneficiaries were supposed to have completed their houses by that time. The research used several methods of data collection including interviews with a 10 per cent sample of women beneficiaries, case studies of women beneficiaries, and participant observation. Secondary data, in particular the results of a baseline survey, were also used.

6.4.4 Findings and Conclusion

Most clearly, the criteria applied appeared to affect women negatively in several ways. First, the cost of the project plots had been based on the assumption that charges would be related to 20-25 per cent of household income. However, 63 per cent of the applicants appeared to work in the informal sector and had, by consequence, irregular incomes. Of the women applicants less than a fifth worked in the formal sector, one-half were self-employed (selling vegetables and charcoal), while the remaining third earned money from subletting rooms. Thus, many of these women did not have a cash income to report when applying for the project, and the underlying assumption regarding the household income was unrealistic. Working in the informal sector adversely affected women as regards the sixth criterion as well: few women were able to meet the requirement of evidence of employment. Second, the down payment required to cover the cost of water connection and loans for building materials proved to be too high for the vast majority of women applicants. Many women had no savings of their own and had therefore to incur extra debts with informal money-lenders or relatives in order to meet this requirement. Third, applicants had to be heads of households. This criterion adversely affected women in a rather curious way. In order to be a candidate for the project, women who had been left by their husbands had to prove that they were separated and had to support children. But they were often reluctant to change their title because of the status inherent to being married. But married women were assumed not to be household heads. Fourth, women whose husbands owned property were excluded from allocation. But these women often had no control over this property, because their husbands could have sold their plot without their wife's consent. Some husbands sold the house secretly and disappeared with the money. In consequence, the wife only became aware of the transaction when the new owner came to declare his ownership and evict the resident family. Fifth, it was often difficult for women to confirm their residence in Nairobi. When they came to the capital with their husbands, it was only the husband who registered as resident. In addition, women had often returned to their rural homes at harvest times or to help their families because of economic pressure. Therefore, the length of residency was unclear. Apart from the criteria of selection, other problems for women-headed households concerned the process of house construction and the financing of housing construction.

A first bottle-neck resulted from the gendered conception of house building. In urban areas building is a male-dominated profession: 'Men's domain is the building site and women provide support'. In consequence, many women cleared the plot, carried stones, mixed concrete, and cleared the debris after construction. But these activities were perceived as extensions of domestic work and not acknowledged as building work.

A second bottle-neck resulted from the structure of the female-headed households, which were generally one-parent family households. While men usually had a wife or other relatives to contribute to building activities and to supervise the site, many women had to combine this with earning a living and thus had to rely on paid skilled or semi-skilled labour. In addition, because of the high building standards prescribed by the authorities, women could not utilize their own skills. Not surprisingly, women appeared to use twice as many craftsmen and labourers as men did and, in consequence, they had to exceed loans for materials and to incur heavy debts. It also made them liable to financial abuse and to the theft of building materials. Financial provisions were insufficient to complete the house and all plot owners needed additional financial arrangements. Most women borrowed from relatives and friends, or joined a building group. But some women could not rely on relatives or friends, nor could they appeal to official funds because of their irregular earnings. In addition, women preferred small and successive loans to large and once-only loans which were most cost-effective for banks. All in all, the extra interest caused by multiple loans appeared to be a heavy burden on household budgets. Participation in building groups alleviated the women's burden in the building process. The digging of foundation trenches were usually carried out by mutual assistance. Group building facilitated raising the large amounts of money needed for construction and brought the hiring of contractors considerably more within reach. According to the author, the main difficulty for such building groups was to maintain group cohesion and to ensure that all members could afford to stay in the group. Members were previously unacquainted and their only common interest was in the building. Such factors endangered the continuance and at least the effectiveness of these groups. For brevity's sake, we have to leave other information on the project aside.

6.5 Key Study: Living Arrangement by Choice or by Constraint in Mexico

6.5.1 Introduction

For several reasons Miraftab's study (1997; 1998) is quite interesting. From a practical point of view, the study is of interest because in Mexico - as in many other Latin American countries - the economic flaw in the 1980s contributed to an increase of households headed by women (Chant, 1996a; Miraftab, 1997). According to Chant, in Mexico the proportion of female-headed households to all households tripled from 1960 to 1990.

Next, from a theoretical point of view, the study is of interest because it criticizes Turner's theory on the housing trajectories of the urban poor, which implies that a household's consolidation and advancements in the life-cycle necessarily leads to a preference for home-owning in a peripheral settlement. It considered renting as a transitional mode of housing and thus attributed only a minor role to this tenure status.

6.5.2 Regional Developments

Miraftab mentions several developments which have taken place in many Latin American countries since the early 50s. Irregular settlements of the informal sector came to play an increasingly major role in meeting the housing needs of the poor. The rental sector - originally constituting the primary housing alternative for urban populations - became marginal in the housing market. Governmental policy centred on facilitating home ownership through self-help.

At the same time, economic changes affected household dynamics and composition. Women's education and their participation in the labour force strongly increased, supposedly leading towards an increased number of female-headed households. While in most other Latin-American countries the average size of households shrank, in Mexico it increased from 4.9 to 5.1 between 1970 and 1990, in spite of declining fertility. Some households brought in new members and established extended or mixed households to share the costs of living. Increased economic power and increased self-awareness made women less dependent on their male partners.

6.5.3 Data and Analysis

The study was carried out in 1992-1993 in the Metropolitan Area of Guadelajara, the second largest city of Mexico with over 2.8 million inhabitants. The majority of the city's housing stock is owner-occupied.

Miraftab chose three areas which embraced a range of housing alternatives common among poor households in that city. The first area was in the city centre, and included renters of the multi-tenant 'vecincidades', characterized by a series of rooms surrounding a common courtyard. Each household rented their own room, but they shared the courtyard, the sanitary services, and washing areas. The second area was a newly developing irregular settlement located on the northern edge of the Metropolitan Zone. It predominantly constituted owner-occupied units constructed through self-help activity, but lacked basic services such as sewerage, pavements, water and electricity, and had only limited transportation facilities to other parts of the city. The third area was a 'colonia' in which the author had previously lived and worked. It was located between the other two areas, less than ten kilometres from the city centre and fairly accessible to other parts of the city. It had obtained basic urban services and - being an older working-class neighbourhood - contained a mix of renters and owners.

In a first phase, Miraftab conducted in each area 30 random surveys with adult female members of households in order to explore the relations between the gender of the household head, the location of the housing, the housing tenure, and the spatial arrangement of the residences. In a second phase, in-depth interviews were conducted with 30 female heads of households in different stages of their life-cycles and in different types of housing.

6.5.4 Findings and Conclusion

The housing situation of low-income family households and their composition based on the gender of the household head appeared to be clearly correlated. Differences referred to location within urban space, tenure status and living arrangement.

First, as to location, more women-headed households' housing was located in the inner-city 'vecincidades', somewhat less in the peripheral settlements and considerably less in the so-called 'colonia' in-between, compared to male-headed (including two-parent) households. Half of all residents of the inner-city 'vecincidades' were in households headed by women alone. In the peripheral locations, less than a third and in the 'colonias' just a quarter of all households were headed by women.

Next, as to tenure status, female-headed households more often rented their dwelling, while male-headed households more often were owners. Among female householders who owned a home, a considerable number had achieved home-ownership prior to their becoming the head of household, the percentage of female household heads achieving home ownership as single mothers being probably considerably lower.

Third, differences between male-headed and female-headed households were largest as to living arrangement: 'shared and semi-shared housing',[1] was considerably more common among female-headed households, while a 'single-family residence' was relatively often occupied by male-headed households, independent of their tenure status.

Miraftab's crucial question was: do these differences exist by constraint or by choice? If both types of households would appear to differ considerably by income, then financial constraints might be supposed to prevail. If they did not differ or differed only slightly, then financial considerations were unlikely to have a main role and choice might be assumed to prevail.

On this question, the research findings are quite clear. Female householders in the sample earned 33% less than male householders. But considering the total - or per capita - income of household members, no substantial differences between both household types emerged (the earnings of women-headed households were only 3.9% lower). Strategy was at the root of these differences: female householders launched more family members into the work force. In consequence, residential location of female-headed households appeared not to be determined by constraints - at least financial constraints - but rather by choice or preference.

What makes these preferences understandable? Miraftab's in-depth interviews revealed an interesting range of concerns which influenced the decisions on location made by the female-headed households. The most important refers to the opportunity to combine domestic and income-generating activities. This concern supposedly burdened in particular young single mothers, who expressed a strong preference for living in the centrally located 'vecincidad' with its shared housing-configuration. The author mentions several reasons: these young single mothers could not rely on the support of grown-up children. Closeness to the location for earning money was particularly important, considering the distance and bad transportation facilities to peripheral areas, and the lack of basic services. Further, the inner-city 'vecincidad' offered more social tolerance for single motherhood and for pregnancy out of wedlock, supposedly because of the many single mothers living in this area.

Another important concern for female-headed households involved the evidently better opportunities for informal-sector earnings offered by the specific location. For the same activities, in the vecincidad the earnings of unskilled women were clearly highest compared to the earnings of women in both the peripheral area and the 'colonia'. The women in the inner-city areas had a wider and wealthier pool of customers to sell to in the streets and markets downtown than the women in the other areas had. This might explain why in the 'vecincidades' the proportion of female householders - being primary maintainers - was much larger than in the other areas.

The author mentions some additional reasons which concern dimensions of the housing arrangements. The shared courtyards of the 'vecincidades' facilitated both the exchange of child-care responsibilities and the development and maintenance of a stable network of social support among the residents. Moreover, the fact that housing construction was considered a male activity in Mexico made self-construction by women in peripheral settlements rather improbable. In consequence, they were relatively dependent on the inner-city areas.

Miraftab concluded that it was in particular the combination of location, tenure, and spatial configuration which was decisive rather than each of these conditions singly. Female households appeared to have a different set of resources and constraints concerning housing compared to male-headed households. Informal-sector home-ownership could not be considered a universally acceptable shelter for the poor. Therefore, government or semi-government efforts should not focus just on facilitating the self-help production of owner-occupied units.

6.6 Conclusions and New Directions for Research

6.6.1 Conclusions

Both key studies offer a first answer to the main question: why does housing supply fail? Nimpuno-Parente's study exemplified the way in which the characteristics of the situation of women-headed households clashed with the institutional system, more particularly its criteria applied in housing distribution. These criteria were presumably not discriminating against women versus men or against one-parent versus two-parent households in a direct way. To put it more precisely, the criteria were not discriminatory by intention but by their effects.

Miraftab's research findings exemplify the way in which situational characteristics of women-headed households explain their specific demand, more particularly their priorities as to housing and housing location. For instance, sharing of residence and of residence arrangements implies the sacrificing of autonomy and privacy and - in consequence - lowers the physical housing standard. But this sacrifice is understandable considering the characteristics of the situation of these households and of their prevailing housing options.

Evidently, to policy-makers it is crucial to distinguish among specific groups of demanders and to conceive of their housing priorities in terms of their life-strategies. Some underlying dimensions deserve further elaboration as 'new directions' for research.

6.6.2 New Directions for Research

To the processes of housing production, housing distribution and housing demand, several basic dimensions may be distinguished. A first concerns the role of ideology as to the distribution process. A second refers to the relationship between a household's social position and its access to the housing market. Our third suggestion concerns the influence of the legal position, particularly of women-headed households, on access to the housing market. Finally, we will consider the meaning of housing tenure in relation to household strategies.

1 Distribution of dwellings and ideology In so-called welfare states, the level of state intervention is high. Where public authorities are involved, some legitimized way of discerning and judging the housing needs of applicants has to be developed. Such ways of discerning needs may be expressed in formal policies and explicit practices, or in informal decision-making processes within organizations, for instance regarding the centrality of the nuclear family unit (Henderson and Karn, 1984; Watson, 1986; Heenan and Gray, 1997). According to Henderson and Karn (1984), most promising is an approach which focuses on understanding perceptions and practices of personnel, not so much in themselves, but as the result of the organization and its personnel being part of an inegalitarian social structure. Being part of such a social structure leads to the reproduction of ideological beliefs and stereotyping of particular social 'types', for instance 'respectability' categories.

In less-industrialized countries the distribution of housing may be less dependent on public authorities and more on informal contacts and other resources. Apart from renters and owners, a (housing) class may be distinguished consisting of so-called rent-free consumers or family housers with family rights to housing or obtaining land either via inheritance or the favour of a living owner, framed within a specific ethnic group (Tipple and Willis, 1991; Korboek, 1992, in Arimah, 1997).

Therefore, future research on the way in which ideological beliefs and ethnic identities influence formal and informal practices of housing distribution is highly relevant. The chapter on the *Power Approach* offered a conceptual framework.

2 Social position and access to the housing market Generally speaking, the less the resources a household disposes of, the weaker its position on the housing market. Poorer people are allocated less popular housing than better-off people (Clapham and Kintrea, 1986). The lowest-income households are excluded in several ways: by refusal of building societies to provide relatively small loans, by standards which result in unaffordable construction costs, and by insecurity of employment or income. Competing for scarce housing facilities, middle-income households and employed heads-of-households with stable wages - being often male - will be in a advantageous position in case of allocation (Rakodi with Withers, 1995).

However, the issue of social position includes more than just household income and income stability. First, sitting tenants will benefit in several ways. They may benefit from the sale of rental housing, and former eligibility criteria concerning specific social-economic characteristics will thus remain effective. As a sitting tenant, a household may be able to offer a dwelling (which they will leave) when moving into a new dwelling. Where there is a waiting list, a family household also may or may not be able to refuse a housing offer, dependent on the urgency of their actual housing need (Henderson and Karn, 1984; 1987; Clapham and Kintrea, 1986). In addition, its position seems to be stronger, if its actual housing is endangered by public authorities' programmes, e.g. for housing clearance or housing improvement. In this regard, homeless people and illegal immigrants are disadvantaged. Further and no less important, in both highly-industrialized and less-industrialized countries, a household's position in the housing market seems to depend on its members' participation or non-participation in the economic system, particularly in key economic enterprises (Clapham and Kintrea, 1986). In China, only those formally employed by the public sector had the right to public housing. The allocation of housing was based largely on work status (Wang, 1995). Also in service-and-sites programmes, a substantial number of plots were allocated to employers for their employees (Rakodi, 1995).

Further research is required on the implications of a household's social position, and on the relationships between its social position, its housing preferences and its access to the housing market.

3 Legal position and gender Apart from the key studies we presented, other studies give evidence of the disadvantaged position of women-headed households and of indirect discrimination in both less-industrialized countries and in highly-industrialized countries (Machado, 1987; Watson, 1988; Crow and Hardey, 1991). Despite the fact that the concept of female-headed households refers to an extremely complex and varied reality (Lewis, 1993; also Hardey and Crow, 1991), in many cases women-headed households seem to be handicapped by a weak legal position. Some instances may elucidate the issue.

Married women have a weak position in relation to property. They are not allowed to own a house or to own assets without their husband's consent (Schlyter, 1988; Bruce and Lloyd, 1995; Smith, 1988), and building societies can insist that a married woman be assisted by her husband in all her transactions. As he is asked to sign the building contracts, he is regarded as the only owner of the house.

As to access to land, where patrilineal inheritance prevails women usually only gain access to land through husbands (Chant, 1997). Under Islamic rules of inheritance, daughters can only inherit half as much land from their parents as sons, and only one-eighth of their husband's property, if they have children. In Bangladesh, women normally sacrifice their landholding rights in exchange for the right to visit their parents' house after marrying, thus weakening their social position substantially (Lewis, 1993).

Future research should also be directed to legal rules and social norms which impede equal access to the housing market of men-headed households and women-headed households.

4 Housing tenure and household strategy Home ownership tends to be preferred by a large majority of households and is an important determinant of housing satisfaction (Machado, 1987; Crull et al., 1994; Kumar, 1996; Rakodi, 1995b). In addition, some planners regard renting as a temporary stage in the housing cycle of urban migrants ultimately aiming at ownership, leading to upgrading programmes and service-and-site projects adopted by governments (Kumar, 1996).

However, critical issues concern both the differential accessibility of home ownership across households and the role of home ownership in a household's strategy. Being a tenant may be part of a household's strategy, in particular in case of transitions or other changes in the life-course. Apart from one of our key studies, several other studies show rental housing to be an important solution or to be preferred by women-headed households having a low income (Morris and Cho, 1986; Peake, 1987; Schlyter, 1988). For instance, the renting of a room was in many cases a way of coping with a break between the former life and the more permanent arrangements for the future, e.g. when leaving the family home or after divorce or widowing. Lacey and Sinai (1996) suggest viewing housing as something that helps the poor in generating income.

Therefore, the increased attention of research to the relative cost of owner-occupied and rented housing (Elsinga, 1996), and the gradual emergence of rental housing on the national and international agendas, is hardly surprising (Kumar, 1996; Van der Heijden and Boelhouwer, 1996), in particular regarding women-headed households (Gilroy, 1994).

Further research on the way housing tenure hinders or facilitates households' survival strategies, considering the stage in the family cycle and the inherent transitions, is important. A conceptual framework is offered in the chapter on the *Strategy Approach*.

Note

1. Shared residence included cases where more than one family, or one family with one or more related or non-related individuals, lived under the same roof and shared all living space. A semi-shared residence contained tenants who shared some of the facilities and communal spaces, but who did not live under the same roof. Finally, single-family residence referred to dwellings inhabited

by only one (nuclear or single-parent) family, with no additional members from outside.

7 The Longitudinal Approach

7.1 Introduction

In demography it is customary to make a distinction between cross-sectional and longitudinal approaches. Cross-sectional data provide a picture of a population, or population segment, with regard to specific demographic characteristics at a certain moment or during a limited period (usually a year) in time. Longitudinal data can only be obtained when a population or population segment is followed through time, which requires access to a continuous flow of data. Collecting cross-sectional data is like taking stock. In a well-known introduction to demography, the subject of fertility, for instance, is treated both ways. There is a part on period fertility which discusses cross-sectional fertility data and their methods of analysis, and there is a part on cohort fertility, which discusses fertility patterns which evolve over time and their methods of analysis (Newell, 1988).

However, this division is not as clear-cut as it seems. To start with, there is a practical problem: collecting longitudinal data presupposes the kind of data-base that is often not available. Taking stock by doing a survey at a certain moment is much more feasible than collecting data over time. To solve this problem, in demography, cross-sectional data are manipulated in such a way that they seem to yield a longitudinal picture. The construction of the Total Fertility Rate (TFR) is a case in point. Contrary to what the term seems to convey, the TFR does not give the actual average total number of live-born children of women at the end of their child-bearing period, because it is calculated by summarising the age-specific fertility rates of women in all age-groups which together comprise the whole child-bearing period. These rates are period statistics, cross-sectional data collected for a certain year. Formally, the TFR is the number of children a woman would have if she survived to age fifty and if throughout her reproductive life she experienced exactly the age-specific fertility rates as for the year in question, which is why the TFR is referred to as describing a synthetic cohort.

For comparative purposes the total fertility rate is appropriate, in spite of the fact that it refers to a synthetic cohort and uses a spurious time dimension. However, for explanatory purposes its artificial character is a serious drawback.

The discussion above on the problem of time, and its synthetic solution for computing total fertility, brings the essence of this chapter into focus. This chapter is about real time, as incorporated in a longitudinal approach to the study of family households. In such an approach the temporal dimension is an integral part of the description and explanation of family household phenomena. As there are more ways to go about this than just one, it follows that there are several longitudinal approaches.

What is meant by the expression temporal (or time) dimension is not self-evident. There are several sorts of time: historical time (*longue durée*), daily time (*durée*), individual time (age, or phase in the life course), and - perhaps - household time, or Hareven's invention (see below): family time. These different ways of looking at time are captured by three of the four themes that Elder sees as central in the evolving life course paradigm: lives and historical time; the timing of lives; and linked lives (Elder, 1994). Given the subject matter of the book, in the approaches to be discussed here the emphasis will be on the categories of time which concern the individual and the household or family, though at the same time attention will be paid to the context of historical time.

In the next section the relevance of longitudinal approaches for the study of family households will be discussed. Then follow sections about important theoretical approaches and concepts: the cohort or generation approach, the life cycle or life course approach, and the concepts of family life cycle and family time. Tamara Hareven's study of the labourers of the Amoskeag Mills in Manchester (New Hampshire) and their families will be presented as a key study to highlight the latter concept. Subsequently, the life course approach as developed by Elder will be discussed in more detail. Then an application of this approach to the subject of migration will be analysed in the second key study. The chapter concludes with a discussion about possible new directions of research.

7.2 The Relevance of Longitudinal Approaches for the Study of Family Households

In causal explanations the temporal dimension is inherent. To prove that X is caused by Y, it is not sufficient to prove co-variation. It is also necessary to prove that Y precedes X (Miller, 1986). One can sometimes get around this requirement by demonstrating that when there is no Y, there is also no X, but often this will not suffice. An example is the inverse relationship found between women's own income from economically productive activities on the one hand and level of fertility on the other. At an aggregate level this relationship can suggest two sequences. The first is that women with no or few children are more disposed to take up work outside the home, which makes the level of fertility the explanatory variable. The second is that working women want to keep their job and income and are inclined to limit their fertility. In this case having a job and an own income is the explanatory variable. A study design aimed at exploring the relationship between the two variables has to take their sequential order into account. The Demographic Institute of the University of Indonesia in Jakarta set up such a study:

> The study will examine whether family planning use affects a woman's decision to enter the labour force and whether labour force participation, in turn, influences a woman's bargaining power in household decision-making, specifically with respect to family spending, contraceptive use and plans for children's future (FHI, 1996, p.16).

A longitudinal approach is also warranted when the researcher is primarily interested in uncovering the dynamics of a process. An example is the question whether poverty at household level is self-perpetuating. To investigate this question in the United States, a nation-wide panel study was set up: the Panel Study of Income Dynamics (Elder, 1985). The study showed that poor households develop adaptive strategies to escape from the circle of self-perpetuating poverty.

> Economic adversity prompts adaptations outside the households by having multiple earners in a family and by other means and within the household through alterations in family composition as people leave or enter. These adaptive responses, in turn, serve to modify the family's resources and economic situation which, once again, influence family decisions. In this manner compositional change represents both a determinant and a consequence of change in economic status (Elder, 1985, p.28).

The example shows that households' use and management of resources cannot be assessed by a single sounding, but that understanding requires monitoring the process. The variable of household composition, particularly, plays a double role in relation to household resources, which can only be pictured with the help of longitudinal data. On the one hand household resources have to sustain a household of a given composition, while on the other hand use of labour as a household resource depends on its composition. This provides households with manoeuvring space which can be used for deploying adaptive strategies, as is described by Elder in the quotation above.

The inadequacy of applying only cross-sectional approaches to the study of the dynamics of family households is well captured by the following statement of Tamara Hareven: 'It is important to realise that a profile of a household at a specific point in time obscures the constant movement of family members in and out of different household patterns over their life courses'. She refers to households of her historical study as 'revolving stages on which different members appeared and disappeared, under their own momentum or under the impact of external conditions' (Hareven, 1982, p.154).

Another aspect of household dynamics which benefits from a longitudinal view is household decision-making. Not only do decision-making processes evolve over time, but outcomes of former decision-making also influence present and future decision-making. An example is decision-making about adopting a foster child. In a small-scale study among Dutch foster parents it was shown how the actual decision to adopt a foster child was preceded by other decisions (Pennartz, 1996). Furthermore, decision-making forms part of strategic behaviour, and strategies can be seen as efforts to 'structure, in a coherent way, actions within a relatively long-term perspective' (Anderson et al., 1994, p.48). A time perspective is built into the notion of strategy.

Finally, at macro level, the *longue durée* is important for a proper understanding of contemporary phenomena. Although in this chapter we shall not go into historical approaches to household and family, their relevance for contemporary theory needs to be mentioned here. The persistent misconception that the nuclear family household is a product of industrial society could only be refuted by meticulous historical research. Lingering evolutionistic thinking led to opposing modern (industrial) societies to so-called traditional societies, where the nuclear family household is seen as characteristic of the first type of societies, extended families and pervasive kinship networks of the second (Laslett, 1972). This has led to downplaying the role of kinship in industrial society - tackled among others by Hareven (1982) by demonstrating the opposite - and exaggerating it for so-called traditional societies. Such distorted views, attributable to an obsolete evolutionistic modernisation paradigm, bias the interpretation of observed forms and functions of contemporary family households, particularly in a comparative context (Niehof, 1997). Awareness of and knowledge about historical processes help to place contemporary family households in a proper perspective.

7.3 Longitudinal Approaches in Studying Family Households

7.3.1 The Concepts of Cohort and Generation

Social demography has always struggled with the temporal dimension. Age, or individual time, is a basic variable in demographic description and explanation. At another level, demographic change reflects and brings about social change. For explaining changing demographic patterns, another temporal dimension than that of individual age has to be to considered. In 1965 the sociologist Norman Ryder published his now classic article, entitled 'The Cohort as a Concept in the Study of Social Change', in which he developed a theoretical frame for linking age to historical time. Ryder defines *cohort* as 'the aggregate of individuals (within some population definition) who experienced the same event within the same time interval' (Ryder, 1965). He sees the cohort as a structural category, not a group. It is defined by external criteria. The most common type of cohort is the birth cohort. Another is the marriage cohort.

The birth cohort comprises an aggregate of individuals who were born in the same period. Individuals of one birth cohort share the timing of historical events which impinge on their lives at various ages. In this way historical time is linked to individual time at aggregate level. According to Ryder, social change occurs when specifc cohorts are exposed to radical events at an age when they are both impressionable and at the same time no longer tied to parental authority and influences: the formative years of adolescence and young adulthood. This is referred to as the socialization hypothesis or the socialization model. Triggered by external events, cohorts in their late teens or early twenties are disposed to make a break with the past. Examples are male cohorts who are at an age to be drafted when a war breaks out, or female cohorts at the age of starting their sexual career at a time when the contraceptive pill is freely available for the first time. Whether or not social change ensues, depends, apart from the nature of the external events, also on previous intra-cohort homogeneity.

For fertility research the identification of significant female cohorts is important, for example in relation to new contraception (see above) or new legislation or policies, for instance with regard to subsidized child care. Cross-cultural comparison of fertility phenomena cannot be done properly without using the cohort method. In a study on the ageing of fertility in Europe, life course fertility patterns of birth cohorts of women (1940-1960) were analysed for ten European countries. Differences and similarities between European countries could be identified and explained by comparing the same cohorts (Bosveld, 1996).

In a more indirect way, the study of the impact of changing family values benefits from focusing on cohorts who have their formative years in a period of ideational change. For their analysis of the importance attached to specific family values, Lesthaeghe and Moors (1992) concentrate on the cohorts born in the 1940s and 1950s and socialized in the 1960s and 1970s. Behind values relating to family and marriage are more general value orientations. When *materialist* orientations (law and order, authority, security) are juxtaposed to *postmaterialist* orientations (ideas count more than money, democracy) according to Inglehart's postmaterialism scale, the cohorts born in the 1940s and 1950s (formative years during the 1960s and 1970s) are significantly more postmaterialist compared to earlier cohorts (formative years during the Depression and World War II). The trend stabilizes first and then postmaterialism declines among the cohorts of the 1960s. When comparing the cohorts who produced the baby boom to the ones who produced the baby bust, the latter made a much clearer break with the attitudes of the parental generation than did the baby-boom generating cohorts. The authors relate these ideational changes to a rise in education and secularization, commenting that 'the findings obviously corroborate the usefulness of the model of cohort succession' (Lesthaeghe and Moors, 1992, p.171). In a paper on the subject Inglehart and Abramson (1993) argue that there is evidence of a trend towards postmaterialist values during the period 1970-92 which cannot be attributed to life-cycle effects (cohorts becoming more postmaterialist as they age), but signifies birth cohort effects.

The terms cohort and generation are often used interchangeably, but they have different meanings. The concept of *generation* as it is understood now in sociological literature derives from Mannheim. Like members of a cohort, members of a generation are similarly located in time. However, mere chronological contemporaneity cannot of itself produce a common generation location. 'Only when contemporaries definitely are in a position to participate as an integrated group in certain common experiences can we rightly speak of community of location' (Mannheim, 1952, p.298). A generation thus is more than a mere aggregate of individuals, it has a group identity. As White (1992, p.31) points out the difference:

> Cohorts only become actors when they cohere enough around events, in both their own and others' eyes, to be called generations. A generation is a joint interpretive construction which insists upon and builds among tangible cohorts in defining a style recognized from both outside as well as from inside.

The sociologist Becker (1992, p.20) gives the following working definition of a generation:

> A grouping of a number of cohorts characterized by a specific historical setting and common characteristics on an individual level (biographical characteristics, value orientations and behavioural patterns) and a systems level (size, generational culture and generational organizations).

Becker distinguishes four generations in contemporary Dutch society: the pre-war generation (born 1910-30), the silent generation (born 1930-40), the protest generation (born 1940-55) and the lost generation (born 1955-70). In a recent book, Becker sketches a picture of these generations; their economic prospects and positions, education, attitudes, ideas, and so on (Becker 1996). Becker's framework allows for developing and testing hypotheses about differences between these generations regarding, for example, household and family formation and dissolution, childbearing and child rearing, women's emancipation.

7.3.2 Life Cycle or Life Course

Among anthropologists there has always been a keen interest in the socio-cultural patterning of the life cycle of individuals in non-industrial societies. Particularly in tribal groups, the individual is expected to go through specific stages in the life cycle, which can only be entered after some socio-cultural requirements have been fulfilled. Van Gennep's classic study, orginally published in 1908 and translated into English in 1960, describes how rituals accompany the transition from one stage to the next. These rituals can be divided into rituals which enable the individual to leave a certain stage behind, rituals which highlight the transition itself, and rituals which aim at incorporating the individual into the new stage and confirm his/her new status. This kind of socio-cultural temporal patterning is not so exotic as it seems. In our own society too, marriage used to be surrounded by customs which had almost the same socially obligatory character as Van Gennep's rites of passage. A bachelor's party can be seen as a ritual of the first kind: an exit ritual. Wedding ceremonies, including the honeymoon, are recognizable as transition ritual, and the obligatory social visiting of the young couple as incorporation ritual.

The life-cycle concept presupposes the existence of an unwritten blueprint of the temporal patterning of the life of an individual, in which the various stages, their sequence and duration, and the transitions from one stage to another are given. It is normative in character and provides society with a certain measure of predictability of, and social control over, the individual life course. Not so long ago, in Western society also, it was socially and morally unacceptable to let parenthood precede marriage. Compared to the societies Van Gennep based his study on, however, in Western society the safeguarding of individual interests, freedom, and options has increasingly gained ground at the expense of social control, conformity and predictability. The concept of life cycle proved too constrictive and the concept of life course took its place. Elder (1994) sees *human agency* as a core element of the life course paradigm, implying an actor approach rather than a structural approach.

Apart from the normative connotations adhering to the concept of life cycle as opposed to life course, another difference can be pointed out between the two concepts. The concept of life cycle implies a cyclical conception of time which is apt to apply to societal organization, because the social metabolism underlying it is based on the endless comings and goings of individual members. But from the individual perspective time unfolds in a linear way.

> The individual, from his side, expects to be able to look backward and forward, to remember and to predict, to experience life as a meaningful continuum. Several mechanisms .... are designed to provide this predictability. Their product is the 'life course' as a meaningful sequence of events and decisions (Elchardus, 1984, p.253).

Apart from the fact that in a number of great religious traditions the life course of the individual is perceived to be cyclical, the notion of individual cyclical time does not seem to have disappeared altogether in Western society, bearing in mind the 'ashes to ashes, dust to dust'.

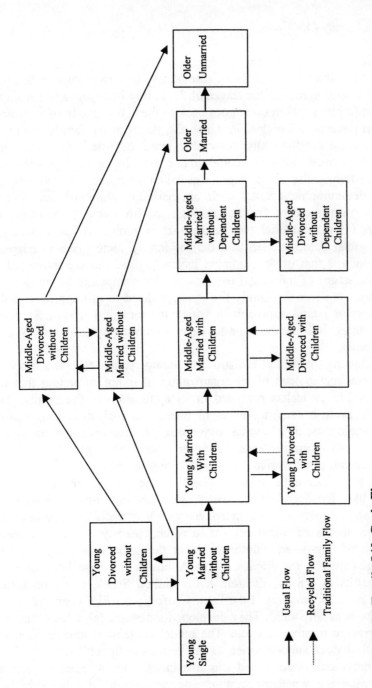

Figure 7.1 Family Life Cycle Flows
Source: Murphy and Staples, 1979, p.17

7.3.3 The Family Life Cycle

The application of the concept of life cycle to the study of the family is long-standing and has a number of disciplinary underpinnings. In the first place, the attention paid to the stages of the family life cycle arose from an interest in family economics. It goes back to the classic study of Rowntree (1906) on poverty in London, in which the stages in the family life cycle that were most economically vulnerable were identified. The consumer sciences developed along this paradigmatic axis. In the second place, the interest in family life cycle stages was taken up by social demography, because demographic events, such as marriage, childbirth and death, propel the movement of families through the life cycle. The studies of Uhlenberg (1969) and Glick (see below), are examples. In this respect, the work of social demographers and that of family sociologists overlap. A third approach is that of development psychologists who are interested in linking the stages of individual psychological development to the familial context and stages in the family life cycle. Related to this approach is the family developmental approach in which the temporal dynamics of the familial context become the main focus, of which the work of Joan Aldous is an example.

Following the lead of Elchardus in seeing cyclical time as a property of the social metabolism of an organization, it is not surprising that the concept of life cycle has persisted in its application to the family. The family life cycle became a subject of interest to such diverse groups as family sociologists, development psychologists, consumer and marketing researchers. Also in this case, however, social change has broadened options and increased variation, thus affecting the blue-print character of the life cycle. The authors of a review article on the subject point to changes like fertility decline, which shortens the family-with-young-children stage, delay of first marriage, which extends the young-single stage, the increased incidence of divorce, leading to an increased proportion of one-parent families, and at the same time a decrease of remarriage (Murphy and Staples, 1979). Although they base their argument on the results of family research in the United States, their conclusion about the need for revision of the Family Life Cycle (FLC) concept seems to be more generally valid. They developed a new model, which they call the modernized family life cycle. The model contains a number of major stages with thirteen subcategories, as can be seen in figure 7.1.

Individual options and circumstances, like whether or not to postpone marriage, whether or not to postpone parenthood or have children at all, can be located in the subcategories and alternative tracks in the model. The authors stress that its efficacy should be judged by its ability to reflect changing demographic trends, rather than exclusively by the absolute numbers of people that it accounts for. At the end of the article the authors give some illustrations of the applicability of the new model. In family sociology, for instance, the current trend toward smaller families may shorten the duration of the life cycle squeeze, the stage when young children are present and family income does not adequately meet family needs.

Another article also provides an update of the family life cycle, but, in addition, goes into the implications of the observed changes for family life. As the author summarizes it: 'The study features an 80-year (1880-1960) perspective on the average ages of mothers at the beginning of five stages in the life cycle, *or life course*, of the family' (Glick, 1977, p.11). The long-time changes in the timing of the stages are shown to be traceable primarily to fluctuations in the birth rate and to improvement in survival rates among adults. Also this author points to the great impact of fertility decline on the family life cycle. The 80-year perspective allows for identifying the influence of historical time on the family life cycle. The data permit the conclusion that:

> .... most of the fluctuations in the starting points of family life cycle stages have occurred when there were closely related changes in economic conditions (notably the economic depression in the 1930s and the decades of affluence after World War II) and longtime demographic changes (Glick, 1977, p.9).

In fact, the study combines a cohort approach with a family life cycle approach. Among the findings used by the author are those of an earlier study in which a similar methodology was applied (Uhlenberg, 1969). In the report of a research project on life cycle differences in housing perspectives of rural households, the issue of change is put right at the beginning:

> The traditional rural family with mother, father, and children working side by side, in or near the home, has changed drastically over the past decades. Rural families now exist in greater patterns of diversity resulting from demographic, technical, social, and cultural changes (Earhart et al., 1994, p.309).

The research question was whether these changes over the life plan affected housing satisfaction and the family's perception of housing needs. The study provides an example of a design in which the differences between the various stages of the family life cycle are treated as explanatory variables.

For the study of family farms, the concept of the family life cycle is most relevant because family labour availability and productivity are strongly related to stages in the family life cycle. The family farm can be defined as a farm which is owned and operated by a family which may include one or more generations (Gasson and Errington, 1993). The family life cycle acquires its significance for farm households particularly in relation to the issue of family labour. Gasson and Errington review several studies to find categorizations of family life cycle stages in relation to farm operation. In a study on southern Ireland the following stages were distinguished: inheritance and marriage, interchangeable in the time sequence; expansion, the period of family building between the birth of the first and the last children; stability, between the birth of the last child and the first migration of offspring; dispersal, with a sub-stage to take account of the death of either spouse. Depending on the prevailing inheritance pattern, the late phase when all the children have left the farm can be seen as part of the normal family cycle, or as a form of family failure (Gasson and Errington, 1993). The variability in labour availability over the family cycle has been recognized as one of the fundamental problems of the family farm business. There is a large range of strategies used by farming families to overcome this problem (Gasson and Errington, 1993).

In the quotation by Glick on the previous page, the concept of life course is, almost casually, put on the same footing as that of life cycle. The family sociologist Joan Aldous, however, makes it a point to preserve the term life course for the individual. In a recent book about rethinking the developmental perspective in the study of the family, she recommends including the life course perspective in family development studies:

> Despite its focus on individuals, it has a number of similarities with a family careers analysis.... As in family development, there is a focus on expectable shifts over time within historical periods, but the emphasis is on the individual, not on families.

And she continues on the relationship between the individual life course and social time:

The social clocks set behavioral expectations associated with particular ages. Family event sequences are linked to age markers. They provide the individual a standard.... Social time includes family time. Together with historical time they provide the three temporal metrics of individual lives (Aldous, 1996, p.19).

The concept of family time mentioned by Aldous will be the subject of the following key study.

7.4 Key Study: Family Time in the USA in Historical Perspective

7.4.1 Introduction

In her now famous study of the labourers of the Amoskeag textile mills in Manchester, New Hampshire, Tamara Hareven set out to 'explore the interrelationships between three different kinds of time: individual time, family time, and industrial time'. She remarks (1982, p.xii) that

.... an understanding of how these kinds of time reinforced each other or conflicted provides insight into the interaction of individuals with the larger historical processes. Under what circumstances did the family respond to external clocks, and under what conditions did it function in accordance with its internal clocks?

In spite of the fact that the study is not a recent one, it deserves its status as a key study, because of the manner in which it deals with the several dimensions of time and their interrelationships.

7.4.2 Key Concepts and Research Questions

As the author remarks, *family* has many meanings and takes many forms. Hareven views the family 'both as a domestic group and as a kinship system that extends beyond the household'. The family provides the immediate context for the individual life course. She describes a life-course perspective as viewing the interrelationships between individual and collective family behavior as they constantly change over people's lives and in the context of historical conditions. The *life-course approach* is concerned with the movement of individuals over their own lives and through historical time and with the relationship of family members to each other as they travel through personal and historical time. The relationship between individual and family time is forged by the timing of life-course events: Family time designates the timing of such life-course events as marriage, the birth of a child, a young adult's departure from the home, and the transition of individuals into different family roles, as the family moves through its life. Individual time and family time are closely synchronized, because most individual life transitions are interrelated with collective family transitions.

In the historical context of this study, in particular, the close integration of individual moves with collective family needs made individual timing dependent on collective family timing. Family time and individual time are both affected by historical time, the overall social, economic, institutional and cultural changes in the larger society. Hareven sees industrial time as an aspect of historical time. It encompasses the industrial culture governing behaviour and relations in the workplace and industrial communities. 'An understanding of the synchronization of these different levels of timing is essential to the investigation of the relationship between discrete lives and the larger processes of social change' (Hareven, 1982, p.6).

This three-dimensional conception of time provided the methodological framework for the study. The research was focussed on the interrelationships between individual time, family time and industrial time. Research questions were:
- How did the family respond to changing working conditions?
- How did industrial work affect family relations?
- How did the family affect conditions in the factory?
- How did individual life course timing depend on collective family needs?

7.4.3 Data Collection

Manchester offered a rich combination of historical sources. More than seventy thousand career files were kept by the Amoskeag Company. These files provided an opportunity for reconstructing work careers over time, and individual and family histories by linking these records with other sources. During the process of reconstructing family histories, former Amoskeag workers and their relatives were interviewed. These oral-history narratives were also published in a separate volume (Hareven and Langenbach, 1978).

7.4.4 Findings and Discussion

Hareven shows the importance of kinship ties, both within and beyond the nuclear family, for labour recruitment and for on-the-job training. The younger ones learnt the tricks from their older relatives working in the factory. Furthermore, kin could fill in for one another. Out of consideration for each other, they rarely exceeded the production quotas that had been informally agreed upon. This type of family work pattern also allowed older workers to hold on to their job.

Industrial work also affected family relations. Sons and daughters moved to Manchester and there set up their own households after marriage instead of coming back to the land. This may have weakened the patriarchal authority of traditional rural families. But migration did *not* result in a breakdown of kinship ties. The relatives remaining behind had a crucial function in providing backup assistance and security for migrating family members. The integration of kin with the factory was also a potential source of conflict. The strike in 1922 set relatives at odds: whether or not to strike divided some families and caused conflicts that took years to overcome.

Hareven emphasizes the interdependencies between family, kin and factory. Kin assistance was essential both in coping with the insecurities dictated by the industrial system, such as unemployment and strikes, and in coping with personal and family crises, especially childbirth, illness, and death (Hareven, 1982). While the first type of insecurities are contingent upon industrial time, the second are events in the individual and family life course. Hareven shows that career choices and economic decisions were made within the family matrix. In this matrix a pivotal role was played by the *kin keeper*. Usually women, kin keepers were helpers, arbiters, and pacifiers (Hareven, 1982).

In the timing of life transitions, the dependency of the individual upon family and factory showed. The large population of boarders in their twenties, for example, reflected postponement of marriage. For women, later marriage also postponed the commencement of childbearing. As regards later life transitions, widowhood was quite common. Widows who wanted to retain the headship of their households had to work. Thus, while married women generally were not employed, nine out of ten widows who continued to head their own households were in the labour force. Hareven (1982, p.166) summarizes the picture as follows:

The synchronization of all the various 'time clocks' that govern the scheduling of individual events - starting and leaving work, leaving home, getting married, setting up an independent household, becoming parents, and launching children from the home - involved the coordination of individual time schedules with those of the family as a group under circumstances shaped by institutional constraints.

Keeping in line with the clock metaphor, one could say that *kin keepers* acted as synchronizers. They played their role as pacifiers and arbiters in situations of conflicting individual and family timing.

7.5 Life Course Dynamics

The development of the Life Course Approach is commonly associated with the work of Glen Elder. He chaired the Committee on Life-Course Perspectives on Human Development, which was established by the Social Science Research Council (United States) in 1977. The committee tried to bring a dynamic life course approach to existing panel data. The results of this effort are presented in the book, of which the theoretical framework will be the subject of this section.

Elder traces the origins of the life course approach to the Chicago School of Sociology (1915), because of its use of life records in the study of social change. It was a time of rapid urbanization, large numbers of immigrants moving to the cities, and family disorganization. The second era of the life course paradigm begins in the 1960s. At that time, a renewed consciousness of and sensitivity to the relationship between individual and social change arose, and the interplay between research and theoretical activities increased. Ryder's essay (1965) brought more sophisticated awareness of the connections between historical and individual life time and, in doing so, provided fresh insight regarding the temporal aspects of life. Elder (1985, p.25) continues to describe this interconnectedness as follows:

> Age represents a basis of historical differentiation through cohorts and of social differentiation according to age-graded statuses and role sequences. Age strata thus order both people and social roles. Socialization and role allocation link people and social roles in the process of aging and cohort succession. This connection between historical age and cohort, on the one hand, and social age in the life course on the other, has alerted investigators to the variable meaning of life events in history.

Trajectories and *transitions* are central concepts in the study of life course dynamics. Transitions are always embedded in trajectories, and each trajectory is marked by a sequence of transitions. Although life transition and life event both entail a change in state, Elder prefers to use the former because it refers explicitly to this change, which may take place over a substantial period of time (Elder, 1985). Events and transitions lead to the concept of duration, the waiting times or spells between a change in state. The consequences of the duration of any event depend on what people bring to the situation, in terms of personal and social characteristics.

Elder's framework allows for much intra- and inter-life course variability about which research questions can be formulated. When conceptualized in this way, the life course approach does not have the normative and standardized character of the life cycle approach. The life course emphasizes human agency (Elder, 1994). Elder (1985) points to the high degree of variation in stage or position across dimensions of the life course of a cross-section of the youth population. However, he also notes that off-timed events in the transition to adulthood in American society are known to have enduring effects. For example, early marriage has proven to increase the odds of divorce. Mulder (1993, p.23) remarks about the concept of the life course that it does not have the normative connotations often associated with the concept of life cycle, but that this is 'not to deny that life courses are, to some extent, normatively structured and standardized'.

Both interdependence and turning points are key features of life course dynamics. 'Interdependence refers to the interlocking nature of trajectories and transitions, within and across life stages' (Elder, 1985, p.23). The angle of interdependence gives a temporal dimension to the problem of conflicting roles. 'The concept of a differentiated life course merely extends in time the familiar notion of multiple roles and their potential cross-pressures. We can thus approach competing life spheres or trajectories from the vantage point of role strain and the allocation of scarce resources' (Elder, 1985, p.33). Interconnectedness over the life course can also be phrased as saying:

....that events and traditions modify life trajectories. Some events are important turning points in life - they redirect paths. The lifetime effects of ordinary events and turning points cannot be appraised without taking into account four sets of variables: (1) the nature of the event or transition, its severity, duration, and so on; (2) the resources, beliefs, and experiences people bring to the situation; (3) how the situation or events is defined; and (4) resulting lines of adaptation as chosen from available alternatives. The first three factors influence lines of adaptation, but the latter links events and the subsequent life course (Elder, 1985, p.35).

An example given by Elder is adolescent childbearing among black people in the United States which leads to persistent economic dependence in later life.

A final aspect of life course dynamics highlighted by Elder is that of control. The trajectory of life can be portrayed as one marked by the recurring loss and recovery of control potential. The extent to which a transition entails loss of control is contingent on the resources or level of preparation people bring to the new situation. Life plans that people make are based on images of the future life course. Revised thinking about the future prompts new life course planning. In this case, we are dealing with forward linkages. Elder says that the life course can be seen as a continuing project of construction and reconstruction as new experience is encountered (Elder, 1985).

7.6 Key Study: A Life Course Approach to Migration Dynamics in The Netherlands

7.6.1 Introduction

In the introduction to her book, Mulder (1993) observes that the significance of migration changes over the life course and that it changes when considered over time, depending on economic circumstances. Questions then arise about how migration patterns are linked to both circumstances in the life course of the individual and the wider social context. The research project addressed these questions. Its aims were to gain better understanding of individual migration behaviour, and to evaluate the appropriateness of different types of data sets for gaining insight into the intersection between individual and historical time. The study was written in the conviction that a better understanding of individual behaviour can be achieved through combining macro and micro approaches, thereby concentrating on the intersection between individual and historical time. The research problem was formulated as: 'How do migration life course patterns in The Netherlands change through time and between birth cohorts; what causes these differences?' (Mulder, 1993, p.15).

We selected this study as a key study because of its consistent application of a life course approach in a field that is relevant to household studies. The methodological problems that Mulder encountered illustrate the difficulties involved in applying a longitudinal approach to the study of family households.

7.6.2 Key Concepts and Research Questions

The study treats migration as 'individual behaviour, counting all within-country changes of usual residence as migration' (Mulder, 1993, p.11). The unit of analysis is the individual:

> No attempt has been made to think of household life courses, or cohorts of households, since this leads to major methodological problems.... Individuals are therefore the units of analysis, even though migration decisions are household decisions. Household characteristics are viewed as influences on individual migration behaviour (Mulder, 1993, p.24).

Mulder specifies four assumptions about human behaviour which underly the study design. First, general goals in life become concrete in the form of specific goals at which people aim. These are expressed through preferences. Second, people pursue their goals rationally, in the sense that they deliberately employ means to reach ends. They do this in a certain decision environment, which codifies decision-making and defines preferences to a certain extent. Third, people's past actions condition future action. People think and act generally with a long-term perspective in mind. A certain degree of biographical continuity is assumed to be important for people's well-being. People may re-define their preferences, but they do so gradually and infrequently. They try to shape their lives along reasonably consistent paths, which Mulder calls careers. Fourth, societies change continually with respect to resources (economic opportunity structures) and the acceptability of certain preferences (social opportunity structures). Because people are inclined to preserve biographical consistency, changes in the social acceptability of preferences are most likely to appear as long-term trends. Such a trend is the increasing centrality of individual goal attainment (individualization) in Western societies.

Key concepts in the study are cohort, career, and life course. Following Ryder, a cohort is defined as 'the aggregate of individuals (within some population definition) who experienced the same event within the same time interval'. Career is defined as a life path. People have several careers simultaneously: household careers, occupational careers, migration careers, and so on. Careers can run parallel courses or intertwine. A life course is then the individual's complex system of careers or, phrased differently, the way in which an individual progresses through various stages or statuses in various careers in life without the normative connotations often associated with the concept of life cycle (Mulder, 1993).

Migration is seen as instrumental behaviour, not as a goal in itself. Migration-related goals can be linked to one or more of the individual's careers which make up the life course. The parallel career producing the goal for which achievement migration is instrumental, is the triggering career. Parallel careers which provide resources and constraints in relation to the migration career are called conditioning careers. The course of the occupational career, for example, determines an individual's income and savings. Through coupling restraints, the household career restricts an individual's mobility.

In the intertwining of the migration career with triggering careers two types of dependence are distinguished: event dependence and state dependence. Event dependence is the effect of the occurrence of an event in a parallel career such as marriage or entering higher education. In most cases, the migration event takes place at about the same point in time as the causal event in the other career. When the event is anticipated, migration can take place prior to it, which illustrates the fact that time ordering does not necessarily reflect causal ordering. State dependence is the (long-term) effect of occupying a certain state in a career. States in a career produce commitments to a location or to a dwelling. Both are stronger when the dwelling is shared with others, and when it is owner-occupied rather than rented. Changes in parallel careers are not evenly distributed over the life course and neither is migration. Because transitional periods are typically concentrated around adolescence and young adulthood, migration behaviour is most prevalent during these periods of the life course as well (Mulder, 1993).

Migration is the dependent variable in the research scheme. Several types of migration can be distinguished according to distance, direction and destination choice. Three clusters of determinants of dynamics in migration behaviour are included in the scheme, one of which is macro-level constraints and opportunities. The other clusters are individual preferences; and parallel, triggering and conditioning careers. Individual preferences are conditioned by socially accepted preferences, parallel, triggering and conditioning careers by macro-level constraints and opportunities. The latter thus influence the dynamics of migration

behaviour directly and indirectly (Mulder, 1993). Based on this scheme Mulder (1993) poses the following research questions:
1. How have age-specific migration patterns, distinguished between short-distance and long-distance patterns, changed through historical time (between periods and cohorts)?
2. How have age-specific triggers for migration and their connection with migration distances changed through historical time (between periods and cohorts)?
3. How has the relationship between migration of distinct types and parallel, triggering and conditioning careers in the life course changed through historical time (between periods and cohorts)?
4. How can the changes in migration behaviour which are the subject of the first three questions be linked to changes in preferences, opportunities, resources, and constraints through historical time?
5. The fifth research question is a methodological one, and will be discussed below.

7.6.3 Data and Analysis

The fifth research question posed by Mulder relates to the suitability of data sets and methods. Three types of data sets are used for answering research questions one to four: aggregate statistics, repeated cross-sectional surveys with some retrospective information, and retrospective surveys.

Macro-level societal change produces migration patterns. For finding the answer to the first research question, the period under study is divided into four parts:
- The reconstruction period (1945-60);
- Increasing mobility (1961-73);
- Economic decline (1974-79);
- The period of recovery (1980-89).

The vital statistics on migration provided by the Central Bureau of Statistics (CBS) are an important source for addressing the first research question. First published in 1948, the CBS inter-municipality migration statistics are published each year and with increasing detail. In addition, literature is reviewed which uses these data as well as census data. Besides using the data for a description of general trends, an Age-Period-Cohort (APC) analysis is applied. The purpose of this method is to separate age, period, and cohort effects (Mulder, 1993).

For answering the second research question additional data are needed. These are found in the CBS Housing Demand Surveys (HDS) of

1981, 1985, and 1989 (second type of data set). The surveys contain information about current housing situation, intended and realized migration behaviour, and motive for the move. The latter is considered the trigger. The assumption that household and housing careers mainly trigger short distance moves, whereas education and occupational career trigger long distance migration, can be put to the test by using these data. Both the time period and age span are more limited in the HDS data compared to the data on inter-municipality migration which were used for answering the first research question. Five variables are used in the analysis: age, period, sex, motive and distance (Mulder, 1993).

The third is the most important of the first three research questions, since it relates to the essential link between migration and individual life courses. For investigating this link, Mulder uses the published results of survey research on migration in addition to the HDS data. At the end of Chapter Six, in which the main answers to the third research question are given, Mulder remarks (1993, p.145) 'In this chapter, individual characteristics were interpreted from a life course perspective. The data, however, were not of the type that first comes to mind when adopting such a perspective. They were cross-sectional in nature, not longitudinal life history data'. Research question four is the leading background question which served as a guideline for the formulation of hypotheses. No new data sets were used for answering this question.

The fifth research question implies an assessment of the usefulness of the data sets for studying migration from a life course perspective. The CBS migration statistics have as their main strength that they are population statistics, meaning that they form a large data base, organized by age and calendar year, thus permitting re-arrangement of the data by period, age, and birth cohort. However, these data have two drawbacks. The first one is that within-municipality moves are not recorded. The second is that they lack information on individual characteristics (Mulder, 1993).

The Housing Demand Surveys provide much richer information, but they are essentially cross-sectional in nature. To a certain extent this limitation is overcome in two ways: first, the surveys are repeated at several points in time; second, retrospective questions are included. As Mulder remarks, any survey including the subject of migration cannot be purely cross-sectional in the sense that it only measures the respondent's characteristics at the moment of the interview. At least some retrospection with regard to the migration event is required. The appropriateness of the data for placing migration in a longitudinal perspective is then determined by the extent to which the observation of the independent variables also was done retrospectively. If this is not the case, the researcher has a major problem when studying the influence of current housing or dwelling characteristics on migration (Mulder, 1993). Fortunately, the HDS surveys contain data on household and housing information before the move.

7.6.4 Findings and Discussion

For the following reasons we will limit the presentation of the research findings and their discussion to the relationship between migration behaviour and household career. In the first place, because the availability of retrospective data on household and housing (see above) made it possible to place the relationship between migration and household career in a longitudinal perspective. Secondly, because of the major importance of the household career in explaining migration behaviour. 'The household career (proved to be) a major triggering career for short distance moves, and, even for moves at longer distance, the triggering effects of the household career are far from negligible' (Mulder, 1993, p.167). A third argument would be that households are, after all, the focus of this book.

Union formation is a major determinant of the household career, and, by implication, also of the migration career. Educational and occupational careers are conditioning factors in relation to union formation. Gender is another differentiating variable. It is to be expected that because of the age difference between partners in heterosexual couples, and the assumed dominance of a man's occupational career over his partner's, less influence from education and working status on moves made for reasons of union formation is expected for females than for males. At the same time, as a consequence of women's increasing emancipation, sex differences in the role of education and working status can be expected to diminish through the periods (Mulder, 1993).

The analysis of the data on the relationship between moves and household career, restricted to those age-groups at the greatest risk, shows both age and period effects. Moves for reasons of union formation were shown to be strongly influenced by state in the household career; there is a marked difference between people living with their parents and singles in their propensity to make a union formation move. This difference is strongly related to age. The educational and occupational careers were shown to have a strongly differentiating effect on union formation moves. A high level of education leads to leaving home alone and postponement of union formation. Age and sex differences proved to be much more pronounced for union formation moves than home-leaving for other reasons. However, even when union formation is not the reason, females were shown to leave home earlier than males.

Looking at period effects, the decrease in the odds of moving for reasons of union formation in the mid-eighties can be attributed to the unfavourable economic conditions during that period. The postponement of home-leaving observed for that period seems to have been a temporary phenomenon. At the same time it could be observed that migration related to union formation is more susceptible to economic influences than forming single-person households. Individualization tendencies showed in the increasing tendency to leave home alone. Apparently, when measured for the entire period under observation, living alone increasingly becomes an extra step in the household career between living with parents and living with a partner (Mulder, 1993).

In the discussion at the end of the book, Mulder points to the limitations of a study design based essentially on cross-sectional data. For example, little information could be obtained about the direct links between migration and the occupational career (job mobility) because of the lack of retrospective data on the latter. As Mulder   (1993, p.222) observes:

> An obvious gain would be achieved by analysing life course data..... Some of the advantages of life course data are that the variables are measured at the right moment; the influence of prior experiences can be studied; a relatively small number of respondents is needed in order to achieve the same number of migrations as in a cross-sectional survey; and individual life course patterns can be reconstructed.

7.7 Conclusions and New Directions for Research

7.7.1 Conclusions

The discussion in this chapter has shown that incorporating a longitudinal perspective in the study of family households is rewarding but methodologically not easy. The methodological complications are fairly inhibiting. At one level there is the relationship between individual age and historical time. Ryder's article on the concept of cohort provided a break-through in this respect. It generated fruitful research in which this concept was applied. The concept of cohort was sociologically further worked out in the concept of generation. The latter concept is less precise with regard to individual time (age), but more sensitive in reflecting historical time. Generation identity can function as an explanatory variable with regard to all kinds of questions relating to household formation, composition, and dissolution.

At another level the relationship between individual time, or the individual life course, and family or household time proves to be problematic. The concept of the family life cycle circumvents some problems by using family life cycle stage as an explanantory variable in relation to individual behaviour. However, the problem of the necessity of synchronizing cannot be ignored, as Aldous and Hareven have pointed out. Elder and Mulder see the individual life course as made up of different trajectories or careers respectively. The household career or family trajectory can then be treated as contextual to other (individual) careers or trajectories. At junctions between trajectories or careers, events or transitions in the one lead to adaptations or discontinuities in the other.

Hareven's historical study uses a design in which the three dimensions of time referred to above are integrated. She distinguishes individual time, family time and industrial (historical) time. She could do so because of the detailed archival materials available, which included family genealogies of workers, and the possibility to interview former workers. When looking at the family household from a longitudinal perspective, family or household time intersects with both individual time and historical time. In Figure 7.2 above these dimensions of time and their intersections are made visible in a hypothetical family household.

As we have seen, in the life course approach the individual life courses are bundles of parallel or intersecting careers (Mulder) or trajectories (Elder). In this kind of research design, the individual life course becomes the dependent variable, household variables become intermediate or independent variables. Household variables mediate the impact of historical time on the life course. In Mulder's study the household career is a major triggering career for the migration career. The housing career is seen as part of the household career. Sometimes it seems as if the household career is reduced to the housing career. An alternative approach would be to focus on the life course of family households. As we have seen, Mulder (1993) refrained from this because of the methodological problems involved. In our opinion, these problems are not fundamentally different from those involved in individual life course approaches. We shall work this out in the next section.

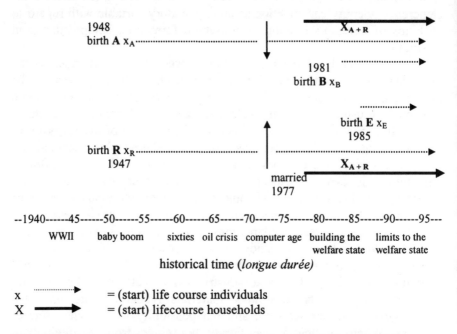

Figure 7.2 A hypothetical family household in longitudinal perspective

A major practical problem is the scarcity of longitudinal data and the constraints in generating them. Panels are expensive. Funding agencies generally do not allow stretching the research beyond the usual time frame of two to five years. The funding infrastructure for social science research thus discourages longitudinal studies. In the key study we presented, the shortcomings of cross-sectional data for a study with a life course perspective were (partly) overcome by using data from repeated surveys and data yielded by answers to retrospective questions. In the concluding chapter of her book on leaving the parental home, Baanders regrets the limitations of having to use cross-sectional data, and stresses the merits of a longitudinal study on the subject:

> A longitudinal approach would enable the researcher to detect the impact of unforeseen events, which may unexpectedly delay or expedite one's departure from the parental home. All this would still further enhance our understanding of the factors affecting the decision to leave home (Baanders, 1998, p.218).

7.7.2 New Directions for Research

In this section we suggest four directions for longitudinal research in the field of family households. The first is in developing a household life course approach. The second is a longitudinal (household) approach in social gerontology. The third direction is about the normative character of the life course. The fourth centres around questions of household control and household strategies

1 A household life course approach As a point of departure for developing a household life course, we distinguish three dimensions of the family household: family or social dimension, dwelling dimension, householding dimension. By the latter we mean those activities that are geared towards the provision for the basic needs and care of the household members, and the generation and management of resources and assets to be able to do so. Within each dimension household careers develop:
1. The family career, under which family time can be subsumed;
2. The household composition career, which indicates the comings and goings of household members through time (Tamara Hareven's household as a revolving stage), including non-family household members. Like the family career, it is part of the social dimension.
3. The housing career, part of the dwelling dimension. It includes moving house. Individual moves will be visible in the household composition career.
4. The household financial career, indicating the household's acquiring financial resources, assets, and obligations through time, is an aspect of the householding dimension.
5. The household economic career, dealing with the household's income generating performance in relation to its spending patterns, is also part of the householding dimension.
6. The household life course starts at the formation of the household and ends with the founders' exit.

Based on this outline, sketchy though it is, several clusters of research questions can be formulated. The first is a cluster of questions relating to household poverty or vulnerability. The relationship between economic household careers and parallel household careers, and the impact of historical time (period effects) on both, would be the line of investigation. The household composition career could be a major triggering career in relation to the economic career of the household. The same applies to questions relating to household consumption patterns. The phenomenon of the 'family squeeze' could be analysed in this way. Actually, the term household squeeze would be more appropriate, since the term refers to an imbalance between family time and household composition on the one hand and household resources on the other, at a certain stage in the household life course.

A second cluster could comprise questions which relate events and states in the family career to the other household careers, for example the housing career, in a truly longitudinal fashion. Not only the leaving home of young people, but also the staying in the own home of elderly people could be studied in this manner.

What all these questions have in common is that they explore the relationships between the several careers that make up the household life course as they develop through time. Period effects influence these relationships through their impact on one or more careers, or affect a relationship directly. Individualization as a macro-social trend, for example, affects the relationship between housing career and household composition career.

2 A longitudinal household approach in social gerontology. As we have seen, in the life course paradigm as developed by Elder the interdependence of trajectories and transitions across life stages is an important element. The focus implied by the life course perspective paradigm on the linkages between events and transitions that are separated in time, is highly relevant for research in social gerontology. Events and transitions in early life shape trajectories and may redirect paths. Empirical evidence seems to suggest that the experience of old age has much to do with early hardship in the adult years and one's responses to it. The extent to which one is able to accumulate assets during the adult years, for example, will be an important factor in determining one's economic autonomy during old age. This holds for tangible assets, such as building up a pension during one's working life, but also for intangible assets, like a sustainable social (kinship) network that one can fall back on for care and emotional support in later life.

Peter Laslett's concept of third age, though interesting enough in its own right, would be far more interesting if it incorporated a life course perspective. Of course, third age refers to a patterning of the life course and thus incorporates the temporal dimension. In Laslett's description first age is an era of dependence, socialization, immaturity and education; second age an area of independence, maturity and responsibility; third age an era of personal fulfilment; and fourth age an era of final dependence, decrepitude and death (Laslett, 1991). In a life course perspective, the shaping of the third age would have to be seen in connection with the previous ages. Hypotheses could be formulated about the effects of household careers in earlier ages on living arrangements, autonomy, and care arrangements in third and fourth age.

3 *The normative character of the (household) life course* A totally different field of longitudinal research on the family household can be subsumed under the heading of the normative character of the life course, whether at the individual or household level. The authors quoted in this chapter do not seem able to resolve the opposition between observed standardization of the life course on the one hand and increasing variability and individualization on the other. The concept of life cycle came to be rejected because of its normative connotations and was replaced by the concept of life course. In the course of the debate, the first became associated with the collective level, the second with the individual level.

Above, we proposed to concentrate on the household life course in longitudinal research on the family household. This is not to deny that there are cyclical aspects to the development of family households, but to avoid taking these as a point of departure. That would unnecessarily narrow our scope. It is also not to deny that there are norms and values pertaining to the way households develop. On the contrary, we assume that there are, and we think that questions about the degree of standardization of the household life course and the norms behind it are most relevant and interesting. What about life course values, which, though not producing iron-cast norms, do seem to yield some sort of an *ideal type* of life course, from which too much deviation might sooner or later lead to problems? Baanders' research (1998) on leaving home by young people shows that norms about when to leave home, in what circumstances and under what conditions, still influence young people's decision-making as regards staying, planning to leave, or leaving home.

Research questions can be formulated on the normative character of life course stages and transitions, as well as on the actual degree of standardization of individual and household life courses. These questions are relevant because standardization evokes anticipation, and the acknowledgement of norms invites expectations.

4 *Control and strategies* The issue of control, raised by Elder, is also involved in the subject of standardization. In studying households confronted with an involuntary break in the life course because of disaster,

this angle should be taken into account. When the anticipated and desired life course cannot be pursued any longer, households lose control. Research along these lines will yield insights into the survival strategies of households in disaster situations, and extremely vulnerable households which are on the brink of disaster. Such an approach would, for example, be relevant to apply to rural households in areas in Sub-Saharan Africa where HIV/AIDS infection is reaching pandemic proportions (see Barnett, 1992/93; Bos et al., 1996).

Research questions can be formulated on the relationship between, on the one hand, the nature of the survival strategies, and, on the other hand, the discontinuities or the gap between the life course pursue before the disaster and the actual situation. Furthermore, the applicabilility of the concept of strategy can be questioned in a situation in which future developments cannot be anticipated. In such a situation, the concept of coping seems more appropriate than that of strategy.

8 The Morality Approach and the Issue of Care

8.1 Introduction

The researchers and studies to be discussed in this chapter have a common emphasis on the moral contents of the relationships between household and family members and the moral motivations for their actions. Morality concerns the distinction between conduct that is right or wrong. Moral judgements presuppose certain standards of what is right and wrong. These standards yield a normative framework within which judgements are made, obligations are formulated, and upon which legitimate expectations are based. But there is no such thing as the morality approach. The authors discussed in this chapter approach the subject of morality in relation to the family household in different ways.

The issue of care plays an important role in this chapter because care is morally motivated and a large part of care practice takes place in the context of the household or family and among kin. Support can be seen as a form of care. Gender is a factor which appears to be interwoven in the discourse about the morality and practice of care and support. The concepts of morality, care, support, and gender feature as key concepts in this chapter. There are several reasons why the context of the family household is bound to generate questions of morality. We will discuss these reasons below by way of an introduction to the theme of this chapter.

A first reason is encapsulated in the prefix family. Family, in the sense of both kinship relationships and the domestic unit,[1] implies ascribed relationships. One does not pick them; one has them. In every society kinship and family relationships are embedded in a normative structure. They can be more or less prescriptive or more or less specific, but there are always norms governing the relationships between relatives and family members. Not adhering to such norms is considered bad conduct and defies expectations. Family obligations are formulated within this normative structure. Depending on the degree of prescriptiveness of the norms and the nature of the relationship involved, there is more or less room for negotiation (Finch and Mason, 1993). Precisely because of the moral contents of kinship and family relationships, a kinship network functions as a resort for social support for the individuals who are part of it. The benefits of a kinship network can be compared to that of an insurance scheme. Insurance schemes depend on the relationship between individual members and an institution whose function it is to inspire trust. Kinship networks can create the same effects, 'precisely because the network of relationships is drawn from a field of relationships characterised by social solidarity and diffuse obligation prior to any actual flows of benefits occurring' (Harris, 1990, p.61).

A second reason lies in the household's domestic mode of production. Within households, goods and services are produced and exchanged. Resources necessary for producing goods and services are to a large extent shared. Household resource management is guided by certain normative principles about intra-household division of resources, benefits, and tasks. Housework is non-commoditised. It is not rewarded in money. It is task-oriented rather than time-oriented (Vogel, cited in Kloek, 1989). The exchange of goods and services within the household does not follow the rules of the market economy, but is based on principles of reciprocity and morality, for example the obligation to support the dependent and care for the weak members of the household. The resulting domestic arrangements thus have a certain moral content. Hence, Cheal (1989), without reducing household economics to moral principles only, speaks about the 'moral economy of the household'.

The notion of the inherent moral contents of family household organisation requires some further explanation. We agree with Anderson et al. (1994) that 'households, like all enduring groups, must have emergent properties which we can treat as existing above the individual level', but we do not assume that the interests of the household as a group always, at whatever expense, prevail over those of its individual members. In this we endorse Naila Kabeer's (1991) attack on the notion of the household economy as a single welfare-maximising agent under the benevolent dictatorship of the household head, a notion which underlies neo-classical economic approaches to the household. By moral contents, then, we do not mean a morality of maximising joint welfare. Rather, we see the moral properties of family household organisation as arising out of the weighting of interests, rights and responsibilities of individual members as against those of the group, or vice versa, on the basis of a certain normative consensus. The norms involved are those that concern relationships (family), status (as based on sex or age), and the desired output of domestic production (well-being, security, etc.).

The conclusion reached above, that a morality of maximising joint welfare is an invention of economists rather than a universal attribute of family household organisation, implies that the actual nature of the moral elements in family household organisation should be a matter for investigation. The facts that the unity of the household tends to be taken for granted (Wilk, 1989), and that, for various reasons, the image of the family household as a natural entity is quite resilient (Harris, 1984), explain the lack of interest in its inner workings. The 'naturalness' seems to add validity to the notion of maximising joint welfare because something that is assumed to be natural is not questioned and seems morally right. But when we do open the black box of the family household, a different picture may emerge. Reading a research report about London working-class families, the sociologist Leonard got the impression that the researchers were disturbed by their findings. In the families described, men and women proved to go their own separate ways, and the mother-daughter relationship rather than the husband-wife relationship proved to be pivotal in the functioning of these households. 'It was somehow not "natural" or "right"', she concludes, summarising the misgivings of the researchers about their findings (Leonard, 1990, p.38).

Although there are normative ideas about the functioning of family households which undoubtedly suffer from a middle-class bias, we have to conclude that there is no moral blue-print for the family household organisation. Neither can it be assumed that maximising joint welfare is the dominant and exclusive guiding moral principle. To members of a family household the moral contents of domestic arrangements and their application in practice are contestable, which makes room for negotiation. Therefore, as one of the key studies for this chapter we selected the book by Janet Finch and Jennifer Mason (1993) about negotiating family responsibilities.

In the next section we will demonstrate the relevance of the morality approach, more particularly in relation to the issues of care and poverty, to be followed by a discussion of Joan Tronto's (1993) work on the ethics of care. As we shall see, the subject of care inevitably raises questions about gender. Subsequently, we will pay attention to the morality of give-and-take within family households, looking particularly at the work of David Cheal. Then the key studies will be presented: one based on the work of Finch and Mason in an English community, the other on research conducted in Kenya. As in the other chapters, conclusions are drawn and new directions for research are indicated in the final section.

8.2 The Relevance of the Morality Approach

The morality approach appears to be particularly relevant for the study of care and household poverty. Poverty and dependency give rise to moral concerns and morally motivated action. Therefore, approaches which highlight the moral element in human interaction are appropriate. We shall substantiate these statements below.

To be able to demonstrate the relevance of the morality approach for issues of care, it is necessary to first go into the concept of the welfare state. De Swaan (1988) described the gestation of the welfare state as a socio-historic construction. He pictures how, over the course of centuries in European countries, personal responsibilities and actions came to be transformed into a responsibility for an impersonal collectivity. Along with this process of social transformation, people's ideas and attitudes about care changed. As an American sociologist phrased it in a paper: the I-will-take-care-of-it mentality was replaced by the it-must-be-taken-care-of or something-ought-to-be-done-about-it mentality (Wiersma, 1997). In an article about the moral underpinnings of the welfare state, Zijderveld (1979) points to the conditions in which welfare states developed: affluence, structural differentiation, and generalisation. In other words, welfare states cannot develop in poor and undifferentiated societies which are characterised by particularism, such as the kind of societies in which patron-client relationships and the moral economy of the peasant (Scott, 1976) prevail, or societies which are mainly structured by kinship and ethnicity. The nature of the moral underpinnings of welfare states obviously go back to particular historical circumstances and traditions. Hence the existence of different welfare-state regimes (Esping-Andersen, 1996).

However, there are cracks in the even most complete welfare state, irrespective of the underlying regime. Also well-functioning welfare states do not seem to have final answers for persistent social problems such as social and political inequity, poverty, and the need for care. The latter is proved by their politicians' call for a 'caring society'. At the same time in these states, women were being drawn increasingly into production outside the home and home-based production was being drawn into the market. Labour-saving appliances in the household relieved women of part of the drudgery with which older generations of women had been burdened. These changes in the division of labour between the sexes solved old problems but created new ones. Fukuyama (1997) even goes so far as to blame modern contraception for women's autonomy and women's autonomy for the breakdown of the family and - in its wake - of the societal order, citing crime and divorce statistics to prove his point. The argument obviously plays into the hands of the New Right, but we will not go into its flaws here.

Marxist feminists challenged the gendered arrangements on which the welfare state was based, pointing to the double oppression of women; by capitalism and by patriarchy. Though proletarians may die out, housewives will not, because they are needed to enable men to engage in wage labour (Von Werlhof, 1984). So, in the welfare-state era, the last vestige of capitalist society, the housewife, comes under feminist fire. During the 1960s and 1970s this expressed itself primarily in efforts to redefine and re-evaluate domestic labour from a gender perspective. Gardiner (1997, p11) defines domestic labour as:

> ....those unpaid household activities which could be done by someone other than the person who actually carries them out or could be purchased if a market for those activities existed. Domestic labour can be distinguished from personal care activities which people perform for themselves.... and leisure activities which cannot be delegated to someone else.

During the 1980s and 1990s the debate centred increasingly on issues of care. Child care became a much debated topic, leading to new legislation and social policies in many countries. Given the association between the ideology of maternalism and the origins of the welfare state (Orloff, 1996), it is not surprising that feminists attacked the welfare state at this point. Challenging the moral underpinnings of the welfare state in this respect unavoidably implied challenging existing gender relations and the gendered division of care labour in the household.

Another field in which the care debate evolved is that of elderly care. As a consequence of steadily declining fertility and increasing life expectancies, populations are ageing. This process has been going on for some time in welfare states. Dependency ratio's changed in composition; from comprising a relatively large proportion of children to comprising a large proportion of elderly.[2] Finch (1989) summarises this trend as follows: 'Changes in the dependency ratio have expanded the need for younger generations to provide care to older people, but also have affected their capacity to do so'. As it is said in an OECD publication on the topic:

.... much of the current concern over caring is driven by anxieties over the rising costs of the health and social care of older people. The assumption is that their needs will have to be met by a greater reliance on the family. However, the capacity of the family itself is under threat from changing demographics.

The author also points to the gendered nature of care patterns: 'Heavy-duty, intimate caring, particularly across generations, tends to fall to women' (Twigg, 1996, p.81).

It has to be concluded that the issue of care, particularly elderly care, seems fraught with moral complexities. First, there is the gender perspective. Why should countless women, apart from having their large share in domestic labour, be expected to provide personal care for the elderly members of their household? Second, there is the question of why policymakers are so fond of evoking the role of the family when they raise the issue of elderly care, while it would be more appropriate to speak about households. After all, households are 'care providers' (Gardiner, 1997). Is this because the term family carries moral weight? What exactly is the division of care labour in family households, and what norms sustain it? Is care labour 'domestic labour' in the sense that it can be delegated to others (Gardiner, 1997), or is it too personal, too intimate? All these questions point to the relevance of applying a moral approach when addressing issues of care.

Another field in which a moral approach seems warranted is that of the study of poverty. How do poor households get by? As is remarked in a study about households during unemployment: 'For the experience of unemployment or unremitting poverty the ground rules seem muddled, idiosyncratic and often non-negotiable' (McKee, 1987, p.116). This is because, as the study showed, the situation of unemployment does not transcend the history and structure of relationships already in existence. These relationships cannot be seen apart from norms about proper marital relationships, economic roles of men and women, obligations towards kin, etc.

McKee notes also that 'there seems to be a deep-seated tension between the need for households to stand alone and for households to support each other, and between individual and collective solutions to crises' (1987, p.115). The choices individuals and households make in a situation of distress can only be properly understood when the moral dimensions and normative underpinnings of their positions and relationships are taken into account. Applying rational choice theory or a classical economic approach will not do because, as is noted in a study about low-income households: 'Economists and their admirers - rational choice theorists in the other social sciences - have trouble with norms'. They fail to recognise that norms are guidelines requiring judgement and discrimination for their application; that they involve negotiation and flexibility for their implementation in everyday social institutions; that they are concerned with aspects of life that are inescapably shared, and resources that are inherently indivisible (Jordan et al., 1992). Thus, for an understanding of how family households cope with poverty and distress it is necessary to identify the normative principles and their application that underlie sharing and reciprocity. We will come back to these issues in the section devoted to the concept of the moral economy of the household, having sufficiently demonstrated the relevance of a moral approach to the issue of household poverty here.

8.3 Tronto's New Ethic of Care

A book was published in 1993 which was an eloquent plea for putting the debate about care on a new footing. The study was prompted by a question the author, Joan Tronto, asked herself: 'Why are essential activities of caring not well regarded, theorised, supported, and respected in our society?' (Tronto, 1993, p.19). Tronto proposes a new paradigm, one which centres around care. In this section we will discuss Tronto's ideas extensively, because of their relevance to the subject of this chapter.

The title of the book is: *Moral Boundaries, a Political Ethic of Care.* Tronto uses the metaphor of boundaries because boundaries make you reflect on what they include and exclude, and what happens when you draw them differently. By drawing the boundaries differently a new paradigm can be created. Tronto observes that throughout the twentieth century the argument that women are more moral than men has been put to the fore. In spite of the strong appeal of this women's morality, however, its political success has been nil. Women's morality has not wielded power. The ideas which underlie the concept of women's morality are the values of caring, nurturance, and the importance of human relationships. These ideas are the starting points for Tronto's vision of the 'good society'. She says:

> The core argument of this book, then, can be expressed in paradoxical terms: I argue that we need to stop talking about 'women's morality' and

188 _The Domestic Domain_

start talking about a care ethic that includes the values traditionally associated with women (1993, p.3).

Moral arguments are interpreted within a political context, which includes and excludes through moral boundaries that have been constructed. Tronto distinguishes three crucial moral boundaries. The first one is the *boundary between morality and politics*. In Western society morality and politics seem to concern quite different aspects of human life. The first has to do with considerations as to what one thinks is important to do and in what ways; the second with the allocation of public resources and maintaining the public order. Because of the existing boundary between morality and politics, 'either politics becomes a means to achieve moral ends, or morality becomes a means to achieve political ends. But the notion that politics and morality are similar ends and means is incomprehensible' (Tronto, 1993, p.8). As a consequence, it is extremely difficult for moral arguments ever to gain political power. In Tronto's view, the concept of care can bridge the separation.

The second moral boundary is the *moral point of view boundary*. According to this boundary, morality is an abstraction, formulated by philosophers on the basis of abstract reasoning, far removed from the world of daily life and human emotion. In morality, according to the moral point of view, the types of concerns raised by women's morality are of a secondary order, marginal, or irrelevant.

The third boundary is the *boundary between public and private*. The line between public and private life in Western society is drawn in such a way that women's moral arguments are placed in the private sphere of household, family and friends, and are regarded out of place in the public sphere. The private sphere is primarily associated with women and the public sphere with men. Politics is part of the public sphere. This particular boundary and its implications are central to the argument of the book. We would like to add here that the artificiality and culture-specific character of the boundary between private and public have been highlighted in other discourses as well. For instance, the fact that we define paid work outside the home as belonging to the public sphere and the formal economy leads to classifying home-based production and industries as belonging to the so-called informal sector. The latter term is not only a misnomer with little explanatory value, but also carries the connotation of being unimportant. The opposite is true: this so-called informal sector is of tremendous economic importance, particularly in developing countries.

Tronto continues to argue that, in her opinion, feminist theory does not provide a solution for the problem of boundaries and the undervaluation of care. The reason is that feminist theory faces a strategic dilemma: either it has to acknowledge the differences between women, which goes against the core of the theory, or it keeps positing the sameness of women, which makes it inadequate and marginal.

After explaining why an alternative paradigm of care is needed, why feminist theory as it is does not provide it, and how the crucial boundaries became to be gradually drawn, Tronto outlines the contours of the new paradigm she proposes. She views care as

> ....a species activity that includes everything that we do to maintain, continue, and repair our 'world' so that we can live in it as well as possible. That world includes our bodies, our selves, and our environments, all of which we seek to interweave in a complex, life-sustaining web (1993, p.103).

Important features of this definition are that care does not just concern human interaction but also caring for others, objects, environment, that it is not only dyadic and between individuals, that defining care is culture-specific, and, finally, that caring is ongoing. In spite of the fact that her definition is very broad, in Tronto's view not all human activity is care: 'In general, then, I will use care in a more restricted sense, to refer to care when *both the activity and disposition of care are present*' (Tronto, 1993, p.105, our emphasis). Tronto sees care as having four separate but analytically interconnected phases:

1. *Caring about*: The recognition that care is necessary, which involves assuming the position of another person or group. Caring about is culturally shaped and can take place at an individual and social or political level.

2. *Taking care of*: Involves assuming responsibility for the identified need and determining how to respond to it. It implies notions of agency and responsibility.

3. *Care-giving*: The direct meeting of the needs for care, involving physical work and face-to-face contact. Giving money is not a form of care-giving, because money does not solve human needs, though it provides the resources by which human needs can be satisfied.

4. *Care-receiving*: 'It is important to include care-receiving as an element of the caring process because it provides the only way to know that caring needs have actually been met' (Tronto, 1993, p.108). The object cared for has to respond to the care received, for the activity to be called caring.

Participation in the phases of care reflects the distribution of power in society: 'Caring about, and taking care of, are the duties of the powerful. Care-giving and care-receiving are left to the powerless' (Tronto, 1993, p.114).

Tronto distinguishes several crucial aspects of good care. The first one is practice. Care involves both thought and action. The four phases of care can serve as an ideal for the practice of care to test whether it forms an integrated, well-accomplished act of care, and whether it is provided in an integrated and holistic manner. The second one is conflict, which is likely to be within each of the phases and between them. An example is that the way the physician 'takes care' of the patient may not always agree with the care-giving nurse. Care-givers may also be confronted with conflicting demands. How they resolve these affects the quality of care. The third point is that there are particular and universal aspects of care. The construction of adequate care varies from culture to culture, and also among different groups in society; 'yet despite the fact that the meaning of care varies from one society to another, care is nonetheless a universal aspect of human life' (Tronto, 1993, p.110). Tronto adds that good care requires adequate resources, such as goods, time, skills, the allocation of which may involve conflicts (see above).

Tronto points to four crucial mechanisms to which make care marginalized:

1. Care is seen as a disposition rather than a practice. If care is only seen as a disposition or an emotion it is easily sentimentalised and privatised. To avoid this we have to think of care in terms of a practice, without ignoring emotion and disposition in care.

2. Care is declared a private activity. Care is conceived as a private concern, and is supposed to be provided in the household, which prevents it from becoming a social concern so that adequate resources can be provided for those with caring tasks.

3. There is a disdain for care receivers because neediness is conceived as a threat to autonomy. Thus, people who need care become pitiful and are not respected.

4. To the powerful, care implies privileged irresponsibility. Those who are privileged can ignore hardships that others have to face. The privileged take care of problems because they have the means to do so, but they do not interact directly with those who need care. In Tronto's new ethic of care the tables are turned. The points of departure of this new ethic of care are, first, that we should not understand care's moral qualities as abstract

principles but as contained in practice. The second, that we should revise
our notions about autonomy:

> Throughout our lives, all of us go through varying degrees of dependence
> and independence, of autonomy and vulnerability. A political order that
> presumes only independence and autonomy as the nature of human life
> thereby misses a great deal of human experience, and must somehow hide
> this point elsewhere. For example, such an order must rigidly separate
> public and private life (Tronto, 1993, p.135).

Instead, we should acknowledge that thoughout their lives, all
people need care. There are five essential interrelated elements in this new
ethic of care, which can be related to the four phases mentioned earlier:
1. The first element is *attentiveness*. It relates to the phase of 'caring
about'. Neglect and inattentiveness are immoral. Modern society, in which
virtually all human needs can be met through the market, creates
inattentiveness. 'That "others" matter is the most difficult moral quality to
establish in practice' (Tronto, 1993, p.130).
2. The second one is *responsibility*. It relates to the phase of 'taking care
of'. 'Taking care of' requires responsibility, which is different from
fulfilling obligations. The latter is embedded in formal rules, the former in
cultural practices and individual disposition.
3. The third element is *competence*. It relates to the phase of 'care-giving'.
Making certain that the caring work is done competently must be a moral
aspect of care because it ensures adequacy. Those who are taking care of
should guarantee the competence of the care-givers and should see to it
that care-givers have adequate resources.
4. The fourth one is *responsiveness*. It relates to care-receiving. Caring
challenges the notion that individuals are autonomous. Vulnerability belies
this notion. Responsiveness requires empathy. It presupposes attentiveness.
5. The fifth element is the *integrity of care*. It requires that the other moral
elements are integrated into an appropriate whole. Only then can proper
judgements be made and proper strategies designed.
    In an earlier publication by Fisher and Tronto (1990), in which the
conceptualization of care as outlined above already features, it is
emphasized that the household mode of caring 'that is precapitalist in its
origins and centers on families based in communities', works in an
integrative and egalitarian way. 'Because caring about, taking care of, and
care giving are communally shared values and activities, household and
family membership confers a sort of equality on participants'. They
contrast this with the marketplace, which alters household- and

community-based caring and creates new forms for giving care outside the household and community. The care process becomes reduced to the idiom of exchange, and is regulated by demand and purchasing power. Bureaucratic caring grows out of a political process. Much of it is fragmented and inadequate. The conclusion is that, 'although the central instutions of modern life claim to promote caring, both marketplace and bureaucracy seriously distort and fragment caring activities' (Fisher and Tronto, 1990, p.46-50).

Hence, the need for a new approach to care, a new paradigm as proposed by Tronto in her book. The elements of care as outlined therein, the vision of care as a process and as a practice, together will enable us to formulate new criteria for the quality of care and to valuate care justly. Still, as Tronto points out, there are moral pitfalls that we should beware of. One of them is the problem of parochialism and partiality. Because care is concrete and operates at close distance, we may become indifferent to the needs of those outside our own circle. A related problem is that of detached care and otherness. If we only take care through charity or paying taxes, we easily become deluded about the nature of care. There is the problem that people who need care are easily alienated and treated as others and unequals. Care givers are inclined to say what care receivers need. Then there is the problem of privileged irresponsibility of the relatively powerful. These problems should be approached by acknowledging that 'throughout their lives, all people need care; so the inequality that emerges when some are care-givers and others are care-receivers should not be so morally significant' (Tronto, 1993, p.145-147).

8.4 Cheal's Moral Economy and the Morality of Give-and-Take

While Tronto's new ethics of care embrace the whole social and political order and the moral principles upon which they are based, this section will focus on morality within the context of the family household. There is a difference in level of abstraction, but not in the importance of the role of morality.

Within households there is an exchange of goods and services, the latter including care and support. When considered at a particular moment, these exchanges are more often than not unbalanced. Some household members give more than they receive in return, while for others it may be the other way around. When we follow these exchanges during the household's life course, these imbalances will even out to some degree. In common parlance: there is a lot of give-and-take in households. In its common understanding the expression implies that the amount and nature of what is given does not necessarily have to equal that of what is taken, and vice versa. At some point, all people give some and all people take some. It is implicitly assumed that all giving and taking will more or less even out in the end, and that they together serve some common good. Give-and-take behaviour takes place within closely knitted networks or groups: in households, between relatives and neighbours, on the workfloor. Abstaining from give-and-take relationships while being a member of a group where such behaviour is common, will be considered a-social, egoistical, or even immoral. But it is also felt wrong to be too much at the giving end or too much at the receiving end. On the basis of her study of unemployed households, McKee (1987, p.115) observes:

> Unemployed households were not always in a position of receiving or depending upon others for resources but sought actively to reciprocate in kind. Unemployed households fought hard against dependency and against the stereotype of 'always being at the receiving end'.

It has to be concluded that there is evidently a morality to give-and-take. Our understanding of the non-economically motivated part of the household economy, the exchanges and transactions that seem to follow moral rather than economic rules, has gained a lot from the work of David Cheal. Cheal, in turn can be considered to owe much to the work of economic anthropologists, notably Marshall Sahlins' work on the concept of reciprocity. To characterize this aspect of the household economy, Cheal uses the term moral economy, acknowledging the important earlier application of the concept in a study about Asian peasants by James Scott (1976). Cheal defines the concept as follows: 'By a *moral economy* I mean a system of transactions which are defined as socially desirable (i.e. moral), because through them social ties are recognized, and balanced social relationships are maintained' (1988, p.15). The gift economy, which is the subject of the book cited here, is defined by Cheal as a system of redundant transactions within a moral economy. After defining the concept of moral economy, Cheal continues to localize moral economies:

> In the contemporary world system, moral economies exist alongside political economies. The systems of relationships within which moral economies are grounded are therefore only part-societies. These part-societies typically consist of small worlds of personal relationships that are the emotional core of every individual's social experiences (1988, p.15).

In Cheal's view, trust and commitment are important factors in the sustainable functioning of the moral economy. Both are generated through intensive interaction between its participants and result from sharing the routine of everyday life. Harris (1990) also points to the commitment and solidarity that result from the intensive interaction that takes place on a day-to-day basis in the household context.

In another publication, Cheal applies this line of thinking specifically to the question of the moral-economic versus political-economic contents of household resource management. Cheal (1989) characterizes the moral and political economy in this article by five interrelated characteristics, which are given in Table 8.1. on the next page.

We will not discuss the appropriateness of the characterizations in detail here, but accept the models as validly portraying two different modes of management of resources at household level. The question that arises then is: are they mutually exclusive? Cheal says they are not: 'We may find when all the evidence is in, that structures of moral economy and political economy are typically parallel systems of household organization' (Cheal, 1989, p.19). The implication is that we cannot make a division of societies into ones in which households will be organized according to the mode of the moral economy and other societies in which households follow the model of the political economy. For any society then, the organization of resources at the level of the household becomes a subject of empirical investigation, in which the kind of rules that are invoked and their effects on different categories of household members cannot be assumed *a priori*.

8.5 Key Study: Negotiating Family Responsibilities in Britain

8.5.1 Introduction

The research on which the book by Janet Finch and Jennifer Mason (1993) is based was carried out between 1985 and 1989. The research project was known as the Family Obligations Project. The research area was the area known as Greater Manchester, which covers the cities of Manchester and Salford and a ring of small towns around it, an area thought to be reasonably representative of the UK in terms of social, economic and ethnic composition.

Table 8.1 Characteristics of moral economics and political economics

Moral Economy	Political Economy
1. The actions of individual household members are motivated by a desire to produce socially preferred (i.e. moral) relationships between them which define the domestic division of labour.	1. The actions of individuals are motivated by the rational pursuit of their self interests.
2. Insofar as all members act this way, transactions between them will take the form of ritualised interaction in which the possibility of conflict is minimised. The felt need to maintain enduring relationships of co-operation results in explicit ideologies of mutual support between household members.	2. Participants in exchanges seek to obtain the best possible outcomes for themselves, and exchange relations are therefore competitive. The opposition of interests in the exchange process will lead to negotiation, bargaining, or open struggle.
3. Within a moral economy, a rational individual will use all available means to maintain these because they are a source of long term economic security.	3. The net gains and losses individuals receive or suffer will be determined by differences in manipulative skills and the possession of resources.
4. Resources become available to individuals through a socially defined process of mobilisation and distribution. The forms of institutionalised interactions structure the directions in which resources flow. These, and the rules of category membership, determine the net gains and losses of individuals in transactions.	4. Resources become available to individuals through a process of the division of labour and its products. Modes of production and appropriation structure the resource flows.
5. In order to ensure the participation of others in such transactions, household heads engage in verbal and non-verbal discourses that construct the meaning of the household as the natural centre of economic life. Within this context, the pattern of resource flows is accepted as taken-for-granted reality.	5. In order to ensure the collusion of the powerless in unequal exchanges, those who possess resources expound ideologies which mystify the true nature of exchange transactions. If necessary, force will be used to maintain existing systems of relations.

Source: Cheal, 1989, p.14-16

8.5.2 Conceptual Framework

The research built upon Janet Finch's earlier study (1989) in which the concept of family responsibility was explored. In this study she rejects the idea that these responsibilities are shaped by rules associated with particular genealogical relationships and positions. She argues instead that people handle family responsibilities by acknowledging certain guidelines (Finch, 1989). What these guidelines are, whether there is a consensus on these guidelines, and how they are applied, become questions for empirical investigation, which is precisely what was done in the Family Obligations Project.

The study consisted of two main parts, a large-scale survey and an in-depth qualitative study. The aim of the survey was to find out whether, in Britain of the 1980s, a consensus could be identified about family responsibilities and obligations. In the survey, 978 people were interviewed, a representative sample from the electoral register in 40 wards in Greater Manchester. The reasearch issues addressed in the survey were about the norms and beliefs to which people give public assent.

The second part of the study was designed to understand how people develop commitments and responsibilities towards their relatives in practice. The proposition underlying the qualitative part of the study was that such commitments are the result of processes of negotiation.

8.5.3 Data Collection

In total, the survey contained 69 questions, or parts of questions, which focused on normative issues. The questions were asked by using a vignette technique, meaning that respondents were asked to consider example situations. They were not asked what they themselves would do in such a situation, but what would be the proper thing to do, what the people pictured in the situation *should* do. The following is an example:

> Suppose that a young couple with a small child have returned from working abroad and and can't afford to buy or rent anywhere to live until one of them gets a job. Should any of their relatives offer to have the family in their home for the next months? (Finch and Mason, 1993, p.12).

In the second part of the study 88 people were interviewed using semi-structured interviewing techniques. A complex procedure was followed to select the respondents. Initially, a selection was made from the survey respondents. Subsequently, some of the selected respondents were asked permission to approach persons identified by the respondents as her or his close family to be interviewed as well.

8.5.4 Findings and Discussion

Findings of the survey For determining the consensus in the answers to the survey questions, a rule of thumb was developed. It was decided to use the principle that, where an answer attracted at least one-and-a-half times the simple majority, this would be taken to indicate significant agreement. Of the 69 questions, 48 percent had a pattern which reached the so-called consensus baseline (significant agreement), and 52 percent did not.

The overall conclusion from the survey data is that 'norms and beliefs about family responsibilities are not easily recognized or clearly agreed upon among the British population' (Finch and Mason, 1993, p.17). An interesting finding is that although it is known from other sources that women are more likely to give practical and personal support to relatives than men, there is no difference between women and men as regards the publicly endorsed beliefs and values regarding support to relatives. Similarly, there proved to be little systematic difference in answers given by people with different social backgrounds. The rather mixed and apparently contradictory patterns of answers in the survey could therefore not be explained by different groups of respondents giving different answers (Finch and Mason, 1993).

The survey showed that people make judgements about the appropriateness of family assistance in the light of the circumstances which were outlined in each case. Although there are circumstances in which most people do agree that the family should take responsibility, there is no evidence in the survey data of a general feeling that the family should normally be the first port of call for most people. When looking at the data from the angle of when, according to the majority of the respondents, family assistance should or should not be given, several significant findings emerge. A first one is that people will endorse family responsibilities in deserving cases where the need is presented as entirely legitimate and the person who needs assistance is not at fault in any way. The second feature that emerged from the data is that people are more likely to accord responsibility when the assistance needed is fairly limited, in terms of time, effort or skill. These two significant features seem to represent procedural guidelines for deciding whether to take responsibility for assistance or not. Thirdly, the survey data support the view that responsibilities between parents and children are accorded special status, without, however, seeing parent-child responsibilities as automatic or unlimited. The survey also shows that parent-child relationships should not be treated as symmetrical in terms of responsibilities. Parents' continuing responsibility to help their children seems to be endorsed more strongly than any other type of family responsibility.

Findings of the qualitative study Appendix C of the book provides a detailed account of the findings of the qualitative study as regards 'who does what for whom'. An interesting finding is the more important role of the mother's mother in looking after young children compared to that of the father's mother. A more general finding is that parent-children exchanges dominate over all others as regards financial help, providing a home, and emotional support. Parents' support for their children is much more common than the reverse for the above mentioned areas of assistance (Finch and Mason, 1993). This finding corroborates the finding in the survey of the strong norm endorsing parents' support to children.

While within the relationship between parents and children an imbalance is apparently accepted, it appears from the case studies that, in general, the parties involved in exchange of support strive to maintain a proper balance. One of the ways in which this can be achieved is by direct payment, a form of exchange especially found among siblings: 'Indeed it seems particularly characteristic of sibling relationships that a debt should be repaid in the same currency' (Finch and Mason, 1993, p.41). This applies to women and men more or less equally. As regards forms of indirect repayment, a different picture emerges from the case studies. The term indirect can refer to different kinds of assistance that are exchanged or to exchanges involving a third party through whom repayment is done. The indirect exchanges of the first type require agreement on the right 'currency' for the exchange and this necessitates negotiation. The gender balance is different here: women dominate in indirect exchanges. Furthermore, such exchanges appear to be often found between persons of different generations. The cases show that the type of indirect exchange which involves generalised reciprocity, also bridges generations. It is formulated as: I want to do for my children what my parents did for me. The parents are repaid, as it were, by supporting their grandchildren.

The negotiation processes which are involved in all forms of exchange except direct payment develop over time. This is how commitments are built up. Negotiation can take explicit and implicit forms. Open round-the-table discussions are of the first type. These are prompted by specific needs and events. Finch and Mason (1993) say about implicit negotiations that although there is no open discussion, people somehow inform each other about what kinds of responsibility they regard as reasonable for themselves and for others. Thus, when a specific need arises it seems obvious who will help. The case studies provide a wealth of examples of such processes. Not only does the use of the concept of negotiation lead to paying attention to commitments in family responsibilities, but it also makes clear 'the entrenching of *moral* commitment and responsibilities within the kin group' (Finch and Mason, 1993).

An important implication of the moral character of commitment and responsibilities of kinship relations is that not taking responsibility at a particular moment is only acceptable when there is a legitimate excuse. It appears that inability, rather than unwillingness, is generally considered a valid excuse, provided it is convincingly demonstrated. More specifically, valid excuses appeal to lack of competence or resources and geographical distance. The ability to have excuses accepted as legitimate varies according to gender and genealogical distance. As regards the first variable, the case studies material proves that for women to appeal to employment as an excuse is less acceptable than for men.

The importance of the legitimacy of excuses when not taking responsibility shows that the kin group is like an *audience* to people's negotiations with their kin. Moral judgements are made before this audience. An intriguing finding in this respect is what could be called the norm of 'not expecting'. Although there is a certain logic to the view that a responsibility to give help does imply a correspondingly right to expect it, the survey and interview data (case studies) do not confirm this. As the researchers note:

> Indeed we get strong messages that the majority of our respondents see it as wrong to expect assistance from relatives in time of need, even to expect recompense for assistance given previously, in the sense of *assuming* it will automatically be given (Finch and Mason, 1993, p.135).

They suggest that the norm of not expecting is related to the moral identity of being 'independent', which is important for both young and old. Finch and Mason call the negotiated moral identity of the individual in the kingroup reputation. By doing so they make three claims: first, that there is a shared image of each individual within a kin group; second, that this image is stable over time; third, that these shared images matter in the sense that they affect people's behaviour. The interview data attest to the existence of reputation. Reputations provide the basis on which exchanges of assistance can be negotiated. There were several examples in the data where people are asked to do things because they have the reputation for doing them. Some people, notably women, have the reputation of being the 'family carer'.

Discussion When we place the findings of the study of Finch and Mason in the light of Tronto's conceptualization of care and Cheals' concept of the moral economy of the household, several comments can be made. A first comment is that Tronto's definition of care, also in its restricted sense which requires the presence of a disposition of care, is obviously applicable to the activities described by Finch and Mason. Second, Tronto's emphasis on care as practice makes it amenable to identifying it in the morally motivated exchanges of money, goods, and services within kin groups.

Tronto's concern about dependencies and power inequalities involved in caring is also proven right by Finch and Mason's data. Finch and Mason (1993, p. 58) say about this:

> Issues of power and control are closely intertwined with the negotiation of the balance between dependence and independence. If a person's position gets defined as imbalanced, so that they are treated as 'too dependent' upon another relative, they end up in a position of subordination to that person.

The issues of dependency, control, and power obviously occupy a key position in the thinking about and the actual provision of care between kin. Finch and Mason point to the differences in women's and men's biographies. They emphasize that biographies form part of negotiation processes (Finch and Mason, 1993). The differences in the biographies of men and women can be considered to reflect the gender-based division of roles and positions in society. As we have seen, Tronto (1993) distinguishes four phases of care. Her observation that women dominate in the third phase, that of care giving, and that the gender difference is less prominent in the phases of caring about and taking care of, could be confirmed by applying the distinction in phases to Finch and Mason's case material. Their observation that there is a gender difference between direct compared to indirect caring already points to the gendered nature of specific forms of care.

When we look at the research of Finch and Mason in the light of Cheal's concept of the moral economy of the household, several comments can be made. A first one is about the more or less clear boundaries of the household as compared to the flexible boundaries of family and kin. As the study of Finch and Mason proves, the moral economy extends beyond the boundaries of the household. Another point is the important role by Cheal attached to the household head. Finch and Mason's emphasis on negotiation yields a different picture than Cheal's household as a natural economic entity with the household head as the moderator. In this sense, Finch and Mason's study is more modern. Cheal's concept still suffers from the stereotypical image of the household as a unity and the household head as a benevolent dictator.

The concept of reputation that Finch and Mason develop on the basis of their case studies is promising because it explains why some people have a more significant role than others in exchange between kin. It also allows for the position of household head to be part of such a reputation. The term 'family helper' which Finch and Mason coined to refer to women who have the reputation of being available for assistance to relatives and being good at it, brings to mind Hareven's (1982) concept of 'kin keeper' for women who have a reputation as helpers, pacifiers, and arbiters in the kin group.

8.6 Key Study: The Morality of Family in Kenya

8.6.1 Introduction

The study discussed in this section is based on a new analysis of data collected in 1972-1973 at the Child Development Research Unit of the University of Nairobi. In spite of the fact that the data were not recently collected, the findings of the analysis yield insights which are valid and relevant today as well.

We selected this study because it shows both how opinions about family obligations are anchored in values and norms, and that such opinions are not 'automatically' derived from the endorsed moral principles. It is also an interesting study because it shows the role of the cultural factor. By this we mean that the contents of the moral principles that provide the framework for opinionating clearly have to be placed in a cultural context, in this case that of the Kipsigis and Abuluyia communities in Kenya.

8.6.2 Data Collection and Research Questions

The study design of the research project that was carried out during 1972-1973 was heavily based on the work by Kohlberg. The social psychologist Kohlberg interviewed a sample of students of the University of Chicago about moral choices and formulated a theory of moral development on the basis of the research findings (Kohlberg, 1981, 1984). Like in Kohlberg's study, the respondents of the present study were confronted with moral dilemmas in the form of short narratives and were asked questions about what would be the proper course of action for the proponents in the narratives. The narratives in the Kenya study used for the new analysis were the following:

> *Moral Dilemma 1: Daniel and the School Fees*
> A man, Daniel, managed to complete his secondary school education (Form 4) on the basis of school fees given him by his brother. Afterwards he married and took his wife to live with his parents in the rural area, while he got a job in the city. Eight years later, when his first son was ready to go to primary school, his mother and father came to him and said: 'Your brother who educated you has been in an accident and cannot work, so you must begin to pay for the education of your brother's child'. This child was the same age as his own son. The man, Daniel, did not have enough money to pay school fees for both his own son and his brother's child. His wife said he must put his own son first.

> *Moral Dilemma 2: James and the Nairobi Show*
> James is a 14-year-old boy who wanted to go to the Nairobi Show very much, His father promised him that he could go if he saved up the money himself. So James worked hard and saved up the shillings it cost to go to the Show, and a little more besides in case he saw something at the Show he wanted to eat or drink or buy to take home. But just before the Show was going to start, his father changed his mind. Some of his father's friends decided to go to town to drink beer, and James's father was short of money. So he told James to give him the money he had saved. James did not want to give up going to the Nairobi Show, so he thought of refusing to give his father the money. (Pope Edwards, 1997, p.50).

Five key questions were formulated with regard to the two dilemmas. The questions were put to a group of community leaders from the Kipsigis community and from the Abaluyia community and, likewise, to young adults (students), also from both communities. All respondents were men. Students of the University of Nairobi did the interviews in their home areas. Interviewer and respondent were matched according to ethnicity. The interviewers were equipped with tape recorders to record their interviews, which lasted one to two hours. At that time four moral dilemmas were put to the respondents. Of these four, the two narratives quoted above proved best in eliciting familial values. Hence, the analysis was based on these two. The sample used for the analysis consisted of six Kipsigis elders, five Kipsigis students, eight Abaluyia elders, and six Abaluyia students.

8.6.3 Findings and Discussion

The answers to the questions (mentioned below) by the four groups in the sample are summarized in table 8.2.

Table 8.2 Respondents' responses to questions about moral dilemmas

	Dilemma I			Dilemma II	
Respondents	question 1	question 2	question 3	question 4	question 5
Kipsigis elders (6 persons)	nephew (4) son (2)	parents 4 wife 2	yes (3) sometimes (3)	give (3) refuse (3)	yes (6)
Kipsigis students (5 persons)	nephew (3) son (2)	parents 3 wife 2	no (3) sometimes (2)	give (2) refuses (3)	yes (2) no (2) yes/no (1)
Abaluyia elders	nephew (1) son (4) both (2) son/both (1)	parents (2) wife (3) both (2) no ans. (1)	yes (3) sometimes (4) no (1)	give (4) refuses (4)	yes (4) no (4)
Abaluyia students (6 persons)	nephew (3) son (2) both (1)	parents (2) wife (2) both (2)	yes (2) no (2) sometimes (2)	give (2) refuse (4)	yes (2)

Source: Based on C. Pope Edwards, (1997), table 3.3, p.62

The questions were the following:
1. Should Daniel pay school fees for his son or his nephew?
2. Should Daniel prefer harmony with his wife or with his parents?
3. Should a grown son obey his parents?
4. Should James give his father the money he earned himself or refuse?
5. Does James's father have the authority to ask for that money in this situation?

The moral values that stood out in the respondents' answers were those of paternal authority, family harmony, and unity. However, they were emphasized differently. Also, additional principles were evoked, such as respect, responsibility, reasonableness, keeping promises, reciprocity, and the value of education. The latter two refering to the educational value of the Nairobi Show and Daniel's responsibility to provide proper education for his son. Although a clear overlap between the four groups of respondents in their reference to the salient moral values is visible in the verbatim answers, the patterns of answers show differences according to ethnicity and generation (age). The Kipsigis men put relatively more emphasis on respect and paternal authority; responsibility and reasonableness are more emphasized by the Abaluyia men. Especially regarding the issue of paternal authority (the third and fifth question), the younger generation is more doubtful about its salience than the elders of both groups.

The research was limited to men, as was Kohlberg's project. Kohlberg's theory of the stages of moral development was based on interviews with male students only. Indeed, this was the main criticism levelled against it, and it prompted Gilligan's research on women's morality. Tronto (1993) discusses this issue extensively in her book. But, although it would have been very interesting to have answers from Kipsigis and Abaluyia women on the same questions, this is not our main concern here. The point is not a representative picture of the salient moral principles of particular ethnic groups, but the way moral principles work. The findings of this research confirm the appropriateness of Finch and Mason's view of norms as guidelines rather than rules. Its most important finding is not the existence of salient moral principles that all respondents refer to, but the fact that they do so in different degrees. The situations outlined in the moral dilemmas require the respondents to consider the validity of salient norms for a particular situation and in relation to alternative principles. The balance in the end differs according to age and ethnicity. No doubt, it would also have differed according to gender had this variable been incorporated in the study.

8.7 Conclusions and New Directions for Research

8.7.1 Conclusions

There are several lessons that can be learnt from discussions about the concepts of care, family or household, gender and morality as they feature in the work of authors like Tronto and Cheal and in the key studies we have selected. Let us look at morality first. What the moral approaches we presented have in common is that they relate morality to politics and to practice. Moral principles are not seen as rules but guidelines for practice. Tronto rejects a detached morality which creates otherness. In her opinion there should be a continuity between morality in the private sphere and morality in the public domain, which includes the political sphere.

According to such a view of morality as a set of guiding principles which have to be applied in concrete contexts, care is not just a moral principle. Care as practice is the powerful message of Tronto. It is reflected in the actions of the respondents in the study of Finch and Mason. Sevenhuijsen (1998) emphasizes the need to develop a broad and and diverse perspective of care as a form of *human agency*. This implies that for good care both the moral drive behind it and the actual practice of it are relevant. As Sevenhuijsen (1998, p.20) says:

> The motives behind care, and our judgement of these motives, is certainly not the only factor determining the quality of caring activities them selves. For this we also need to look at the result. 'Bad' motives can also lead to 'good' care, just as a 'good' motive, such as attentiveness to vulnerability, is no guarantee of good care: it can also lead to paternalism or undue protection.

The terms *support* and *care* are sometimes used interchangeably. Finch and Mason use the term care only when they refer to care giving, which is for Tronto just one of the four phases of care. In Tronto's broad definition, the support to family members and relatives as documented by Finch and Tronto could be called care. At first glance, care seems to have stronger moral underpinnings than support. However, if we look at family support, the persons involved in it refer to moral principles. This can also be seen in the answers of the Kenyan respondents in the study of Pope Edwards. We can conclude that giving support is a form of care when it takes place between people who have long-standing relationships in which moral obligations and expectations have been built up.

Another terminological issue that can be noted when looking at the contents of this chapter is that of the overlap in meaning of household and family. At the beginning of this chapter we already alluded to this problem. Cheal's use of the term household follows from his focus on economy and resources. Finch and Mason speak of family in two ways: as members of the family household and as kin or relatives. In the Kenya study, family refers primarily to the patrilineal family, particularly to the relationship between father and son. From the research presented in this chapter it is obvious that the principles of Cheal's moral economy also operate beyond household boundaries. By looking at support and care as evolving over time, and keeping in mind Finch and Mason's concept of reputation, the distinction between household and family looses its significance in the issue of care. We should see household, family, and kinship as providing overlapping moral contexts within which people acknowledge obligations to give or receive support. There also seems to be a consensus that being physically close and sharing daily life reinforces people's moral commitments towards each other. In this way the household can be seen as a context of *condensed morality*. As we have already commented, we do not agree with the importance Cheal attaches to the position of the household head. We prefer not to attach *a priori* importance to this position, but to see it as a form of reputation instead.

A last conclusion concerns the views on the relationship between care and gender. Sevenhuijsen points to a crucial division here. She observes that the production of knowledge about gender and care has proceeded along two different tracks. The first one is the extensive work on care as an activity, a 'labour of love'. This track produces studies on women carers, women's needs for care, etc. A recent example is a study on family care in which gender differences in coping strategies of carers were investigated. As it turned out, women deploy a broader range of coping strategies and are more likely to involve social relationships in their coping than men (Nolan et al., 1996). No reference to Tronto is made. For Sevenhuijsen this would not be surprising as Tronto's work belongs to the second track: the extensive debate among feminist theorists about the ethics of care at the intersection of psychology, ethics, political theory and feminist jurisprudence (Sevenhuijsen, 1998). No doubt, the fact that these discourses proceed along separate tracks has to do with the boundaries Tronto has called to our attention. In the next section we shall return to this point in the elaboration of new directions for research.

8.7.2 New Directions for Research

As we see it, a morality approach in the study of family households could be further worked out in three directions. The first direction could be summarized as research on standards of care. The second as an application of the life course perspective to the issue of care. The third comprises a comparative morality approach. We will discuss these three new directions for research below in this order. We will not refer to gender specifically in the sections below. It goes almost without saying that, in any research about care and about moral principles in household and family organization, gender is an indispensable variable.

1 Standards of care In an article about ethics of care and social policy in Scandinavia the authors observe that research on care of elderly people often has a decision-maker perspective. In research that is aimed at measuring and securing the quality of care, there is very seldom discussion about what care is and what its necessary conditions are (Eliasson Lappalainen and Nilsson Motevasel, 1997). Given the two-tracked discourse about care and its ethics which Sevenhuijsen pointed at (see above), this situation is probably not limited to Scandinavia.

Research about quality of care suffers from the lack of a solid and well-argued methodological base in which ethical and moral points of view are made explicit. Since Kuhn pointed our attention to paradigms, social scientists are well aware of the role values and context play in social research. Particularly in research about something so heavily ethically loaded as care, the trap of a naïve assumption of value-neutralness should be avoided. This is possible by starting from the premise of the dual character of care as a moral principle and as practice, and by using the outlines of Tronto's 'new paradigm' as a methodological base.

For research about measuring quality of care or research that is to yield standards of care, Tronto's four phases of care can be the starting point. As we have shown in section 8.3, Tronto attaches the following qualities to these four phases and their interrelationship: *attentiveness* (caring about); *responsibility* (taking care of); *competence* (care-giving); *responsiveness* (care-receiving); and *integrity of care* (interrelationship of the phases). These qualities lend themselves to operational definitions in given contexts. The Scandinavian authors quoted above do not refer to Tronto. They do not seem to know her work. Still, their conclusion about the essence of good care comes close to Tronto's vision: '...care can be described as a balance act between responsibility for the other .... and a respect for the integrity of the other' (Eliasson Lappalainen and Nilsson Motevasel, 1997, p.191). Respect for integrity of the other is captured by Tronto's quality of responsiveness. Tronto's framework of qualities is more comprehensive, taking attentiveness and competence into account as well. We propose to use it as the methodological base for innovative research about the quality and standards of care.

2 The life course perspective and the issue of care If care is viewed as a process which involves interaction of people over time, as it seen by the authors quoted in this chapter, the life course perspective becomes relevant. In Chapter 7 this perspective was extensively discussed. The point here is that moral obligations and moral reputations not only evolve over time and thus imply a time dimension, but that obligations and rights and relation to care and support are also linked to life course-related social positions in the family household. In an earlier publication, Finch (1987) speaks of the life course as a *normative* timetable, as it shapes normative choices people make and the negotiation processes that take place among family members and relatives.

In our opinion, this view is worth more systematic application in research about household and family care and support. In the moral dilemma presented by the case of Daniel in the study of Pope Edwards, the life course perspective is clearly present, though not explicitly referred to. The morality of care provided by households and families when placed in a life course perspective works in two ways. In the first place it is important to assess which obligations and norms are phase- or position-specific, and what the implications for care and support are. In other words, care obligations and practices have to be related to family and household time. In the second place is historical time. Phase- and position-specific obligations and practices will be affected by processes of social, economic and technological change. It is particularly relevant to apply this dual time perspective systematically to the subject of elderly care in rapidly ageing societies.

3 A comparative morality approach In developing her alternative paradigm for an ethic of care, Tronto shows her alertness to the role of the cultural context. Given her weariness of universalistic moral claims, this is to be expected. Her vision of care as practice paves the way for a comparative approach to care practices and the moral principles by which they are guided. We would like to endorse such an approach, believing it to provide a rich ground for exciting research. The basic elements of the Tronto's methodological framework (the integrated four phases and the corresponding qualities) is applicable in a comparative manner. The way the phases work out and what qualities are emphasized will depend on the cultural context.

However, for such research to yield valid and interesting results, there are several requirements that should be kept in mind. In the first place there is the matter of the level of comparison. Since Louis Dumont's heroic efforts to apply a comparative approach to whole societies in his two studies Homo Hierarchicus (about India) and Homo Equalis (about France), social scientists have not attempted comparison at that level anymore. When we make a plea for a comparative approach, we have a comparison at the level of the family household in mind, not a comparison at the level of societies. In our approach, the societal level functions as a context.

In the second place we should be on our guard for our own implicit assumptions and ethnocentric biases. Ideally, in a comparative research project not only the research subjects should have different cultural backgrounds, the researchers as well. Comparative research is too often narrowly understood as Western researchers doing research in non-western societies. In an interesting research project, Indian anthropologists did research about elderly care in the Netherlands. After having done depth-interviews with elderly people in an old people's home, they admitted that when they started their research they assumed that in a modern society like the Netherlands moral principles of kinship solidarity and respect for the elderly would have disappeared. Not only did they have to conclude otherwise on the basis of their interviews, but they also learned about the importance elderly people attach to values like autonomy and privacy (Van der Veen, 1995).

A comparative approach to issues of family and household care is extremely relevant in societies with a high degree of cultural pluriformity. In such a context, comparative research can yield valuable theoretical insights about the role of culture in shaping care practices and the moral principles underlying these, and it can provide a valuable basis for responsible and appropriate policy-making in the field.

Notes

1. In Dutch there are two terms. The term *familie* denotes the network of kinship relationships, while the term *gezin* refers to the domestic unit of the nuclear family. This facilitates the discussion about kinship and family considerably.
2. The dependency ratio pictures the number of dependants, defined as persons under 15 and above 64, in relation to the number of persons aged 15-64, in a population.

9 Synthesis and a View Ahead

9.1 A Bird's Eye View of the Previous Chapters

In the foregoing chapters we presented seven different theoretical approaches and applied each of these to divergent aspects of the functioning of family households. The approaches may be considered as complementary to one another rather than competing. Like a spotlight, each approach highlights a specific side of reality which is largely left in the dark by the other approaches. Taken together, they may illuminate the reality of family households comprehensively, which is just what we intended to do in this book.

A bird's eye view may make some main lines apparent. The second chapter of the book highlights the Theory of Reasoned Action and the Theory of Planned Behaviour. Both theories imply a step forward compared to regular rational choice theories in that they explicitly attribute explaining power to social norms. The Theory of Planned Behaviour implies, in addition, a recognition of people's life-situation by inserting control beliefs into the theoretical model. They both, however, leave the objective structure comprising facilitating conditions and macro-structural conditions in the dark. In addition, behaviour is explained by cognitive factors instead of being understood as an outcome of goal-oriented action.

The latter aspect is incorporated in the Strategy Approach (Chapter 3), which focuses on the actor-centered perspective and at the same time inserts a long-term time perspective. Here, we focus on migration behaviour as embedded in life-strategies of households. However, this approach also leaves several important questions unanswered. A first one refers to the ambivalence of human existence as being goal-oriented versus 'way of being'. A second question relates to the concept of a family household as a unity or as a conglomeration of individuals and individual interests.

This issue is explicitly dealt with in Chapter 4, which represents the Organizational Approach. It highlights the interactions between household members, particularly regarding the allocation of financial resources. The chapter clearly demonstrates the necessity of perceiving the household both as an entity and as a conglomeration of competing individuals in which inequality may persist. Normative expectations fulfill a key role.

In Chapter 5, the issue of inequality, which emerged in the previous chapter, is now viewed from a power angle. The focus is on inequity in the division of household production, partly in farming activities, partly in domestic work. The Power Approach transcends the foregoing one in that it definitively incorporates the impact of ideology as a collective phenomenon, thus breaking with the dominating paradigm of Popper's methodological individualism in the social sciences. The focus on ideology, however, overshadows the explanatory power of a household's situation (Chapter 2) and of social-structural factors, among others.

Chapter 6, on the Opportunity Structure Approach, elucidates the role of these structural factors and uses the issue of access to the housing market for exemplification. We staged objective structures as containing opportunities for action. Opportunities, however, still have to be recognized and seized by family households.

In Chapter 7, a dimension is taken up which had more or less remained in the dark in the previous chapters: the time dimensions of family households, being implied in the Longitudinal Approach. We demonstrated its explanatory power by using key studies, firstly on the interaction between family relations, industrial work, and family needs, and secondly on patterns of migration. At the end of this chapter we propose to use the concept of household life course as a heuristic device.

Finally, Chapter 8 deals with what in particular in Chapter 3 (on the Strategy Approach) remained rather obscure: the issue of morality. Care appears to be a key issue for exemplifying this approach.

Thus, in a sense we closed the circle which was opened by the (improved) rational choice theories. By no means does this imply that the chapters cover all possibly relevant approaches. Both time and space were limitations to further elaboration upon other approaches here. Some key issues, however, need further clarification. We shall focus in particular on the role family households may fulfill in processes of social change.

9.2 Households as Mediating Agencies

In terms of Giddens' structuration theory (1996), households may be considered as mediating agencies between structure and the active, individual subject. Structure refers to both generative rules and resources that are both applied in and constituted out of action. Households may be conceived as systems which are produced and reproduced in the social interaction of its members, a process in which rules and resources are conceived as media as well as outcomes. In Giddens' (1996, p.101) own terms: 'Structure is the generative source of social interaction but is reconstituted only in such interaction'. As social systems, households are dynamic and fluid (Davidson, 1991), which implies that fundamentally they must be created and recreated continuously. Nor should households be conceived as 'things'; they are flexible and vary according to time and culture.

In processes of social change, the importance of the mediating role of family households increases. Being a household's member is just one role most people have. In most cases, household members have roles in external systems as well: as an employee in the labour market, as a pupil in the school system, as a neighbour, as a volunteer in a local welfare organization, and so on. Hence, one and the same person participates in different social systems. These systems do not necessarily connect with one another and, in modernizing societies, they may even be increasingly divergent. Furthermore, the external systems themselves are in a continuous state of change: rules, resources, and practices continuously change in educational systems, in labour markets, and so on. Both traditions and renewals are transmitted through family households as mediators.

Wolf's (1992) research in Indonesia nicely elucidates the process of mediation. She describes the way in which women's participation in industrial capitalism mediates both family change and industrial growth as they travel from village to factory. The factory work accelerates changes that occur more slowly in the broader society. Increasing numbers of factories in rural and suburban areas in Central Java offer employment opportunities for girls. These girls are young and single and come from poor households. They constitute an attractive workforce to the employers because they are cheap and docile. But, whether commuting or boarding, these girls strive to become independent. They become more assertive and they feel less obligated to submit to parental authority. In fact, they do not contribute much to the parental household economy (Wolf, 1993; Niehof, 1998). More in general, Niehof (1998) observes a trend toward a greater diversity of women's roles, varying according to rural-urban differentials, social class, and age. Furthermore, the public domain for women has become larger and more accessible; the mobility of rural women has increased due to more and better roads and transport facilities.

Nevertheless, women's roles develop within a framework of tradition, Islam, and state ideology. Thus,

> ....women can make use of all the emancipatory loopholes tradition, Islam and state ideology provide, but they can only do so within the boundaries of women's natural destiny, the idea of the kodrat wanita (Niehof, 1998, p.253).

In the area of family households, new individual roles and ambitions collide with traditional collective rules and regulations. In order to survive, family households have to search continuously for compromises, have to coordinate the changing beliefs, ambitions, and behaviours of its members, and mould them into new forms. Thus, it may be true, as Castells (1997) states, that patriarchy is rooted in the family, but families may reproduce as well as destroy it at the cost of an eventual divorce. In addition, transformations such as waning ideologies or ideological hegemonies have to pass family households and the connected informal social networks in order to gain support in civil society at large. Family households may keep traditions alive as well as participate in the undoing of traditions. They may learn their members to obey to public authorities as well as to revolt against the law. They may do so for utilitarian reasons, but also for achieving better life-chances of their members or their companions. Thus, it is unjustified to regard family households just as bulwarks of tradition. This leaves us with the question if whether there is any creativity implied in the functioning of households which operates beyond the activities of individual members.

9.3 Family Households as Creative Agencies

The discussion in Chapter 8 made the importance of creativity to normative expectations apparent: action cannot be deduced from the norms themselves in everyday life. Creativity is required in order to 'give norms and values a concrete form in practice' (Joas, 1996, p.233). Hence, in addition to rational action and normatively oriented action, Joas argues in favour of a third dimension of human action. He designates this dimension as 'the creativity of human action'. In his view, this creative dimension is inadequately expressed in the other models.

Circumstances may force people to use their creativity and 'bend the rules'. Chen's (1990) research in Bangladesh, for example, showed the rules which constrain women's labour to post-harvest and domestic work in other households or to the lowest levels of trade. It showed also how sheer poverty forces women to enter the public domain, despite the patriarchical rules which deny their access to it. This connects with some further issues. First, severe constraints force people to invent new ways of action. Inventions may involve technological innovations, but may concern social innovations as well. They emerge from the dimension which Joas denoted as 'the creativity of action'. Social innovations surpass the boundaries of rationality, as framed by the prevailing ideology. They imply breaking through the prevailing *frame of rationality*, in the same way that creativity in science is not derived from pre-existing knowledge and cannot be logically derived from pre-existing knowledge (Damasio, 1994). Second, while innovations are commonly attributed to the elite in society, they appear to be produced by marginalized groups as well, and in particular by the poorest people, albeit by necessity. Ideological hegemony thwarts innovations which emerge 'from below'. But as both Hetler's study about Indonesia (Chapter 3), and Chen's study about Bangladesh show, innovations from below should by no means be considered as less valid, compared to innovations which arise from other social strata. Third, the emergent property of the creativity of family households is implied in the commonality of interests: rules are not bent for the sake of the individual actor but for the benefit of the household as a group. However, the question may arise: are family households able to be creative in a authentic sense?

9.4 Life-World's Values

According to Habermas (1981), the life-world is the taken-for-granted universe of daily social activity. Communicative reasoning prevails over instrumental or strategic reasoning, satiated with tradition, habitual ways of carrying out activities, and pre-interpreted frames of interpretation. Communicative action and reasoning result not only in shared frames of interpretation, but also in group solidarity and accountability of individual subjects. In the process of modernization, however, traditions are giving way and thus liberate individuals from their binding force. At the same time, the disappearance of tradition gives way to what Habermas calls the process of colonization by the economic system and the state system. If modernization does indeed proceed in this manner and if traditions fade away, it is of crucial importance to delineate what is really substantial (if there is something substantial) to people's life-world, including family households, which can resist such colonization. The moral aspects of caring as proposed by Tronto (1993) may qualify: attentiveness, responsibility, competence, and responsiveness. Similar values emerged from research on the grounds of 'feeling-at-home' in divergent settings. Such values were termed as, for instance, 'being in control', 'mutual trust', 'mutual availability', 'commonality of interests' (Pennartz, 1981). Research on urban barrio movements in Latin America by Friedmann (1989) delivered related qualities which he termed life space values: neigbourliness, good citizenship (living up to the common code within the barrio), relations of personal trust and reciprocity, solidarity, etc. Such qualities are evidently not exclusive to family households. They are not gender-specific, class-specific, or age-specific. They prevail in primary and lasting relationships within people's life-world. If the life-world is able to resist the process of colonization by the economic system and the state system, as mentioned by Habermas, then this is due to these values. Even household production, which we framed in terms of power (in Chapter 5), may be reframed in terms of responsibility, moral developmen, self-control, family commitment, altruistic and prosocial behaviour (see Ahlander and Bahr, 1995). Life-world values are associated with 'way of being'. They balance on the sharp edge between feelings and ideology. In addition, they can hardly be measured appropriately, cannot be enforced by external agencies, and are barely predictable. Nevertheless, they should have a substantial role in studying family households.

9.5 Family Households in a State of Change

Not only external systems, but households themselves are nowadays in a continuous state of change. On the one hand, this certainly implies discontinuity in the life-world of its members. It also offers, however, an increasing freedom of choice and, as a consequence, may be a counterforce to the process of colonization.

Two intertwined processes are particularly relevant to family households: diversification and de-standardization. As to diversification, Castells (1997, pp.138-149) mentions several trends which are relevant: the increasing frequency of marital crises, the growing difficulty of making marriage, work, and life compatible, delaying coupling, and setting up partnerships without marriage. His statistics show high percentages of first marriages dissolved through separation, divorce, or death among women aged 40-49 in less-developed countries in Asia, Latin America/Caribbean,

Middle East/North Africa, and Sub-Saharan Africa. Generally, percentages of women aged 20-24 who have never been married are increasing, which indicates delayed coupling. Non-marital births as a percentage of all births by region in developed countries are on the increase. Statistics show a similar trend concerning the proportion of single-parent households in relation to all households with dependent children and at least one resident parent in developed countries. The percentage of households headed de jure by women in countries in Asia, Latin America/Caribbean, Middle East/North Africa, and Sub-Saharan Africa increases. Additionally, crude divorce rates during 1971-1990 increased, varying by 26 per cent (USA) to 157 per cent (Mexico). Castells also mentions findings from the US Bureau of the Census that households in 1990 in the United States were classified as: married couples with children (26.3 per cent), married couples without children (29.8 per cent), other families with children (8.3 per cent), other families without children (6.5 per cent), men living alone (9.7 per cent), women living alone (14.9 per cent), and other non-family households (4.6 per cent). The nuclear family thus represents just a substantial minority among all households. In highly industrialized countries, co-residential groups arise as alternatives to nuclear family households (Kesler, 1989).

De-standardization also implies increased opportunities for individuals to structure their own living arrangements and to deviate from prevailing rules. According to Cheal (1991), there has been a secular trend of standardization until the early 1970s, which implied the strengthening of the normative pattern of getting married, having children, and surviving until at least age 50 in an intact first marriage. But after the early 1970s, at least in most Western countries, the process of standardization stopped or reversed, resulting in an increase of different household configurations and sequences which deviate from the normative pattern of family life (Cheal,1991; Te Kloeze et al., 1996). Scanzoni (Scanzoni et al., 1989) proposes the concepts of close relationships or primary relationships for relationships previously defined as family or conjugal relations. Somewhat later, Scanzoni and Marsiglio (1989) identify sets of interdependencies, three of which reflect behavioural interdependencies and a fourth one represents a formal interdependency, namely, legal marriage. Thus, they all try to transcend the connotations related to 'the normal family' and to avoid the difficulty of conceiving of alternatives as deviations of this normal family (Cheal, 1991). Such broad concepts, however, obscure a clear view of those configurations which this book focuses on: the domestic domain, comprising a dwelling unit, an economic unit, and a reproductive unit.

As to public policy, processes of de-standardization are difficult to deal with. Meeting the needs of different types of households is complicated. Importantly, as the previous chapters showed, some types of households are disfavoured compared to other households and therefore need particular attention. Nimpuno-Parente's study illustrated the limited access women-headed households may have to new housing projects. Miraftab's research illuminated the particular priorities of women-headed households and their residential location characteristics. Further, the research of Gonzáles de la Rocha showed the relevance of the phase in a household's life-cycle, and the relevance of the income/expenditure ratio which is related to the life-cycle.

Insight into the needs of people living in different living arrangements is important to be able to support those whose needs are most urgent. In addition, such insight is important because it lays bare the hidden assumptions which implicitly favour prevailing living arrangements to alternative ones.

The informal sector, and family households within it, is responsible for the welfare of its subjects and that of future generations. It interacts with the physical environment and provides the basis for society at a macro-level. But first and for all, the informal sector *is* society, in particular civil society.

Bibliography

Ahlander, N.R. and Bahr, K.S. (1995), 'Beyond Drudgery, Power, and Equity: Toward an Expanded Discourse on the Moral Dimensions of Housework in Families', *Journal of Marriage and the Family*, vol. 57, pp. 54-68.

Ajzen, I. (1987), 'Attitudes, Traits, and Actions: Dispositional Prediction of Behavior in Personality and Social Psychology', *Advances in Experimental Social Psychology*, pp. 1-63.

Ajzen, I. (1988), *Attitudes, Personality, and Behaviour*, Open University Press, Milton Keynes.

Ajzen, I. (1991), 'The Theory of Planned Behavior', *Organizational Behavior and Human Decision Processes*, vol. 50, pp. 179-211.

Ajzen, I. and Fishbein, M. (1980), *Understanding Attitudes and Predicting Social Behavior*, Prentice Hall, Inc., Englewood Cliffs, NJ.

Ajzen, I. and Madden, T. (1986), 'Prediction of Goal-Directed Behavior: Attitudes, Intentions and Perceived Behavioral Control', *Journal of Experimental Social Psychology*, vol. 22, pp. 453-474.

Aldous, J. (1996), *Family Careers, Rethinking the Developmental Perspective*, Sage Publications Inc., Thousand Oaks/London.

Anderson, M. (1980), *Approaches to the History of the Western Family, 1500-1914*, MacMillan Press, London.

Anderson, M., Bechhofer, F. and Gershuny, J. (eds) (1994), *The Social and Political Economy of the Household*, Oxford University Press, Oxford.

Anderson, M., Bechhofer, F. and Kendrick, S. (1994a), 'Introduction', in M. Anderson, F. Bechhofer, and J. Gershuny (eds), *The Social and Political Economy of the Household*, Oxford University Press, Oxford, pp. 1-18.

Anderson, M., Bechhofer, F. and Kendrick, S. (1994b), 'Individual and Household Strategies', in M. Anderson, F. Bechhofer, and J. Gershuny (eds), *The Social and Political Economy of the Household*, Oxford University Press, Oxford, pp. 19-67.

Arimah, B.C. (1997), 'The Determinants of Housing Tenure Choice in Ibadan, Nigeria', *Urban Studies*, vol. 34, pp. 105-124.

Askham, J. (1975), *Fertility and Deprivation; A Study of Differential Fertility amongst Working-Class Families in Aberdeen*, Cambridge University Press, Cambridge.

Baanders, A. (1998), *Leavers, Planners and Dwellers. The Decision to Leave the Parental Home*, PhD Thesis, Landbouwuniversiteit Wageningen.

Bachrach , P. and Baratz, M.S. (1970), *Power and Poverty, Theory and Practice*, Oxford University Press, New York.

Bagozzi, R.P. and Dabholkar, P.A. (1994), 'Consumer Recycling Goals and their Effect on Decisions to Recycle: a Means-End Chain Analysis', *Psychology and Marketing*, vol. 11, pp. 313-340.

Bankart, C.P. and Bankart, B.M. (1985), 'Japanese Children's Perceptions of their Parents', *Sex Roles*, vol. 14, pp. 679-690.

Barlett, P.F. (1989), 'Introduction: Dimensions and Dilemmas of Householding', in R.R. Wilk (ed), *The Household Economy*, pp. 1-10.

Barnett, T. (1992/93), *On Ignoring the Wider Picture: Aids Research and the Jobbing Social Scientist*, Rural Development Studies, Institute of Social Studies, The Hague.

Becker, G.S. (1981), *A Treatise on the Family*, Harvard University Press, Cambridge, Mass.

Becker, H. (1992), 'Introduction', in H.A. Becker (ed), *Dynamics of Cohort and Generations Research*, Thesis Publishers, Amsterdam, pp. 19-27.

Becker, H. (1996), *Generaties en hun Kansen*, Meulenhoff, Amsterdam.

Behrman, J.R. (1990), 'Peeking into the Black Box of Economic Models of the Household', in B.L. Rogers and N.P. Schlossman (eds), *Intra-Household Resource Allocation*, pp. 44-50.

Bentler, P.M. and Speckart, P. (1979), 'Models of Attitude-Behaviour Relations', *Psychological Review*, vol. 86, pp. 452-464.

Bentley, J.W. (1989), 'Eating the Dead Chicken: Intra-Household Decision Making and Emigration in Rural Portugal', in R.R. Wilk (ed), *The Household Economy, Reconsidering the Domestic Mode of Production*, Westview Press, Boulder, pp. 73-90.

Berry, S.S. (1984), 'Households, Decision Making, and Rural Development: Do We Need to Know More?', *Development Discussion Paper 167*, Harvard Institute for International Development, Cambridge, Mass.

Blain, J. (1994), 'Discourses of Agency and Domestic Labor: Family Discourse and Gendered Practice in Dual-earner Families', *Journal of Family Issues*, vol. 15, pp. 515-549.

Blair, S.L. (1993), 'Employment, Family, and Perceptions of Marital Quality among Husbands and Wives', *Journal of Social Issues*, vol. 14, pp. 189-212.

Blair, S.L. and Johnson, M.P. (1992), 'Wives' Perception of the Fairness of the Division of Household Labor: the Intersection of Housework and Ideology', *Journal of Marriage and the Family*, vol. 54, pp. 570-581.

Blaisure, K.R. and Allen, K.R. (1995), 'Feminists and the Ideology and Practice of Marital Equality', *Journal of Marriage and the Family*, vol. 57, pp. 5-19.

Blood R.O. jr. and Wolfe, D.M. (1960), *Husbands and Wives, the Dynamics of Married Living*, The Free Press, Collier-MacMillan Ltd, New York/London.

Bolak, H.C. (1997), 'When Wives are Major Providers, Culture, Gender, and Family Work', *Gender and Society*, vol. 11, pp. 409-433.

Bos, F., Leutscher, M. and Niehof, A. (1996), 'Aids in Afrika: Rampspoed of Aanzet tot Sociale Verandering' (Aids in Africa: Disaster or Motor for Social Change), *Medische Antropologie*, vol. 8, pp. 169-184.

Boss, P. (1988), *Family Stress Management*, SAGE Publications, Newbury Park, CA.

Boss, P.G. and Gurko, T.A. (1994), 'The Relationships of Men and Women in Marriage' in J.W. Maddock, M.J. Hogan, I. Antonov and M.S. Matskovsky (eds), *Families before and after Perestroika, Russian and U.S. Perspectives*, The Guilford Press, New York/London, pp. 36-75.

Bosveld, W. (1996), *The Ageing of Fertility in Europe. A Comparative Demographic-Analytical Study*, Thesis Publishers, Amsterdam.

Bourdieu, P. (1986), 'The Forms of Capital', in J.G. Richardson (ed), *Handbook of Theory and Research for the Sociology of Education*, Greenwood Press, New York.

Brannen, J. and G. Wilson (eds) (1987), *Give and Take in Families, Studies in Resource Distribution*, Allen & Unwin, London.

Brannen, J. and Moss, P. (1987), 'Dual Earner Households: Women's Financial Contributions after the Birth of the First Child', in J. Brannen and G. Wilson (eds), *Give and Take in Families, Studies in Resource Distribution*, Allen & Unwin, London, pp. 75-95.

Brenner, J. and Laslett, B. (1986), 'Social Reproduction and the Family', in U. Himmelstrand (ed), *The Social Reproduction of Organization and Culture*, SAGE Publications, London, pp. 116-131.

Brines, J. (1994), 'Economic Dependency, Gender, and the Division of Labor at Home', *American Journal of Sociology*, vol. 100, pp. 653-688.

Bruce, J. and Lloyd, C. (1995), 'Finding the Ties that Bind; Beyond Headship and Household', in A. van den Avort, K. de Hoog and P. Kalle (eds), *Single Parent Families*, Proceedings of the Conference (on) Single Parent Families, The Netherlands Family Council, The Hague, pp. 60-92.

Bubolz, M.M. (1991), 'Theory, Research, and Practice in Home Economics', *Journal of Theory in Home Economics, Themis*, vol. 1, pp. 1-14.

Burgoyne, C.B. (1990), 'Money in Marriage: How Patterns of Allocation Both Reflect and Conceal Power', *The Sociological Review*, vol. 38, pp. 634-665.

Burie, J.B. (1982), *Het Machtsspel van Mensen, over Organisaties en Hoe die met Elkaar Omgaan*, Van Loghum Slaterus, Deventer.

Burns, S. (1975), *The Household Economy, its Shape, Origins & Future*, Beacon Press, Boston.

Butler, R. (1991), *Designing Organizations, A Decision-Making Perspective*, Routledge, London and New York.

Carroll, J.S. and Johnson, E.J. (1990), *Decision Research, a Field Guide*, SAGE Publications, Newbury Park.

Castells, M. (1997), *The Power of Identity*, Blackwell Publishers, Malden, Mass./ Oxford, UK.

Chant, S. (1987), 'Domestic Labour, Decision-making, and Dwelling Construction: the Experience of Women in Querétaro, Mexico', in C.O.N. Moser and L. Peake (eds), *Women, Human Settlements, and Housing*, pp. 33-54.

Chant, S. (1997), *Women-Headed Households, Diversity and Dynamics in the Developing World*, Macmillan Press Ltd., Houndmills.

Cheal, D. (1988), *The Gift Economy*, Routledge, London/New York.

Cheal, D. (1989), 'Strategies of Resource Management in Household Economies: Moral Economy or Political Economy?' in R.R. Wilk (ed), *The Household Economy. Reconsidering the Domestic Mode of Production*, Westview Press, Boulder/San Francisco/London, pp. 11-23.

Cheal, D. (1991), *Family and the State of Theory*, Harvester/Wheatsheaf, New York.

Chen, H. (1996), *The Role of Gender in Farming Household Decision-Making in Yaan, South-Western China*, Landbouwuniversiteit, Vakgroep Huishoudstudies, Wageningen.

Chen, M. (1990), 'Poverty, Gender and Work in Bangladesh', in L. Dube and R. Palriwala (eds), *Structures and Strategies, Women, Work and Family*, SAGE Publications, New Delhi, pp. 201-220.

Clapham, D. and Kintrea, K. (1986), 'Rationing, Choice, and Constraint: the Allocation of Public Housing in Glasgow', *Journal of Social Policy*, vol. 15, pp. 51-67.

Coleman, M. and Ganong, L.H. (1989), 'Financial Management in Stepfamilies', *Life-styles: Family and Economic Issues*, vol. 10, pp. 217-232.

Coltrane, S. (1992), 'Men's Housework: a Life Course Perspective', *Journal of Marriage and the Family*, vol. 54, pp. 43-57.

Coltrane, S. (1996), *Family Man, Fatherhood, Housework and Gender Equity*, Oxford University Press, New York/Oxford.

Coltrane, S. and Ishii-Kuntz, M. (1992), 'Men's Housework: a Life Course Perspective', *Journal of Marriage and the Family*, vol. 54, pp. 43-57.

Cook, C.C., Bruin, M.J. and Laux, S. (1994a), 'Housing Assistance and Residential Satisfaction', *Housing and Society*, vol. 21, pp. 62-75.

Cook, C.C., Bruin, M.J. and Winter, M. (1994b), 'Housing Cost Burden among Female Heads of Households', *Housing and Society*, vol. 21, pp. 16-31.

Cornell, L.L. (1987), 'Where Can Family Strategies Exist?', *Historical Methods*, vol. 20, pp. 120-123.

Corral-Verdugo, V. (1996), 'A Structural Model of Reuse and Recycling in Mexico', *Environment and Behavior*, vol. 28, pp. 665-696.

Cromwell, R.E. and Olson, D.H. (eds) (1975), *Power in Families*, John Wiley and Sons, New York.

Crow, G. (1989), 'The Use of the Concept of "Strategy" in Recent Sociological Literature', *Sociology*, vol. 23, pp. 1-24.

Crow, G. and Hardey, M. (1991), 'The Housing Strategies of Lone Parents', in M. Hardey and G. Crow (eds), *Lone Parenthood, Coping with Constraints and Making Opportunities*, Harvester, New York, pp. 47-65.

Crull, S.R. (1994), 'Housing Satisfaction of Households at Risk of Serious Housing Problems', *Housing and Society*, vol. 21, pp. 41-51.

Dahl, R.A. (1958), 'A Critique of the Ruling Elite Model', *American Political Science Review*, vol. 52, pp. 463-469.

Damasio, A.R. (1994), *Descartes' Error, Emotion, Reason and the Human Brain*, MacMillan General Books, London and Basingstoke.

Danes, S.M. and Rettig, K.D. (1993), 'Farm Wives' Business and Household Decision Involvement in Times of Economic Stress', *Home Economics Research Journal*, vol. 21, pp. 307-333.

Danes, S.M., Doudchenko, O.N. and Yasnaya, L.V. (1994), 'Work and Family Life', in J.W. Maddock, M.J. Hogan, A. Antonov and M.S. Matskovsky (eds), *Families before and after Perestroika, Russian and U.S. perspectives*, Guilford Press, New York/London, pp. 156-185.

Daneshvary, N., Daneshvary, R. and Schwer, K.R. (1998), 'Solid-Waste Recycling Behavior and Support for Curbside Textile Recycling', *Environment and Behavior*, vol. 30, pp. 144-161.

Darke, R. (1989), 'Housing and Spatial Policies in the Socialist Third World', *The Netherlands Journal of Housing and Environmental Research*, vol. 4, pp. 51-66.

Davidson, A.P. (1991), 'Rethinking Household Strategies', in D.C. Clay and H.K. Schwarzweller (eds), *Household Strategies, Research in Rural Sociology and Development; A Research Annual*, vol. 5, pp. 11-29.

Davis, H.L. (1981), 'Decision Making within the Household', in H.H. Kassarjian and T.S. Robertson (eds), *Perspectives in Consumer Behavior*, Scott, Foresman, and Company, Glenview Ill., pp. 357-379.

Deacon, R.E, and Firebaugh, F.M. (1988), *Family Resource Management, Principles and Applications*, Allyn and Bacon, Inc., Boston.

Deacon, R.E. (1996), 'Visions for the 21st Century', in C.B. Simerly et al. (eds), *A Book of Readings*, pp. 41-50.

DeMaris, A. and Longmore, M.A. (1996), 'Ideology, Power, and Equity, Testing Competing Explanations for the Perception of Fairness in Household Labor', *Social Forces*, vol. 74, pp. 1043-1071.

Derksen, L. and Gartrell, J. (1993), 'The Social Context of Recycling', *American Sociological Review*, vol. 58, pp. 434-442.

De Oliveira, O. (1991), 'Migration of Women, Family Organization and Labour Markets in Mexico', in E. Jelin (ed), *Family, Household and Gender Relations in Latin America*, Kegan Paul, Intern., UNESCO, London, pp. 101-118.

De Swaan, A. (1983), *De Mens is de Mens een Zorg, Opstellen 1971-1981*, Meulenhoff, Amsterdam.

De Swaan, A. (1988), *In Care of the State*, Oxford University Press, Oxford/New York.

223

De Swaan, A. (ed) (1994), *Social Policy beyond Borders, the Social Question in Transnational Perspective*, Amsterdam University Press, Amsterdam.

De Young, R. (1990), 'Recycling as Appropriate Behavior: A Review of Survey Data from Selected Recycling Education Programs in Michigan', *Resources, Conservation and Recycling*, vol. 3, pp. 1-13.

Diekmann, A. and Preisendörfer, P. (1992), 'Persönliches Umweltverhalten, Diskrepanzen zwischen Anspruch und Wirklichkeit', *Kölner Zeitschrift für Soziologie und Sozialpsychologie*, Jrg.44, Heft 2, pp. 226-251.

Dietz, Th., Stern, P.C. and Guagagno, G.A. (1998), 'Social Structural and Social Psychological Bases of Environmental Concern', *Environment and Behavior*, vol. 30, pp. 450-471.

Dobbelsteen, S. (1996), *Intrahousehold Allocation of Resources; a Micro-econometric Analysis*, PhD-thesis, Landbouwuniversiteit Wageningen, Vakgroep Huishoudstudies.

Drèze, J. and Sen, A. (1995), *India, Economic Development and Social Opportunity*, Oxford University Press, Delhi.

Dube, L. and Palriwala, R. (eds) (1990), *Structures and Strategies, Women, Work and Family*, SAGE Publications, New Delhi.

Dwyer, D. and Bruce, J. (eds) (1988), *A Home Divided, Women and Income in the Third World*, Stanford University Press, Stanford.

Earhart, C.C., Weber, M.J. and McCray, J.W. (1994), 'Life Cycle Differences in Housing Perspectives of Rural Households', *Home Economics Research Journal*, vol. 22, pp. 309-324.

Edwards, R. and Ribbens, J. (1991), 'Meanderings around "Strategy": A Research Note on Strategic Discourse in the Lives of Women', *Sociology*, vol. 25, pp. 477-489.

Elchardus, M. (1984), 'Life Cycle and Life Course: The Scheduling and Temporal Integration of Life', in S. Feld and R. Lesthaeghe (eds), *Population and Societal Outlook*, Koning Boudewijnstichting, Brussels, pp. 251-267.

Elder, G.H. (1985), *Life Course Dynamics. Trajectories and Transitions. 1968-1980*, Cornell University Press, Ithaca/New York.

Elder, G.H. (1994), 'Time, Human Agency, and Social Change: Perspectives on the Life Course', *Social Psychology Quarterly*, vol. 57, pp. 4-15.

Eliason Lappalainen, R. and Nilsson Motevasel, I. (1997), 'Ethics of Care and Social Policy', *Scandinavian Journal of Social Welfare*, vol. 6, pp. 189-196.

Elsinga, M. (1996), 'Relative Cost of Owner-Occupation and Renting: A Study of Six Dutch Neighborhoods', *Netherlands Journal of Housing and the Built Environment*, vol. 11, pp. 131-150.

Engle, P.L. (1990), 'Intra-Household Allocation of Resources; Perspectives from Psychology', in B.L. Rogers and N.P. Schlossman (eds), *Intra-Household Resource Allocation: Issues and Methods for Development Policy and Planning*, United Nations Press, pp. 63-79.

Esping-Andersen, G. (1996), *The Three Worlds of Welfare Capitalism*, Polity Press, Cambridge.

Fapohunda, E.R., and Todaro, M.P. (1988), 'Family Structure, Implicit Contracts, and the Demand for Children in Southern Nigeria', *Population and Development Review*, vol. 14, pp. 571-594.

Ferree, M. M. (1991), 'The Gender Division of Labor in Two-Earner Marriages', *Journal of Family Issues*, vol. 12, pp. 159-180.

FHI (1996), *The Impact of Family Planning and Reproductive Health on Women's Lives: A Conceptual Framework*, Family Health International, Research Triangle Park, North Carolina.

Finch, J. (1987), 'Family Obligations and the Life Course', in A. Bryman et al. (eds), *Rethinking the Life Cycle*, The MacMillan Press LTD, Houndmills/ London.

Finch, J. (1989), *Family Obligations and Social Change*, Polity Press, Cambridge.

Finch, J. and Mason, J. (1993), *Negotiating Family Responsibilities*, Tavistock/ Routledge, London and New York.

Firebaugh, F. (1995), 'Single Parents and Parenting: A Life Course Perspective', in A. van der Avort, K. de Hoog and P. Kalle (eds), *Single Parent Families*, Nederlandse Gezinsraad, The Hague.

Fisher, B. and Tronto, J. (1990), 'Towards a Feminist Theory of Caring', in E.K. Abel and M.K. Nelson (eds), *Circles of Care, Work and Identity in Women's Lives*, State University of New York Press, Albany, pp. 35-62.

Folbre, N. (1987), 'Family Strategy, Feminist Strategy', *Historical Methods*, vol. 20, pp. 115-118.

Folz, D.H. (1991), 'Recycling Programme Design, Management, and Participation: A Rational Survey of Municipal Experience', *Public Administration Review*, vol. 51, pp. 222-231.

Foucault, M. (1986), 'Disciplinary Power and Subjection', in S. Lukes (ed), *Power*, Basil Blackwell Ltd., Oxford, pp. 229-242.

Frederick, A.J. and Dossett, D.L. (1983), 'Attitude-Behaviour Relations: A Comparison of the Fishbein-Ajzen and the Bentler-Speckart Models', *Journal of Personality and Social Psychology*, vol. 45, pp. 501-512.

Friedmann, J. (1989), 'The Latin American *Barrio* Movement as a Social Movement: Contribution to a Debate', *International Journal of Urban and Regional Research*, vol. 13, pp. 501-510.

Frijda, N.H. (1986), *The Emotions*, Maisons des Sciences de l'Homme and Cambridge University Press.

Fukuyama, F. (1997), *The End of Order*, The Social Market Foundation, London.

Gamba, R. and Oskamp, S. (1994), 'Factors Influencing Community Residents' Participation in Commingled Curbside Recycling Programmes', *Environment and Behavior*, vol. 26, pp. 587-612.

Gans, H.J. (1972), *People and Plans. Essays on Urban Problems and Solutions*, Penguin Books Ltd., Harmondsworth.

Gardiner, J. (1997), *Gender, Care and Economics*, Macmillan Press, London.

Gasson, R. and Errington, A. (1993), *The Farm Family Business*, CAB International, Wallingford.

Gershuny, J. (1996), 'Veränderungen bei der Arbeitsteilung im Haushalt: Mikro-Soziologische Analysen', in K. Zapf et al. (eds), *Lebenslagen im Wandel: Sozialberichterstattung im Längsschnitt*, Campus Verlag, Frankfurt/New York, pp. 97-124.

Gershuny, J. and Brice, J. (1996), *Change in the Division of Domestic Work: Micro-Sociological Evidence from Three Countries*, Essex University for Project PACO, pp.1-15,

Gershuny, J., Godwin, M. and Jones, S. (1994), 'The Domestic Labour Revolution: A Process of Lagged Adaptation', in M. Anderson et al., *The Social and Political Economy of the Household*, pp. 151-197.

Giddens, A. (1991*), Modernity and Self-Identity, Self and Society in the Late Modern Age*, Polity Press, Cambridge.

Giddens, A. (1994), *Sociology*, Polity Press, Cambridge.

Giddens, A. (1996), *In Defence of Sociology, Essays, Interpretations, and Rejoinders*, Polity Press, Cambridge, UK.

Gilbert, A. (1981), 'Pirates and Invaders: Land Acquisition in Urban Colombia and Venezuela', *World Development*, vol. 9, pp. 657-678.

Gilbert, A. and Gugler, J. (1992), *Cities, Poverty and Development, Urbanization in the Third World*, Oxford University Press, Oxford/New York.

Gilroy, R. (1994), 'Women and Owner Occupation in Britain, First the Prince, then the Palace?', in R. Gilroy and R. Woods (eds), *Housing Women*, Routledge, London and New York.

Glick, P.C. (1977), 'Updating the Life Cycle of the Family', *Journal of Marriage and the Family*, vol. 39, pp. 5-15.

Goldenhar, L.M. and Connell, C.M. (1993), 'Understanding and Predicting Recycling Behaviour: An Application of the Theory of Reasoned Action', *Journal of Environmental Systems*, vol. 22, pp. 91-103.

Goldsmith, E. (1996), *Resource Management for Individuals and Families*, West Publishing Company, Minneapolis/ St.Paul.

González de la Rocha, M. (1991), 'Family Well-being, Food Consumption, and Survival Strategies during Mexico's Economic Crisis', in M. González de la Rocha and A. Escobar La Tapí (eds), *Social Responses to Mexico's Economic Crisis of the 1980s*, Center for U.S.-Mexican Studies/University of California, San Diego, pp. 115-127.

González de la Rocha, M. (1994), *The Resources of Poverty, Women and Survival in a Mexican City*, Blackwell, Oxford, UK & Cambridge, USA.

Goody, J. (1972), *Production and Reproduction, a Comparative Study of the Domestic Domain*, Cambridge University Press, Cambridge.

Gottman, J.M. (1991), 'Predicting the Longitudinal Course of Marriages', *Journal of Marital and Family Therapy*, vol. 17, pp. 3-7.

Graham, H. (1987), 'Being Poor: Perceptions and Coping Strategies of Lone Mothers', in J. Brannen and G. Wilson (eds), *Give and Take in Families, Studies in Resource Distribution*, Allen & Unwin, London, pp. 56-74.

Gramsci, A. (1971), *Selections from the Prison Notebooks*, edited and translated by Q. Hoare and G.N. Smith, Lawrence and Wishart, London.

Granzin, K.L. and Olsen, J.E. (1991), 'Characterizing Participants in Activities Protecting the Environment: A Focus on Donating, Recycling, and Conservation Behaviours', *Journal of Public Policy and Marketing*, vol. 10, pp. 1-27.

Green, K.B. (1996), 'Our Intellectual Ecology: A Treatise on Home Economics', in C.B. Simerly et al. (eds), *A Book of Readings*, pp. 1-8.

Greenstein, Th.N. (1996a), 'Husbands' Participation in Domestic Labor: Interactive Effects of Wives' and Husbands' Gender Ideologies', *Journal of Marriage and the Family*, vol. 58, pp. 585-595.

Greenstein, Th.N. (1996b), 'Gender Ideology and Perceptions of the Fairness of the Division of Household Labor: Effects on Marital Quality', *Social Forces*, vol. 74, pp. 1029-1041.

Grindle, M.S. (1989), 'The Response to Austerity: Political and Economic Strategies of Mexico's Rural Poor', W.I. Canak (ed), *Lost Promises: Debt, Austerity, and Development in Latin-America*, Westview Press, Boulder, Colo, pp. 129-153.

Gross, I.H., Crandall, E.W., and Knoll, M.M. (1973), *Management for Modern Families*, Prentice Hall, Englewood Cliffs.

Guagagno, G.A., Stern, P.C. and Dietz, T. (1995), 'Influences on Attitude-Behavior Relationships, a Natural Experiment with Curbside Recycling', *Environment and Behavior*, vol. 27, pp. 699-718.

Guyer, J. (1988), 'Dynamic Approaches to Domestic Budgeting: Cases and Methods from Africa', in D. Dwyer and J. Bruce (eds), *A Home Divided, Women and Income in the Third World*, Stanford University Press, Stanford, pp. 155-172.

Habermas, J. (1981), *Theorie des Kommunikativen Handelns, Teil II Zur Kritik der Funktionalistischen Vernunft*, Suhrkamp, Frankfurt am Main.

Hakansson, N.Th. and LeVine, R.A. (1997), 'Gender and Life-Course Strategies among the Gusii', in Th.S. Weisner, C. Bradley, and Ph.L. Kilbride (eds), *African Families and the Crisis of Social Change*, Bergin & Garvey, Westport, pp. 253-267.

Hall, P. (1989), 'Arcadia for Some: the Strange Story of Autonomous Housing', *Housing Studies*, vol. 4, pp. 149-154.

Hallin, P.O. (1995), 'Environmental Concern and Environmental Behaviour in Foley, a Small Town in Minnesota', *Environment and Behavior*, vol. 27, pp. 558-578.

Hamid, P.N. and Cheng, S.T. (1995), 'Predicting Antipollution Behavior, the Role of Molar Behavioral Intentions, Past Behaviour, and Locus of Control', *Environment and Behavior*, vol. 27, pp. 679-698.

Hantrais, L. and Letablier, M.T. (1996), *Families and Family Policies in Europe*, Addison Wesley Longman Ltd., London and New York.

Hardesty, C. and Bokemeier, J. (1989), 'Finding Time and Making Do: Distribution of Household Labor in Nonmetropolitan Marriages', *Journal of Marriage and the Family*, vol. 51, pp. 253-267.

Hardey, M. and Crow, G. (1991), *Lone Parenthood, Coping with Constraints and Making Opportunities*, Harvester/Wheatsheaf, New York.

Hardon-Baars, A. (1994), 'The Household, Women, and Agricultural Development Revisited', in K. de Hoog and J.A.C. van Ophem (eds), *Changes in Daily Life*, Wageningen Agricultural University, Department of Household and Consumer Studies, Wageningen, pp. 101-116.

Hardon-Baars, A. (1996), 'User/use-oriented Approach to Technology Assessment and Innovation: Some Lessons for Marketing Research', *UPWARD, Into Action Research*, Partnerships in Asian Rootcrop Research and Development, Los Banos, Philippines, pp. 203-216.

Hardoy, J.E. and Satterthwaite, D. (1981), *Shelter Need and Response-Housing, and Settlement Policies in Seventeen Third World Nations*, John Wiley and Sons, Chichester.

Hareven, T.K. (1982), *Family Time and Industrial Time, the Relationship between the Family and Work in a New England Industrial Community*, Cambridge University Press, Cambridge/New York.

Hareven, T.K. and Langenbach, R. (1978), *Amoskeag: Life and Work in an American Factory-City*, Pantheon, New York.

Harris, C.C. (1990a), *Kinship*, Open University Press, Buckingham.

Harris, C.C. (ed) (1990b), *Family, Economy and Community*, University of Wales Press, Cardiff.

Harris, O. (1984), 'Households as Natural Units, in K. Young et al. (eds), *Of Marriage and the Market, Women's Subordination Internationally and its Lessons*, Routledge and Kegan Paul, London, pp. 136-157.

Hartmann, H.I. (1981), 'The Family as the Locus of Gender, Class and Political Struggle: The Example of Housework', *Signs: Journal of Women in Culture and Society*, vol. 6, pp. 366-394.

Heenan, D. and Gray, A.M. (1997), 'Women, Public Housing and Inequality: A Northern Ireland Perspective', *Housing Studies*, vol. 12, pp. 157-171.

Henderson, J. and Karn, V. (1984), 'Race, Class, and the Allocation of Public Housing in Britain', *Urban Studies*, vol. 21, pp. 115-128.

Henderson, J. and Karn, V. (1987), *Race, Class and State Housing Inequality and the Allocation of Public Housing in Britain*, Gower Publ. Cy. Ltd., Aldershot.

Hetler, C.B. (1990), 'Survival Strategies, Migration and Household Headship', in L. Dube and R. Palriwala (eds), *Structures and Strategies, Women, Work and Family*, SAGE Publications, New Delhi, pp. 175-199.

Hill, P.P. and C.A. Solheim (1993), 'Home Economists as Environmentalists: Setting a Research Agenda', in R. Von Schweitzer (ed), *Cross Cultural Approaches to Home Management*, pp. 51-64.

228

Hira, T.K. (1997), 'Financial Attitudes, Beliefs and Behaviors: Differences by Age', *Journal of Consumer Studies and Home Economics*, vol. 21, pp. 271-290.

Hochschild, A.R., with Machung, A. (1989), *The Second Shift*, Avon Books, New York.

Homer, M., Leonard, A., and Taylor, P. (1985), 'The Burden of Dependency' in N. Johnson (ed), *Marital Violence*, Routledge and Kegan Paul, London.

Hopper, J.R. and Nielsen, McC. J. (1991), 'Recycling as Altruistic Behaviour, Normative and Behavioural Strategies to Expand Participation in a Community Recycling Programme', *Environment and Behavior*, vol. 23, pp. 195-220.

Horrell, S. (1994), 'Household Time Allocation and Women's Labour Force', in M. Anderson et al. (eds), *The Social and Political Economy of the Household*, pp. 198-224.

Horrell, S., Rubery, J., and Burchell, B. (1994), 'Working-Time Patterns, Constraints, and Preferences', in M. Anderson et al., *The Social and Political Economy of the Household*, pp. 100-132.

Howenstine, E. (1993), 'Market Segmentation for Recycling', *Environment and Behavior*, vol. 25, pp. 86-102.

Inglehart, R. and Abramson, P.R. (1993), *Affluence and Intergenerational Change: Period Effects and Birth Cohort Effects*, Paper presented at the conference on 'Solidarity between the Generations?', University of Utrecht, Utrecht, vol. 7-8.

Ishii-Kuntz, M. (1993), 'Japanese Fathers, Work Demands and Family Roles', in J.C. Hood (ed), *Men, Work, and Family*, SAGE Publications, Newbury Park, pp. 45-67.

Jelin, E. (1990), 'Household Organization and Expenditure in a Time Perspective: Social Processes of Change', in B.L. Rogers and N.P. Schlossman (eds), *Intra-Household Resource Allocation: Issues and Methods for Development Policy and Planning*, United Nations University Press, Tokyo, pp. 114-127.

Jelin, E. (ed) (1991), *Family, Household and Gender Relations in Latin America*, Kegan Paul International Ltd., London.

Joas, H. (1996), *The Creativity of Action*, Polity Press, Cambridge.

Jones, R.E. (1990), 'Understanding Paper Recycling in an Institutionally Supportive Setting: An Application of the Theory of Reasoned Action', *Journal of Environmental Systems*, vol. 19, pp. 307-321.

Jordan, B., James, S., Kay, H. and Redley, M. (1992), *Trapped in Poverty? Labour-Market Decisions in Low-Income Households*, Routledge, London and New York.

Kabeer, N. (1991), *Gender, Production and Well-Being: Rethinking the Household Economy*, Discussion Paper 288, Institute of Development Studies, Sussex.

Kamo, Y. (1994), 'Division of Household Work in the United States and Japan', *Journal of Family Issues*, vol. 15, pp. 348-378.

Kesler, B.E.Th.A. (1989), 'Dwelling Communities as a New Lifestyle: A Report on an Innovatory Movement in Social Housing in The Netherlands', in J.Brech (ed), *Neue Wohnformen in Europa*, Bd.II, Verlag für Wissenschaftliche Publicationen, Darmstadt.

Key, R.J. and Firebaugh, F.M. (1989), 'Family Resource Management: Preparing for the 21st Century', *Journal of Home Economics*, vol. 81, pp. 13-17.

Kingsbury, N.M. and Scanzoni, J. (1989), 'Process Power and Decision Outcomes among Dual-Career Couples', *Journal of Comparative Family Studies*, vol. 20, pp. 231-246.

Kirchler, E. (1990), 'Spouses' Influence Strategies in Purchase Decisions as Dependent on Conflict Type and Relationship Characteristics', *Journal of Economic Psychology*, vol. 11, pp. 101-118.

Kirchler, E. (1993), 'Spouses' Joint Purchase Decisions: Determinants of Influence Tactics for Muddling through the Process', *Journal of Economic Psychology*, vol. 14, pp. 405-438.

Kirchler, E. (1995), 'Studying Economic Decisions within Private Households: A Critical Review and Design for a "Couple Experiences Diary"', *Journal of Economic Psychology*, vol. 16, pp. 393-419.

Klijn, E.H. and Koolma, H.M. (1987), 'Coalitievorming in de Volkshuisvesting, het Spel om de Knikkers', *Stedebouw en Volkshuisvesting*, vol. 68, pp. 18-25.

Kloek, E. (1989), *Gezinshistorici over Vrouwen*, Sua, Amsterdam.

Kluwer, E. (1998), *Marital Conflict over the Division of Labor: When Partners Become Parents*, PhD Dissertation Rijksuniversiteit Groningen, Groningen.

Kohlberg, L. (1981), *Essays on Moral Development: vol 1. The Philosophy of Moral Development*, Harper Row, San Francisco.

Kohlberg, L. (1984), *Essays on Moral Development: vol. 2. The Psychology of Moral Development*, Harper Row, San Francisco.

Kok, G. and Siero, S. (1985), 'Tin Recycling: Awareness, Comprehension, Attitude, Intention and Behaviour', *Journal of Economic Psychology*, vol. 6, pp. 157-173.

Komarovsky, M. (1967), *Blue Collar Marriage*, Vintage Books, New York.

Komter, A. (1985), *De Macht van de Vanzelfsprekendheid, Relaties tussen vrouwen en mannen*, VUGA Uitgeverij B.V., s' Gravenhage.

Komter, A. (1989), 'Hidden Power in Marriage', *Gender & Society*, vol. 3, pp. 187-216.

Kumar, S. (1996), 'Landlordism in Third World Urban Low-Income Settlements: A Case for Further Research', *Urban Studies*, vol. 33, pp. 753-782.

Lacey, L. and Sinai, I. (1996), 'Do Female-Headed Households have Different Shelter Needs than Men? The Case of Monrovia Liberia', *Journal of Comparative Family Studies*, vol. 27, pp. 89-108.

Lansana, F. M. (1992), 'Distinguishing Potential Recyclers from Nonrecyclers: A Basis for Developing Recycling Strategies', *Journal of Environmental Education*, vol. 23, pp. 16-23.

Lansana Margai, F.M. (1997), 'Analyzing Changes in Waste Reduction Behaviour in a Low-Income Urban Community Following a Public Outreach Programme', *Environment and Behavior*, vol. 29, pp. 769-792.

Laslett, P. (1991), *A Fresh Map of Life. The Emergence of the Third Age*, Harvard University Press, Cambridge, Massachusetts.

Laslett, P. with Wall, R. (1972), *Household and Family in Past Time*, Cambridge University Press, London/New York.

Leira, A. (1987), 'Time for Work, Time for Care: Childcare Strategies in a Norwegian Setting', in J. Brannen and G. Wilson (eds), *Give and Take in Families*, pp. 175-191.

Lennon, M.C., and Rosenfield, S. (1994), 'Relative Fairness and the Division of Housework: The Importance of Options', *American Journal of Sociology*, vol. 100, pp. 506-531.

Leonard, D. (1990), 'Sex and Generation Reconsidered', in C.C. Harris (ed), *Family, Economy and Community*, University of Wales Press, Cardiff, pp. 35-52.

Lesthaeghe, R. and Moors, G. (1992), 'Rationality, Cohorts, and Values', in H.A. Becker (ed), *Dynamics of Cohort and Generations Research*, Thesis Publishers, Amsterdam, pp. 165-187.

Levin, I. (1993), 'Family as Mapped Realities', *Journal of Family Issues*, vol. 14, pp. 82-91.

Lewis, D.J. (1993), 'Going it Alone: Female-Headed Households, Rights and Resources in Rural Bangladesh', *The European Journal of Development Research*, vol. 5, pp. 23-42.

Lloyd C.B. and Desai, S. (1992), 'Children's Living Arrangements in Developing Countries', *Population Research and Policy Review*, vol. 11, pp. 193-216.

Lukes, S. (1974), *Power: A Radical View*, The Macmillan Press Ltd., London and Basingstoke.

Lyson, T.A. (1985), 'Husband and Wife Work Roles and the Organization and Operation of Family Farms', *Journal of Marriage and the Family*, pp. 759-764.

Macey, S.M. and Brown, M.A. (1983), 'Residential Energy Conservation, the Role of Past Experience in Repetitive Household Behavior', *Environment and Behavior*, vol. 15, pp. 123-141.

Machado, L.M.V. (1987), 'The Problems for Women-Headed Households in a Low-Income Housing Programme in Brazil' in C.O.N. Moser and L. Peake (eds), *Women, Human Settlements, and Housing*, pp. 55-69.

Mannheim, K. (1952), 'The Problem of Generations', in K. Mannheim (ed), *Essays on the Sociology of Knowledge*, Oxford University Press, Oxford, pp. 276-322.

Matsushima, C. (1992), *A Philosophical Stance for Home Economics*, Life Course Institute, Tokyo.

Mauldin, T. and Meeks, C.B. (1990), 'Time Allocation of One- and Two-Parent Mothers', *Life-styles: Family and Economic Issues*, vol. 11, pp. 53-69.

McCarty, J.A. and Shrum, L.J. (1994), 'The Recycling of Solid Wastes: Personal Values, Value Orientations, and Attitudes about Reycling as Antecedents of Recycling Behaviour', *Journal of Business Research*, vol. 30, pp. 53-62.

McCrone, D. (1994), 'Getting by and Making out in Kirkcaldy', in M. Anderson, F. Bechhofer, and J. Gershuny (eds), *The Social and Political Economy of the Household*, Oxford University Press, Oxford, pp. 68-99.

McIntosh, W.A., and Zey, M. (1989), 'Women as Gatekeepers of Food Consumption: A Sociological Critique', *Food and Foodways*, vol. 3, pp. 317-332.

McKee, L. (1987), 'Households during Unemployment: The Resourcefulness of the Unemployed, in J. Brannen and G. Wilson, *Give and Take in Families: Studies in Resource Distribution*, Allen & Unwin, London, pp. 96-117.

Mennell, S., Murcott, A., Van Otterloo, A.H. (1992), *The Sociology of Food, Eating, Diet and Culture*, SAGE Publications, London.

Miller, B.C. (1986), *Family Research Methods, Family Studies Text Series 4*, SAGE Publications, Beverly Hills, California.

Mingione, E. (1994), 'Life Strategies and Social Economies in the Postfordist Age', *International Journal of Urban and Regional Research*, vol. 18, pp. 24-45.

Miraftab, F. (1997), 'Revisiting Informal-Sector Home Ownership:The Relevance of Household Composition for Housing Options of the Poor', *International Journal of Urban and Regional Research*, pp. 303-322.

Miraftab, F. (1998), 'Complexities of the Margins: Housing Decisions by Female Householders in Mexico', *Environment and Planning: Society in Space*, vol. 16, pp. 289-310.

Moch, L. (1987), 'Historians and Family Strategies', *Historical Methods*, vol. 20, p. 113-115.

Morgan, D.H.J. (1996), *Family Connections: An Introduction to Family Studies*, Polity Press, Cambridge.

Morris, E.W. (1991), 'Household, Kin and Nonkin Sources of Assistance in Home-Building: The Case of the City of Oaxaca', *Urban Anthropology*, vol. 20, pp. 49-65.

Morris, E.W. and Cho, J. (1986), 'Logit Models for Housing References, Demographic Variables and Actual Housing Conditions', *Housing and Society*, vol. 13, pp. 118-135.

Morris, E.W. and Winter, M. (1976), 'Housing and Occupational Subcultures', *Housing Educators Journal*, vol. 3, pp. 2-16.

Morris, E.W. and Winter, M. (1978), *Housing, Family, and Society*, John Wiley and Sons, New York.

Morris, L. (1990a), 'The Household and the Labour Market', in C.C. Harris (ed), *Family, Economy and Community*, University of Wales Press, Cardiff, pp. 79-97.

Morris, L. (1990b), *The Workings of the Household, a US-UK Comparison*, Polity Press, Cambridge.

Morris, L. (1994), 'Informal Aspects of Social Division', *International Journal of Urban and Regional Research*, vol. 18, pp. 112-126.

Moser, C.O.N. (1987a), 'Introduction', in C.O.N. Moser and L. Peake (eds), *Women, Human Settlements and Housing*, pp. 1-11.

Moser, C.O.N. (1987b), 'Women, Human Settlements, and Housing: a Conceptual Framework for Analysis and Policy-making', in C.O.N. Moser and L. Peake (eds), *Women, Human Settlements and Housing*, pp. 12-32.

Moser, C.O.N. (1987c), 'Mobilization is Women's Work: Struggles for Infrastructure in Guayaquil, Ecuador', in C. Moser and L. Peake (eds), *Women, Human Settlements and Housing*, pp. 166-194.

Moser, C.O.N. and L. Peake (eds) (1987), *Women, Human Settlements, and Housing*, Tavistock Publications, London and New York.

Mulder, C.H. (1993), *Migration Dynamics: A Life Course Approach*, Thesis Publishers, Amsterdam.

Murphy, P.E. and Staples, W.A. (1979), 'A Modernized Family Life Cycle', *Journal of Consumer Research*, vol. 6, pp. 12-22.

Netting, McC.R. (1989), 'Smallholders, Householders, Freeholders: Why the Familyfarm Works Well Worldwide', in R.R. Wilk (ed), *The Household Economy*, pp. 221-244.

Netting, McC.R., Wilk, R.R., and Arnould, E.J. (eds) (1984), *Households, Comparative and Historical Studies of the Domestic Group*, University of California Press, Berkeley.

Neuman, K. (1986), 'Personal Values and Commitment to Energy Conservation', *Environment and Behavior*, vol. 18, pp. 53-74.

Newell, C. (1988), *Methods and Models in Demography*, John Wiley & Sons, Chichester/New York.

Niehof, A. (1985), *Women and Fertility in Madura (Indonesia)*, PhD Thesis, Rijksuniversiteit Leiden, Leiden.

Niehof, A. (1994), *Het Duveltje uit de Zwarte Doos, de Ongemakkelijke Relatie tussen Gender en Huishouden*, WAU, Wageningen.

Niehof, A. (1995), 'Who Benefits from Income Generation by Women? Some Theoretical Considerations and Evidence from West Java', The 3rd WIVS Conference on Indonesian Women's Studies, Leiden.

Niehof, A. (1997), 'Ouderen, Zorg en Welzijn: een Pleidooi voor een Vergelijkende Benadering', *Medische Antropologie*, vol. 9, pp. 7-23.

Niehof, A. (1998), 'The Changing Lives of Indonesian Women, Contained Emancipation under Pressure', *Journal of the Humanities and Social Sciences of Southeast Asia and Oceania*, BKI 154-II, pp. 236-258.

Nimpuno-Parente, P. (1987), 'The Struggle for Shelter: Women in a Site and Service Project in Nairobi, Kenya', in C.O.N. Moser and L. Peake (eds), *Women, Human Settlements and Housing*, Tavistock Publications, London and New York, pp. 70-87.

Nolan, M., Grant, G. and Keady, J. (1996), *Understanding Family Care. A Multidimensional Model of Caring and Coping.* Open University Press, Buckingham, Philadelphia.

Oatley, K. and Jenkins, J.M. (1996), *Understanding Emotions*, Blackwell Publishers Inc., Cambridge/Oxford.

Obudho, R.A. and Aduwo, G.O. (1989), 'Slum and Squatter Settlements in Urban Centres of Kenya: Towards a Planning Strategy', *The Netherlands Journal of Housing and Environmental Research*, vol. 4, pp. 17-29.

Olson, D.H. and Cromwell, R.E. (1975), 'Power in Families', in D.H. Cromwell and R.E. Olson (eds), *Power in Families*, pp. 3-14.

Orloff, A. (1996), 'Gender in the Welfare State', *Annual Review of Sociology*, vol. 22, pp. 51-78.

Oskamp, S., Harrington, M.J., Edwards, T.C., Sherwood, D.L., Otuda, S.M., and Swanson, D.C. (1991), 'Factors Influencing Household Recycling Behavior', *Environment and Behavior*, vol. 23, pp. 494-519.

Oskamp, S., Zelezny, L., Schultz, P.W., Hurin, S., and Burkhardt, R. (1996), 'Commingled versus Separated Curbside Recycling, Does Sorting Matter?', *Environment and Behavior*, vol. 28, pp. 73-91.

Owens, S. (1990), 'Land Use Planning for Energy Efficiency', in J. Cullingworth (ed), *Energy, Land and Public Policy*, Transaction Press, New Brunswick, NJ.

Pahl, J. (1983), 'The Allocation of Money and the Structuring of Inequality within Marriage', *Sociological Review*, vol. 31, pp. 237-262.

Pahl, J. (1989), *Money and Marriage*, MacMillan Education Ltd., Houndmills.

Pahl, J. (1995), 'His Money, Her Money: Recent Research on Financial Organisation in Marriage', *Journal of Economic Psychology*, vol. 16, pp. 361-376.

Pahl, R. (1975), *Whose City? And Further Essays on Urban Society*, Penguin Books Ltd., Harmondsworth.

Pahl, R. (1985), 'The Restructuring of Capital, the Local Political Economy and Household Work Strategies', in D. Gregory and J. Urry (eds), *Social Relations and Spatial Structures*, MacMillan, Basingstoke, pp. 242-264.

Palriwala, R. (1990), 'Introduction', in L. Dube and R. Palriwala (eds), *Structures and Strategies*, pp. 15-56.

Paolucci, B., Hall, O.A., and Axinn, N. (1977), *Family Decision Making: An Ecosystem Approach*, John Wiley and Sons, New York.

Peake, L. (1987), 'Government Housing Policy and its Implications for Women in Guyana', in C.O.N. Moser and L. Peake (eds), *Women, Human Settlements and Housing*, pp. 113-138.

Pennartz, P.J.J. (1981), *De Kern van het Wonen op het Spoor*, Coutinho, Muiderberg.

Pennartz, P.J.J. (1986), 'Atmosphere at Home: A Qualitative Approach', *Journal of Environmental Psychology*, vol. 6, pp. 135-153.

Pennartz, P.J.J. (1989), 'Semiotic Theory and Environmental Evaluation: A Proposal for a New Approach and a New Method', *Symbolic Interaction*, vol. 12, pp. 131-149.

Pennartz, P.J.J. (1996), 'Besluitvorming in Huishoudens als Proces', *Huishoudstudies*, vol. 6, pp. 11-19.

Pennartz, P.J.J. and Elsinga, M.G. (1990), 'Adults, Adolescents, and Architects, Differences in Perception of the Urban Environment', *Environment and Behavior*, vol. 22, pp. 675-714.

Perry-Jenkins, M. and Folk, K. (1994), 'Class, Couples, and Conflict: Effects of the Division of Labor on Assessments of Marriage in Dual-earner Families', *Journal of Marriage and the Family*, vol. 56, pp. 165-180.

Pope Edwards, C. (1997), 'Morality and Change: Family Unity and Paternal Authority among Kipsigis and Abaluyia Elders and Students, in Th.S. Weisner, C. Bradley, and Ph.L. Kilbride (eds), *African Families and the Crisis of Social Change*, Bergin & Garvey, Westport, Connecticut and London, pp. 45-85.

Presvelou, C., De Hoog, C., and Cuyvers, P. (1996), 'Primary Life Patterns as an Object of Study: The Case of The Netherlands', *Marriage and Family Review*, vol. 23, pp. 535-574.

Priemus, H. (1998), 'Housing Research and the Dynamics of Housing Markets', in A.J.H. Smets and T. Traerup (eds), *Housing in Europe: Analysing Patchworks*, Utrecht University/Danish Building Research Institute, Utrecht/Horsholm, pp. 34-43.

Qureshi, H. and Simons, K. (1987), 'Resources within Families: Caring for Elderly People', in J. Brannen and G. Wilson (eds), *Give and Take in Families*, pp. 117-135.

Rakodi, C. (1995a), 'Housing Finance for Lower Income Households in Zimbabwe', *Housing Studies*, vol. 10, pp. 199-227.

Rakodi, C. with Withers, P. (1995b), 'Home Ownership and Commodification of Housing in Zimbabwe', *International Journal of Urban and Regional Research*, vol. 19, pp. 250-271.

Richards, L. (1989), 'Family and Home Ownership in Australia, the Nexus of Ideologies', *Marriage and Family Review*, vol. 14, p.173-193.

Roberts, B. (1994), 'Informal Economy and Family Strategies', *International Journal of Urban and Regional Research*, vol. 18, pp. 6-23.

Rogers, B.L. (1990), 'The Internal Dynamics of Households: A Critical Factor in Development Policy', in B.L. Rogers and N.P. Schlossman, *Intra-Household Resource Allocation*, pp. 1-22.

Rogers, B.L. and N.P. Schlossman (eds) (1990), *Intra-Household Resource Allocation: Issues and Methods for Developmental Policy and Planning*, Nations University Press, Tokyo.

Rogers, E.M. (1983), *Diffusion of Innovations*, The Free Press, New York.

Roldan, M. (1988), 'Renegotiating the Marital Contract: Intrahousehold Patterns of Money Allocation and Women's Subordination among Domestic

Outworkers in Mexico City', in D. Dwyer and J. Bruce (eds), *A Home Divided, Women and Income in the Third World*, Stanford University Press, Stanford.

Ross, L. and Nisbett, R.E. (1991), *The Person and the Situation, Perspectives of Social Psychology*, McGraw-Hill, New York.

Rowntree, B.S. (1901), *Poverty: A Study of Town Life*, Macmillan, London.

Rudolph, R.L. (1992), 'The European Family and Economy: Central Themes and Issues', *Journal of Family History*, vol. 17, pp. 119-138.

Ryder, N.B. (1965), 'The Cohort as a Concept in the Study of Social Change', *American Sociological Review*, vol. 30, pp. 843-861.

Safilios-Rothschild, C. (1976), 'A Macro- and Micro-Examination of Family Power and Love: An Exchange Model', *Journal of Marriage and the Family*, vol. 38, pp. 355-364.

Safilios-Rothschild, C. (1988), 'The Impact of Agrarian Reform on Men's and Women's Incomes in Rural Honduras', in D. Dwyer and J. Bruce, *A Home Divided*, pp. 216-228.

Sanchez, L. and Kane, E.W. (1996), 'Women's and Men's Constructions of Perceptions of Housework Fairness', *Journal of Family Issues*, vol. 17, pp. 358-387.

Sarver jr., V.T. (1983), 'Ajzen and Fisbein's Theory of Reasoned Action: A Critical Assessment', *Journal for the Theory of Social Behaviour*, vol. 13, pp. 155-163.

Scanzoni, J. (1979), 'Social Processes and Power in Families', in W.R. Burr, R. Hill, F.I. Nye, I.L. Reiss (eds), *Contemporary Theories about the Family*, The Free Press, New York, pp. 295-316.

Scanzoni, J. and Szinovacz, M. (1980), *Family Decision-Making, a Developmental Sex Role Model*, SAGE Publications, Beverly Hills/London.

Scanzoni, J., Polonko, K., Teachman J., and Thompson, L. (1989), *The Sexual Bond: Rethinking Families and Close Relationships*, SAGE Publications, Newbury Park, CA.

Schifter, D.B. and Ajzen, I. (1985), 'Intention, Perceived Control, and Weight Loss: An Application of the Theory of Planned Behaviour', *Journal of Personality and Social Psychology*, vol. 49, pp. 843-851.

Schlyter, A. (1988), *Women Householders and Housing Strategies, the Case of George, Zambia*, The National Swedish Institute for Building Research, Gävle.

Schlyter, A. (1989), *Women Householders and Housing Strategies, the Case of Harare, Zimbabwe*, The National Swedish Institute for Building Research, Gävle.

Schnaiberg, A. (1980), *The Environment: From Surplus to Scarcity*, Oxford University Press, New York.

Schultz, P.W., and Oskamp, S. (1994), 'Environmental Concern and Pro-environmental Behaviors: Do Only the Concerned Recycle?', Paper Presented at the Annual Meeting of the Western Psychological Association, Kona, HI.

Schultz, P.W., Oskamp, S. and Mainieri, T. (1995), 'Who Recycles and When? A Review of Personal and Situational Factors', *Journal of Environmental Psychology*, vol. 15, pp. 105-121.

Scott, J. (1976), *The Moral Economy of the Peasant: Rebellion and Subsistence in Southeast Asia*, Yale University Press, New Haven.

Sevenhuijsen, S. (1998), *Citizenship and the Ethics of Care. Feminist Considerations on Justice, Morality and Politics*, Routledge, London.

Sheng, Y.K. (1989), 'Housing Priorities, Expenditure Patterns, and the Urban Poor in Third-World Countries', *The Netherlands Journal of Housing and Environmental Research*, vol. 4, pp. 5-15.

Sheth, J.N. and Raju, P.S. (1974), 'Sequential and Cyclical Nature of Information Processing Models in Repetitive Choice Behaviour', *Advances in Consumer Research*, vol. 1, pp. 348-358.

Shukla, A. (1987), 'Family Decision Making in India', *Journal of Marriage and the Family*, vol. 49, pp. 621-629.

Simerly, C.B., Light, H. and Midstifer, D. (1996), *A Book of Readings: The Context for Professionals in Human, Family and Consumer Sciences*, The American Association of Family and Consumer Sciences, Alexandria.

Skinner, E.A. (1995), *Perceived Control, Motivation & Coping*, SAGE Publications, Thousand Oaks.

Smith, D.L. (1988), 'Women and Habitat: Nairobi 1985', in W. Van Vliet (ed), *Women, Housing and Community*, Aldershot, Avebury, pp. 185-190.

Soliman, A. (1989), 'Housing Mechanisms in Egypt: A Critique', *The Netherlands Journal of Housing and Environmental Research*, vol. 4, pp. 31-50.

Spiro, R.L. (1983), 'Persuasion in Family Decision-making', *Journal of Consumer Research*, vol. 9, pp. 393-402.

Ssennyonga, J.W. (1997), 'Polygyny and Resource Allocation in the Lake Victoria Basin', in Th.S. Weisner, C. Bradley, and Ph.L. Kilbride (eds), *African Families and the Crisis of Social Change*, Bergin & Garvey, Westport, Connecticut and London, pp. 268-282.

Stack, C.B. (1974), *All Our Kin: Strategies for Survival in a Black Community*, Harper and Row, New York.

Stafford, K. and Avery, A.J. (1993), 'Scheduling Congruity Theory of Family Resource Management: A Basis for Cross Cultural Analysis', in R. von Schweitzer (ed), *Cross Cultural Approaches to Home Management*, pp. 17-41.

Stern, P.C., Dietz, T., Kalof, L. and Guagagno, G.A. (1995a), 'Values, Beliefs and Pro-Environmental Action: Attitude Formation toward Emergent Attitude Objects', *Journal of Applied Social Psychology*, vol. 25, pp. 1611-1636.

Stern, P.C., Dietz, T. and Guagagno, G.A. (1995b), 'The New Ecological Paradigm in Social-Psychological Context', *Environment and Behavior*, vol. 27, pp. 723-743.

Sutherland, D.S. and Ham, S.A. (1992), 'Child-to-Parent Transfer of Environmental Ideology in Costa Rican Families: An Ethnographic Case Study', *Journal of Environmental Education*, vol. 23, pp. 9-16.

Tavecchio, L.W.C., Van IJzendoorn, M.H., Goossens, F.A. and, Vergeer, M.M. (1984), 'The Division of Labor in Dutch Families with Preschool Children', *Journal of Marriage and the Family*, vol. 46, pp. 231-242.

Taylor, S. and Todd, P. (1995), 'An Integrated Model of Waste Management Behaviour, a Test of Household Recycling and Composting Intentions', *Environment and Behavior*, vol. 27, pp. 603-630.

Te Kloeze, J.W., De Hoog, K., Van Bergen, M., Duivenvoorden, M. (1996), *Tussen Vrijheid en Gebondenheid, het Postmoderne Gezin Ontdekt*, Garant, Leuven/Apeldoorn.

Thompson, L. (1991), 'Family Work, Women's Sense of Fairness', *Journal of Family Issues*, vol. 12, pp. 181-196.

Thompson, L. and Walker, A.J. (1989), 'Gender in Families: Women and Men in Marriage, Work, and Parenthood', *Journal of Marriage and the Family*, vol. 51, pp. 845-871.

Tosi, A. (1995), 'Shifting Paradigms, the Sociology of Housing, the Sociology of the Family, and the Crisis of Modernity', in R. Forrest and A. Murie (eds), *Housing and Family Wealth, Comparative International Perspectives*, Routledge, London and New York, pp. 261-288.

Triandis, H.C. (1979), *Interpersonal Behavior*, Brooks/Cole Publishing Company, Monterey, CA.

Tronto, J.C. (1993), *Moral Boundaries. A Political Argument for an Ethic of Care*, Routledge, New York/London.

Turner, J.F.C. (1968), 'Housing Priorities, Settlement Patterns, and Urban Development in Modernizing Countries', *AIP Journal*, pp. 354-363.

Turner, J.F.C. (1976), *Housing by People, towards Autonomy in Building Environments*, Marion Boyars Publishers Ltd., London.

Twigg, J. (1996), 'Issues in Informal Care, in *Caring for Frail Elderly People. Policies in Evolution*, OECD, Paris, pp. 81-92.

Uhlenberg, P.R. (1969), 'A Study of Cohort Life Cycles; Cohorts of Native Born Massachusetts Women, 1830-1920', *Population Studies*, vol. 23, pp. 407-420.

Ungar, S. (1994), 'Apples and Oranges: Probing the Attitude-Behaviour Relationship for the Environment', *Canadian Review of Sociology and Anthropology*, vol. 31, pp. 288-304.

United Nations (1997), *Habitat Agenda and Istanbul Declaration, Second United Nations Conference on Human Settlements, Istanbul Turkey 3-14 June 1996*, United Nations, Dept of Public Information, New York.

Uusitalo, L. (1990), 'Are Environmental Attitudes and Behaviour Inconsistent? Findings from a Finnish Study', *Scandinavian Political Studies*, vol. 13, pp. 211-226.

Van Beek, R. (1997), *Comparison of Household Waste Figures for Various Countries in Europe*, Ministerie van Volkshuisvesting, Ruimtelijke Ordening en Milieubeheer, vol. 1997/36B, Zoetermeer.

Vance, I. (1987), 'More than Bricks and Mortar: Women's Participation in Self Help Housing in Managua, Nicaragua', in C.O.N. Moser and L. Peake (eds), *Women, Human Settlements, and Housing*, pp. 139-165.

Van Dam, H.M. (1988), 'Ecologie van het Wonen, de Ontwikkeling van een Vakgebied tussen Consumptie en Existentie', in J.M. van Dam et al. (eds), *Woonecologie tussen Consumptie en Existentie*, Stichting Voorlichting Huishoudwetenschappen, Wageningen, pp. 9-29.

Van Den Avort, De Hoog, K. and Kalle, P. (eds) (1995), *Single Parent Families, Proceedings of the Conference Single Parent Families Amsterdam 1994*, The Netherlands Family Council, The Hague.

Van Der Erve, H. (1989), 'The Diversity of Work Relationships in the Construction Sector of Semarang', in P. Van Gelder and J. Bijlmer (eds), *About Fringes, Margins, and Lucky Dips, the Informal Sector in Third-World Countries: Recent Developments in Research and Policy*, Free University Press, Amsterdam, pp. 91-111.

Van Der Heijden, H., and Boelhouwer, P. (1996), 'The Private Rental Sector in Western Europe: Developments since the Second World War and Prospects for the Future', *Housing Studies*, vol. 11, pp. 13-33.

Van Der Lippe, A.G. (1993), *Arbeidsverdeling tussen Mannen en Vrouwen, een Interdisciplinaire Studie naar Betaald en Huishoudelijk Werk binnen Huishoudens*, Thesis Publishers, Amsterdam.

Van Der Veen, K.W. (1995), 'Zelfbeschikking in Afhankelijkheid? De Ambiguïteit van Ouderenzorg in Nederland, in S. van der Geest (ed), *Ambivalentie /Ambiguïteit*, Het Spinhuis, Amsterdam, pp. 57-67.

Van Diepen, A.M.L. (1998), 'Spatial Aspects of Housing', in K.J. Noorman and T. Schoot Uiterkamp (eds), *Green Households? Domestic Consumers, Environ-ment and Sustainability*, Earthscan Publications Ltd, London, pp. 101-120.

Van Dongen, W. (1992), 'An Integrated Analysis of the Internal and External Division of Labour in the Family', *Bevolking en Gezin*, vol. 1, pp. 25-54.

Van Gennep, A. (1960), *The Rites of Passage*, The University of Chicago Press, Chicago.

Van Leeuwen, H. (1980), *Ecologie van het Wonen, Algemene Inleiding tot de Leer van de Wisselwerking tussen Mens en Gebouwde Omgeving*, VUGA-Boekerij, s'Gravenhage.

Van Ophem, J.A.C. (1988), *Huishoudens en Inkomensdaling*, PhD-thesis, Landbouwuniversiteit Wageningen, Wageningen.

Van Wezel, R.H.J. (1993), *Woningbeheer, een Onderzoek naar de Sociaal-Culturele Waarden van Huurders en Verhuurders in het Onderhoud van Woningen in de Non-Profit Sector*, Ph.D-thesis, Landbouwuniversiteit Wageningen, Wageningen.

Van Wezel, R.H.J. (1994), *Beyond Tools for Architecture*, Proceedings of the Vth European Full-Scale Modelling Conference 1994 in Wageningen, The Netherlands, Landbouwuniversiteit Vakgroep Huishoudstudies, Wageningen.

Vining, J. and Ebreo, A. (1990), 'What Makes a Recycler? A Comparison of Recyclers and Nonrecyclers', *Environment and Behavior*, vol. 22, pp. 55-73.

Vogler, C. (1994), 'Money in the Household', in M. Anderson, F. Bechhofer and J. Gershuny (eds), *The Social and Political Economy of the Household*, Oxford University Press, Oxford, pp. 225-266.

Vogler, C. and Pahl, J. (1993), 'Social and Economic Change and the Organisation of Money within Marriage', *Work, Employment and Society*, vol. 7, pp. 71-95.

Vogler, C. and Pahl, J. (1994), 'Money, Power and Inequality within Marriage', *The Sociological Review*, vol. 42, pp. 263-286.

Von Schweitzer, R. (ed), *Cross Cultural Approaches to Home Management*, Campus Verlag/Westview Press, Frankfurt am Main/Boulder.

Von Werlhof, C. (1984), *The Proletarian is Dead, Long Live the Housewife?* In: J.I. Wallerstein and Evers, H.D.(eds.) *Households and the World Economy*. Beverly Hills/London/New Delhi: Sage Publications, pp.131-148.

Walby, S. (1986), *Patriarchy at Work*, Polity Press, Cambridge.

Wallerstein, I. and Smith, J. (1991), 'Households as an Institution of the World-Economy', in R.L. Blumberg (ed), *Gender, Family and Economy, the Triple Overlap*, SAGE Publications, Newbury Park, pp. 225-242.

Wallman, S. (1986), 'The Boundaries of Household', in A.P. Cohen (ed), *Symbolising Boundaries, Identity and Diversity in British Cultures*, Manchester University Press, Manchester, pp. 50-70.

Wang, Y.P. (1995), 'Public Sector Housing in China 1949-1988: The Case of Xian', *Housing Studies*, vol. 10, pp. 57-82.

Ward, C. (1976), 'Preface', in J.F.C. Turner (1976), *Housing by People*, pp. 1-4.

Watson, S. (1986), 'Housing and the Family: the Marginalization of Non-Family Households in Britain', *International Journal of Urban and Regional Research*, pp. 8-28.

Watson, S. (1988), *Accomodating Inequality: Gender and Housing*, Allen and Unwin, Sydney.

White, H.C. (1992), 'Succession and Generations: Looking Back on Chains of Opportunity', in H.A. Becker (ed), *Dynamics of Cohort and Generations Research*, Thesis Publishers, Amsterdam, pp. 31-51.

Widegren, Ö. (1998), 'The New Environmental Paradigm and Personal Norms', *Environment and Behavior*, vol. 30, pp. 75-100.

Wiersma, E. (1997), *Reflections on the American Welfare State, Cultural and Theoretical Roots of Recent Radical Welfare Reform*, Unpublished paper.

Wilhelm, M.S. and Keith, J.G. (1987), 'Predictors of Voluntary Simplicity in Consumer Behaviour', *Journal of Consumer Studies*, vol. 11, pp. 113-129.

Wilk, R.R. (1989), 'Decision Making and Resource Flows within the Household: Beyond the Black Box', in R.R. Wilk (ed), *The Household Economy*, pp. 23-54.

Wilk, R.R. (ed) (1989), *The Household Economy, Reconsidering the Domestic Mode of Production*, Boulder, Westview Press.

Wilk R.R. and Netting, McC.R. (1984), 'Households: Changing Forms and Functions', in R.McC. Netting et al. (eds), *Households, Comparative and Historical Studies of the Domestic Group*, pp. 1-28.

Willinger, B. (1993), 'Resistance and Change, College Men's Attitudes toward Family and Work in the 1980s', in J.C. Hood (ed), *Men, Work, and Family*, SAGE Publications, Newbury Park, pp. 108-129.

Wilson, G. (1987), 'Money: Patterns of Responsibility and Irresponsibility in Marriage', in J. Brannen and G. Wilson (eds), *Give and Take in Families, Studies in Resource Distribution*, Allen &Unwin, London, pp. 136-154.

Wolf, D.L. (1992), 'Industrialization and the Family, Women Workers as Mediators of Family Change and Economic Change in Java', in S. Van Bemmelen, M. Jajadiningrat-Nieuwenhuis, E. Locher-Scholten, E. Touwen-Bouwsma (eds), *Women and Mediation in Indonesia*, Verhandelingen van het Koninklijk Instituut voor Taal-, Land- en Volkenkunde 152, KITLV Press, Leiden, pp. 89-108.

Wolf, D.L. (1993), 'Women and Industrialization in Indonesia', in J.P. Dirkse, F. Hüsken, and M. Rutten (eds) *Development and Social Welfare; Indonesia's Experiences under the New Order*, Verhandelingen van het Koninklijk Instituut voor Taal-, Land-, en Volkenkunde 156, KITLV Press, Leiden.

Zick, C.D. (1992), 'Do Families Share and Share-Alike? The Need to Understand Intrahousehold Resource Allocation', *Journal of Family and Economic Issues*, vol. 13, pp. 407-419.

Zijderveld, A.C. (1979), 'Het Ethos van de Verzorgingsstaat. Een Cultuur-sociologische Bijdrage, *Sociale Wetenschappen*, vol. 22, pp. 179-221.

Zimmerman, S.L. (1995), *Understanding Family Policy, Theories and Applications*, SAGE Publications, Thousand Oaks.

Zvonkovic, A.M., Greaves, K.M., Schmiege, C.J. and Hall, L.D. (1996), 'The Marital Construction of Gender through Work and Family Decisions: A Qualitative Analysis', *Journal of Marriage and the Family*, vol. 58, pp. 91-100.

Zwart, S.I. (1990), *Agrarische Huishoudens, Een Onderzoek naar de Veranderende Relatie tussen Gezin en Bedrijf in Oost-Gelderland*, PhD-thesis Wageningen Agricultural University, Wageningen.

241